AL-KEMI

By the same Author:

PHILOSOPHICAL GEOMETRY

André VandenBroeck

AL-KEMI

Hermetic, Occult, Political, and Private Aspects of
R. A. Schwaller de Lubicz

LINDISFARNE PRESS

PUBLISHED BY THE LINDISFARNE PRESS
RR 4, BOX 94A-1
HUDSON, NEW YORK 12534

LIBRARY OF CONGRESS CATALOGUING-IN-PUBLICATION DATA
VANDENBROECK, ANDRÉ.
AL-KEMI: HERMETIC, OCCULT, POLITICAL, AND PRIVATE
ASPECTS OF R. A. SCHWALLER DE LUBICZ
1. SCHWALLER DE LUBICZ, R. A.   2. HERMETIC
PHILOSOPHERS—BIOGRAPHY.   I. TITLE.
BF1598.s33v35   1987   135´.4   [B] 87-17941
ISBN 0-940262-31-2
10 9 8 7 6 5 4 3 2 1

COMPOSITION BY DIX TYPE
PRINTED AND BOUND IN THE UNITED STATES.

1

2

3

4

5

6

A Comment

Discontented, as many of us are, with the prevailing interpretations of reality, interpretations which do not reconcile our inner life with the external world and which deny our most persistent intuitions, André VandenBroeck made contact with R. A. Schwaller de Lubicz, a modern alchemist and Hermetic philosopher (he speaks of him also as a Pythagorean) and under his guidance familiarized himself with what he refers to as "an alternative and unified approach to . . . various disciplines encompassing the earth and its inhabitants." This unified approach, he concedes, might be considered by some as "the wildest of inventions." Nevertheless, his passionate and brilliant book shows de Lubicz to be a source of revolutionary insights. As Mr. VandenBroeck is very evidently a man of independent spirit, not a follower, he does not submit passively to all the teachings of his guide but, as every real thinker must, judges and measures him by appropriate modern standards. (Most esoterists are inclined to avoid the full daunting challenge of the present age.) Although de Lubicz had withdrawn from the contemporary world and its politics he had, in the years immediately after WW1, played a major role in a proto-Fascist French group called *Les Veilleurs,* and while in the last decades of his life he insisted that he was apolitical, he did not entirely repudiate the positions he had taken in the postwar years. VandenBroeck deals forthrightly and bravely with the residue of de Lubicz's reactionary convictions and with the history of the modern mixture of esotericism and politics—a "dangerously explosive" combination. Nazi Germany and Vichy France are never far from his mind as he struggles to distinguish the line between the high spiritual level of de Lubicz's teachings and the political horrors of the Twentieth Century. "The origin of Nazism," VandenBroeck says, "is a weaving of ideas taken from some of the world's most spiritual texts; its sword was honed by acknowledged spiritual exercise. . . ." The personal relationship of these two men ends when VandenBroeck discerns "an unexpected distance" between de Lubicz and his ideas—between his refined spiritual intuitions, his occultism, and the unexplained and unresolved connection with National-Socialism and its conscious and deliberate inhumanity, its self-assigned mission to hack at and sever the ancient human bond that holds our civilization together.

—*Saul Bellow*

For there is nothing covered, that shall not be revealed; and hid, that shall not be known. What I tell you in darkness, *that* speak ye in light: and what ye hear in the ear, *that* preach ye upon the housetops.

Matthew X, 26, 27.

INTRODUCTION

The material underlying the following pages was gathered in 1959 and 1960, years I spent in daily contact with R.A. Schwaller de Lubicz. Thereafter, fifteen years were occupied assessing and corroborating the information that stemmed from this encounter, tracking down neglected and abandoned leads that had opened in our far-flung conversations and needed attention even after direct consultation had become impossible. De Lubicz died several months after I interrupted my work with him.

In 1975, I made a first attempt at my subject, only to find a crucial element of the equation still incomplete. That element was myself. It took another eight years to round out the experience that would capacitate me for this task. It became clear in those last years that an autobiographical aspect was part and parcel of what I was attempting to formulate, and I had hitherto been unable to come to grips with a self that seemed to throw out constantly changing parameters. And so it is a full twenty-five years after the facts and at the ripe age of sixty that I feel confident of telling my story with some chance of success. I can only proffer slight consolation to the reader who might find some of my pages difficult of access: neither was living them easy at times, and both living and writing demanded assiduous efforts. Yet it has been miraculously interesting, and I hope the reader's endeavor will be similarly rewarding.

In previous attempts at committing my story to paper, I had intended to limit myself to the Hermetic aspects of R.A. Schwaller de Lubicz, to what I have come to call the *Hermetic Aor*.[1] Fortuitous encounters and chance discoveries rather than systematic research convinced me that the esoteric aspect could not be sundered from an occultistic one, and that a political component, to my surprise, was barely hidden behind the latter. This sharpened the biographical function and gave prominence to some private aspects I first had no intention of touching. It also brought up a question too speculative to be represented in this factual account, but that must nevertheless be mentioned, as it continues to loom beyond the limits of this book: what is the extent of the responsibility an author shoulders on behalf of his ideas?

As to insights I may have gathered into the personal and even intimate existence of this very seclusive individual, I hope to convey them through the general tone of our relationship rather than by the accumulation of incidents. The relationship, by and large, was based on ideas.

Although these various aspects have all received the attention they deserve, the initial bias has nevertheless prevailed, and we will find ourselves more often than not in the company of the Hermetic Aor, certainly the man with whom I entertained my closest relationship.

Lives lived under the sign of the Hermetic *Oeuvre* are not lived by the standards of society at large; both his and mine were and are lived well removed from the beaten track. As our paths crossed in a far-off region where traffic is scarce, the encounter was intense, total, and not meant for the long term. For Schwaller de Lubicz was an autocratic master, while discipleship, as a condition, is acute for a relatively short time, although it remains chronic thereafter. Indian sages advise the disciple to flit from flower to flower, gathering knowledge at every moment wherever it may be found. Finally, guru is seen everywhere, which means that self has become guru.

The intention here is not a comprehensive presentation of the ideas that motivated the philosopher: this much can be gathered from the published material.[2] As the work progressed and took on a life of its own, it became clear that one single theme had taken precedence over all others in our discussions: the theme of evolution. In itself this fact is hardly surprising, as a definition of evolution is arguably the center of his *Oeuvre* altogether. Yet this theme entered our conversations by an avenue that finds little development in the written work, although the principal elements are present, suitably dispersed as was the author's pedagogic wont. If I were to characterize somewhat simplistically this complex theme and its corollaries by a *term*, I would call its subject *perception;* and I would call its object *form.*

Before reaching these particulars, it must be known that de Lubicz held the traditional conception of an esoteric science and its transmission: true knowledge is inaccessible to the rational mind. This epistemological tenet caused his writings to be spiked with metaphor, innuendo, and at times, obscurity. He mistrusted the written word, disliked writing because truth was inevitably degraded when committed to paper through a profane language. This attitude most clearly ordinates the lineage along which he inscribes himself by his premises and his results. His low regard for "demotic" writing as a means of truth-communication made personal contact with him invaluable, for he had no such reservations concerning the spoken word, the word of gesture. Thus he actively believed in oral transmission of a kind of knowledge best called "gnosis,"[3] and in private, I always found him accessible to leisurely conversation on the most exalted topics. As our relationship soon proved more than casual, his information became increasingly direct, in contrast to his written expression which often presents problems of meaning and referent.

To such an epistemology, personal contact is the kingpin of communication, and I found out later to what extent his frame of reference was tailored to his correspondent. We both had a background in the plastic arts, and I know that his exploration of the theme of perception and form was often initiated by formal and perceptual considerations that referred directly to paint and canvas. Yet I have come to feel that the centrality of these themes was nevertheless mainly a reflection of his own intellectual preoccupations at that moment, and I have become convinced that had he been given time for one more creative outburst, perception and form would have been foremost in his last teaching.

I came to realize, as I have indicated, that it would be sense-less to limit myself to the exposition of de Lubicz's ideas. Concerned with the Hermetic aspects of the man, I feel that it is pertinent to relate how I made contact with him, seeing that at the time he and his work were quite unknown not only to myself, but to the world at large as well. My first attention therefore goes to relating the experience that sensi-tized me to the sphere of thought I subsequently entered, blindly, almost by mistake, inasmuch as such a contact, being made with the unknown, cannot be established at will. These events confirmed for me (should confirmation be in order) a subtler sphere of attraction and affinity in itself reflecting a cosmic organization; and it is the search for cosmological structure that formed the magnet for our interchange.

If up to the time of my meeting with Aor a first part of my enterprise is therefore overtly and purposely autobiographi-cal, the center of the piece, our time in common, is no less prone to subjectivity. On the contrary, as the Hermetic work demanded constant identification of subject and object, and as the difference between them had perforce to be eliminated to achieve abstraction in thought and concreteness in gesture, realization of self deepened accordingly so that its notation again is autobiographical, though now on a different plane. There will be no attempt at objectivity, because the subject does not stand aside from, but rather penetrates the object.

As the work done with Aor did not lie fallow with me, my understanding is now greater than it was at the time. But perennial concerns are timeless, and there is no pretending a return to an understanding I had *then*, when encompassing my subject *now*. If reality exists, it certainly does so in a *present* moment. Truth (or language structured in similarity to such reality, perhaps the very aim of philosophical en-deavor) must therefore look no further than the moment, not further back and not further ahead. The present moment at all times contains the full measure of knowledge.

The question naturally arises: what is that knowledge which can be thus perceived?

It has a name; its name is Al-Kemi, our title. In conformance to a rigorous theory of language which arises from the very discipline that occupies us, our title must be absolutely void of content. As the work is no less than the perfect extension of the title, we must wait until we have read the work before passing judgment on the title's meaning. That is one of the reasons why every seriously constructed text is to be twice read. The first reading will adhere as closely as possible to terminology, and only with the second reading, undertaken after noting the extension of the title, should we begin to let the hitherto undefined terms flower into meaningful words. That is not saying that the term, in its empty comprehension of all content, cannot play a powerful role by itself, by its position in syntax and grammar which makes it a locus in a structural game, and by its identity through etymology.[4] And our title has a venerable etymological background.

Al-Kemi, Aor's central concern throughout his career, stems from a Pharaonic hieroglyph for the Black Land, the Nile valley. Invading Arabs learned the name for the region and added their article: Al-Kemi *means* Pharaonic Egypt, and for a mind steeped in myth, Pharaonic Egypt *is* Al-Kemi. De Lubicz had occupied himself with medieval and Arabic alchemical texts for many years prior to his encounter with Pharaonic Egypt, and his intuition of Al-Kemi as an application of Hermetic gnosis became a certainty with the accumulation of detailed proof in texts and monuments. The significance of this intuition and its impact on history, philosophy, and science; the role of myth in all intellectual and spiritual disciplines in light of the equating of Al-Kemi with Pharaonic Egypt; the relation of myth to mythology, and Egypt and Greece as the twin cradle of an Aquarian Age of civilization in contrast to Greco-Christian Pisces; the possibility of a renaissance through Al-Kemi; and particularly the nature of Al-Kemi itself, explored through the parallel of medieval and Pharaonic expressions—all are topics of great interest that threaded their way through our discussions, but will not be prominently represented in my narrative. My intention in this memoir is to show certain aspects of the man, mainly those I may have been alone to witness, or that have never yet been brought out and discussed. That will allow me to report what he chose to reveal of his intellectual state in the course of our conversations. Furthermore, I have done my best to eliminate material that can be gathered by a thorough study of his published work, even when his oral presentation in my ear is far clearer and more compelling than his printed syntax. In no other way could I guarantee myself the slim volume I desire.

It should be understood that our exchanges took place in French, whereas I shall note them in English. The importance of this divergence from the actual state of affairs can only be appreciated by the bi- or multilingual: it is considerable, and constantly endangers the entire enterprise. Whenever certain expressions are irrevocably wedded to the French in my ear, I shall therefore reproduce them in their original language, and the quotations will always be exact.

The language complication goes further yet, as there was also occasional use of German words or phrases whenever that language provided the correct and irreplaceable term or syntax for a meaning. As a rule, however, we shied away from our common bilingualism as if we felt its dangers, a feeling which events were to confirm. Considerations of language and of theory of language will recur time and again. They are basic to Al-Kemi, as they are basic to the Hermetic controversy of "hiding and revealing," a related topic of consequence. Language and its decipherment is by necessity a basic component in the study of glyph and an aspect of de Lubicz that has to my knowledge hardly been retained in the succession of his ideas. Terminology sustains language, as we have mentioned, but in the Hermetic sciences, terminology is less a syntax than it is a *symbolique*.[5] "*Rien ne marque tant l'esprit que le nombre*,"* was one of Aor's firm contentions, but he usually added that in order for this function of number to inscribe itself, it had to form a symbolic language.[6] And the best example of this process lay in the evidence of Al-Kemi.

At the beginning of my sojourn in his presence, Aor con-

---

* "Nothing stamps the mind more surely than does number."

sidered me practically illiterate for the purpose of the work at hand, and I was put through an intensive course of reading. He was aghast at the fact that I had encountered the Holy Scriptures only in passing, and was not thoroughly familiar with Genesis 1–3, for instance, or the Gospel according to John. I now read, and we discussed all the great texts, from the Emerald Table to Jābir to Basil Valentine and Nicolas Flamel. Based on a lifetime of obedience to the principle of "Ora, lege, lege, lege, relege . . . ," his exegeses guided my first steps in the crucial art of slow reading, then of decipherment as such. Writings hitherto seeming to be but mystifications began to address the objects of my search with utmost clarity. I had learned to read, and I began to realize that *good* texts (of which there are few), far from being exercises in obscurantism, were indeed clear statements concerning perennial questions of cosmic existence. An Hermetic cliché like "as above, so below," at one time a mere posture in pseudophilosophy and devoid of content or proof, now became a living truth everywhere manifest. And this in turn gave meaning to the tantalizing information repeated time and again in all good Hermetic texts that the philosopher's stone indeed could be found anywhere because it was everywhere. What could be its value under those conditions? I came to understand the possibility of a constant moment when everything becomes feasible, the creative putrefaction in the chaos of the beginning. Such concepts ceased being metaphysical and became evident, as if I were studying a science of the obvious. How much can be taken for granted and how much goes without saying: these are questions that must be reconsidered. It is of no greater futility to study the becoming of duality out of oneness, than it is, with Peano and theory of number, to have the number two, and all subsequent numbers, become through the addition of a unit. The difference may simply be that the former point of view has faced the vexing question of the provenance of this ever ready unit at every operation. To that mentality, which we call Pythagorean, once the whole, the All, is given in an all-encompassing oneness, whence this "second" oneness that is conjured in order to make two?

Much goes unseen by a secular mentality, because it goes unquestioned.

We see enormous distances into the past, but the moment is a closed book. We do not reach it; we cannot know it. Meditation alone opens the sesame of intuition. But Aor's meditation was not one of folded hands and erect unmoving spine. His meditation was a gesture, and its result was art. He was proud of having studied with Matisse, but painting was not his chosen manipulation, and I have seen only one work of Aor's hand, a work which survived not in honor of the draftsman, but as a memento of his subject. It is a portrait in pencil, simply and boldly drawn, breathtaking in its similitude: one knows the man without ever having seen him! I can voice this absurdity, for it corresponds to my experience. Concerning the model of this portrait we shall have much to say, as he was frequently present in our conversations. Here I shall only mention his name: "Fulcanelli." I place it in quotes this one time to alert the reader: Hermetic authors always hide behind names. The heaviest burden I carried away from this contact with Hermetic circles was the knowledge I obtained concerning Fulcanelli. It has so far been impossible to transmit. I shall commit it to language and send it to its uncertain future. Perhaps it will disappear, or perhaps posterity will have occasion to judge between truth and fantasy. The future, however, is no longer *my* concern, but the reader's.

1

*Bruges, 1958–1959.—Breakthrough and communication.
—The loan of a book.—Readings: exoteric and
esoteric.—The notion of secret.—The double
reading.—A trip to Grasse.—Isha.—A man
of the right.—Amazement in Lyon.—Some
correspondence.—Upper-case knowledge.*

By training and disposition, I am an artist; to me this means
an involvement with an instrument of knowledge equal in
stature to science and philosophy. After my work with de
Lubicz, I came to understand that the three disciplines had to
join in the practitioner; they had been thus united in antiquity, and most notably in Pharaonic Egypt. For the philoso-
pher-scientist-artist, the object of pursuit is a cosmic
knowledge, a knowledge of the world-as-a-whole, and of the
detail of its becoming. Its subject, however, remains the self.
I have often been hopelessly baffled when examining what art
might represent, and what the relationship might be of that
representation to the original *presentation*. Do we represent
what we see? Or what we know? Or what *is*? Questions of
this sort, when they do not play foremost in the painter's
working mind, are nevertheless implicit in his every working
gesture. In our day, a lack of consensus in the discipline may

be ascertained by the diversity of wagers placed within a large spectrum of possibilities, from nonrepresentation to the most arid and naïve forms of realism.

In the lowlands of Flanders, in the medieval relic of Bruges where I had installed a studio, the questioning made its breakthrough for me. The year was 1958, and I had behind me an intense fourteen years of painting, and thus a steady involvement with these concerns, vague as they might have been in their formulation. The breakthrough took the form of a "logical structure," which I noted down without further research.[1] Problems I had been facing in art revealed their broader implications and a more direct expression in *functional* terms.

That structure of functions presented itself to me as a logical notation of the breakthrough experience; it dealt with knowledge and method, and with the relation between them. As the breakthrough experience steps into the unknown, knowledge must precede method, and the use of method in a search for knowledge never leads to that crucial step. A "method" then, by necessity a syntactic arrangement of knowledge, can at best only express such knowledge in view of its communication. Under those conditions, an intellectual "search for knowledge" begs the question.

Next I attempted to prove the temper of my text by a reading that would *communicate* the experience of breakthrough. The latter would be engendered in my reader and its knowledge could thus be shared. Here every attempt ended in failure and mortification. The content of the piece, a structure of functions and a briefly explanatory syntax in the French language, seemed to escape every one of my readers. It appeared to me as if they hardly even tried, absorbed as they were with irrelevant mathematical or metaphysical interpretations, referring the text to Whitehead, for instance, or to Spinoza, neither of whom I had studied at the time. As I knew the effectiveness of the text by experience, and doubted neither the intelligence nor the erudition of my readers, I could only fault the reading. I concluded that it was indispensable for a theory of language to precede the text. The prospective reader had to be alerted to the existence of such considerations be-

fore he undertook his reading. As a measure of my disappointment, I note that not once after perusing the brief essay (a
mere six pages!) did a reader turn to me with a comment such
as: "Now that I know what is in it, I must read it again."
Reactions pointed to a superficial reading which elicits no
more than the facts of language and exhausts itself in pure
terminology. This exercise failed not only to produce the experience of breakthrough, but any other as well, as the empty
responses showed all too plainly.

Before I could even start work on a theory of language, the
contact I had been searching for was established. It must be
clear by now that my text meant to be vividly experiential
and that no dry incursion into mathematical philosophy was
intended. True, it had been abstracted by a hygiene of language, but only in order to reach the backbone of a live event,
not of a philosophical position. De Lubicz and the actuality
of our encounter proved to me the justice of my intuition.
Only the energy generated by the breakthrough my text described could have made this contact. The blind necessity of
it lacked all method, yet moved knowingly in obscured territory. That is because the "unknown" is the "known" that has
been forgotten. The transition from unknown to known is
therefore always accompanied by the surprise of recognition,
and sometimes by amazement.

My text had proved itself by the events; to obtain a conclu-
sive *reading*, I would yet have to wait for two more years and
for a change of venue. All these events, however, bear telling
in sequence and detail, and I shall begin with the intermediary in my meeting with Aor. The task fell upon an American
poet and bohemian of our generation, whose acquaintance we
made in a Brussels bookstore. It came to light that George
Andrews knew some friends of ours, indeed including my
wife Goldian's first husband, Philip Lamantia, a San Francisco
poet of some renown.

Much could be said at this time not only about George and
our relationship with him, but also of Goldian, my life's companion and indispensable partner in all my enterprises; but as
my title shows, autobiography is here only tangential, albeit

importantly so. Because of that importance, great care must be taken that it not be abused. People and events are introduced only to further my title, and only to the extent to which they assist in that aim. Relationships outside of that framework must wait for a broader format.

At this initial juncture, both Goldian and George are indispensable. I believe it was Goldian to whom George addressed himself. It is doubtful whether any contact would have been made had I been alone. And if so, it would most likely have been contained within the limits of some pleasantries between compatriots in a foreign land. Such is the complementary nature of our characters, Goldian's and mine.

As it was, with friends in common, we talked about books and people, and we exchanged addresses. Before we parted, George offered to lend me a book he was carrying under his arm: *Du Symbole et de la Symbolique,* by R.A. Schwaller de Lubicz.[2] The author was unknown to me, yet later that day, back home in our living room in Bruges when I opened the book, the voice I heard was certainly no stranger. I was particularly struck by the relevance to me of the very first paragraph of the foreword, where the author speaks of two ways of reading and studying "traditional initiatic" texts: the one examines the *exoteric* sense, while the other takes into consideration an *esoteric* meaning. As I was at that time realizing the necessity for a theory of language, I was delighted to feel here a similar need expressing itself in what could be qualified as a "reading lesson." Certainly such a lesson had to be part of a larger theory of language. And I recalled the brilliant Gaston Bachelard, whose lectures I followed in the years after World War II, at the *Collège Philosophique.* They were held evenings in St. Germain-des-Prés; I was at the time a young art student in Paris. Bachelard extolled the merits of *la lecture lente,* a slow dialectic between concept and image; he was also an assiduous reader and interpreter of early scientific texts. And indeed, as in a first approach I skimmed through de Lubicz's book, I noticed a reference to Bachelard's *Nouvel Esprit Scientifique,* published in 1934, when it drew epistemological conclusions from the latest work in physics, a topic which by 1958 had already covered much ground.

Before I return to the details of de Lubicz's first paragraph, I should say that the book had been published in Cairo in 1951. I learned later from the author that the edition had been entirely destroyed during the Cairo riots of that year, and that only a dozen or so copies had survived. How had George Andrews obtained his copy? It had been lent to him by a Belgian Maecenas, Count Philippe d'Arschot, who was visiting Cairo at the time the book came out, met de Lubicz, and obtained a copy from him.

I recognized the idea of a text's double reading as a theoretical statement on written language and was therefore all the more dismayed by the abominable syntax which conveyed the message. Albeit tortured into prose, the gist of that message (though not the detail of its presentation) was yet beautifully close to' my most urgent preoccupation.[3] The exoteric reading is qualified as "historical" and can ("in a general way") be used as a basic foundation of the esoteric meaning. According to the author, it thus becomes a *symbol* for the esoteric meaning, the latter being expressed by the *symbolique*. This esoteric sense could not be transmitted without the exoteric level of comprehension, because it would appear as nonsense to "the multitude," whereas the exoteric sense will present an imaged story or even history, and will be interesting, comprehensible, and thus transmittable. One could conclude (although this is merely implied) that the uninitiated "common people" through the ages will have "peddled" a knowledge that was passing them by.

Particularly striking, and bearing directly on the main theme according to the title of the work, is the clear separation of "symbol," which belongs to the exoteric aspect of the text, and "la symbolique," which expresses the esoteric meaning. This alerts us to the author's personal definition of these terms, so that what de Lubicz means with "la symbolique" can manifestly not be conceived through the term "the symbolic." Far from being a general theory of symbols, the symbolique exists on a level of "reading" which uses symbols merely as support. It does not share its esoteric meaning with the sense that transpires (naturally and with ease so as to be accessible to the many) from the exoteric aggregate of those same symbols. The symbolique is not an extension of the study of symbols; it is a separate language which uses the same symbolic alphabet. The unspoken nature of this language is brought out at the end of the foreword. Hieroglyphs, the silent signs, are a *writing* which uses symbol in order to lead us to the symbolique.

This scheme seemed to echo my differentiation of term and word, with a universe of vocabulary, syntax, and grammar on the one hand (de Lubicz's exoteric sense of the text), and on the other a universe of words where meaning can find its due. Here too, the terminology (the symbolic level in de Lubicz) acted as support for the essential reading which flowered in the words. Here too, one level of reading was generally accessible, and it therefore guaranteed communication. Once this was gained, the "higher" reading became possible.

It is pointed out, furthermore, that the symbol is a sign the reading of which must be *learned*, while the symbolique is a writing the laws of which must be *known*. This again fairly echoes my contention that terminology, the grammar and syntax of language, taught in public schools and accessible to all, guarantees a basic modicum of communication. As to a second reading which would involve a special knowledge (my breakthrough experience), it seemed to fall under the same type of interdict I expressed in my paper on implicit functions: the impossibility of being reached by method. There seemed to be a confirmation of this in de Lubicz's assertion of a symbolique that writes a message accessible only to the few in a writing the laws of which are not learned, but known. This is manifestly a knowledge not preceded by a method, i.e., it is an implicit function such as I defined it in my text.

It is easy to imagine the excitement which de Lubicz's foreword had in store for me. In a way, I was being offered the experimental proof for a "logical structure" I had devised several months earlier: a "theoretical physicist's" dream!

But much more importantly, even a cursory reading of de

Lubicz's pages convinced me that the elusive contact I had been searching for was now at hand. With considerable naïveté I assumed that this author could not but appreciate my essay; he would evidently also have a good many things to tell me. I turned out to be right only in the latter assumption; by then, however, the disappointment of the former no longer mattered.

I sensed a strong basic agreement with the author, and this feeling by far outweighed an equally basic difference in mentalities which from the start became apparent as well. One focus of discussion throughout our future relationship showed itself soon in that portentous foreword: the meaning conveyed by the symbolique was called a *secret* sense, while the somewhat shocking and perhaps childish aspects of "secrecy" were tempered in a parallel with contemporary scientific disciplines. Here also a restricted elite alone has intellectual access to powerful theories and techniques which are virtually holding the general population hostage. De Lubicz then casts this theoretical baggage as scriptures of a "false temple," a "false religion" of materialism.

At the time, before having met Aor, this parallel between Pharaonic Egypt and contemporary science (which is explicated as a contrast between an ancient "constructive and liberating science, a science of genesis" on the one hand, and a "purely rational and analytic science of violent destruction" on the other) struck me as excessively imaged. I was well aware of a possible esoteric sense expressed in the great religious texts of all ages, having long ago abandoned the posture of the hard-nosed (and unexamined!) antireligious atheism of my upbringing.[4] After World War II and the arrival of the Atomic Age, I had given considerable thought to the spiritual possibilities of a non-Newtonian universe such as it was revealed in the works of Einstein, de Broglie, Heisenberg and other physicists with whose world-shaking ideas I had a layman's acquaintance. It had been J. Robert Oppenheimer's much publicized experience that discoveries in the intimate constitution of matter were in some ways congruent with a profound reading of certain religious texts.

But I had always thought the aim of an esoteric meaning in such texts to be psycho-spiritual, and certainly not scientific. The notion that Egyptian hieroglyphs could be relevant *qua scientia* to our scientific establishment was a twist that begged to be documented and confirmed. Discovery of advanced scientific formulae in Pharaonic papyri would at that time have struck me as a good piece of esoteric fiction had it not been for the compellingly, almost primordially authoritative tone of the proposition. This was not written by a writer, a scientist, an Egyptologist, nor by a visionary mystic, but by a judicious mixture of all four.

Scientific rather than mythological content in Pharaonic texts! A remarkable hypothesis, certainly, yet at that time somewhat removed from the main avenue of my preoccupations. Hieroglyphics had never been a subject that drew my attention, and I was for the moment deeply immersed in readings on non-Aristotelian logic. The connection did not strike me then and there; it became compelling only after I had talked to de Lubicz.

Equating the inaccessibility of highly specialized scientific theory with a secret reading in Pharaonic hieroglyphs seemed a specious argument; on the other hand, I wholeheartedly applauded the author's low regard for modern technology, a point of view which only infrequently found its way into print in those years. The reading set me thinking about such topics as *the secret*, the notion of inaccessibility, the unknown. And I could not help thinking about my own text, and what a secret it turned out to be! Its several pseudo-readings had shown it to be quite unapproachable, and even had I nailed the pages to the church door on Sunday, my secret probably would have remained intact. Yet the experience it related, which had afforded me such radical insights and which manifestly had the power to effect change in the living molecular world, I considered of importance at least equal to what could be gotten from dusty Pharaonic papyri, whatever their archaeological value.

As I will eventually be asked to come to more specific terms with my breakthrough experience, I want to avoid the appearance of shirking this task. However, any question on the subject must first be referred to the precise map of the latter which I drew up in *Knowledge and Implicit Functions.* It is only a map, of course, but it is precise as such, and it does the job demanded of any good map: if followed attentively and faithfully, it will inevitably lead to the objective. Errors frequently occur, but it is never the map's fault when we lose our way; it is always human failure.

Beyond the map (and I certainly will be pressed to go beyond), we travel by directives in a language that is mainly the sound of voices. The patter to which language is submitted in modern times has not diminished its potential, but it has eroded our sensitivity. "The *sound* of words has betrayed you," says Bernard de Trévise[5] at being misunderstood. The sound of words rings from the page as surely as from an interlocutor. The faithful map is discarded in favor of imperfectly structured terms and of words with floating extensions. Yet I shall grasp every opportunity in language for meaning and definition, and the notion of "secret" affords such a chance. The term belongs to basic vocabulary, and any English-speaking person comprehends what a secret is. The extension of the word is not quite so comfortable, however. Notwithstanding, I shall say the breakthrough is precisely that: the piercing of a secret. And the power of the experience makes it seem to be *the* secret.

Again, I will never say it better: the breakthrough reaches knowledge without the dubious benefits of method; it reaches knowledge directly, unlearningly. Such knowledge is concrete; it modifies the living being. For years, as a by-product, it allowed me to read any text providing the terms were defined (i.e., could be found in an adequate dictionary) and the laws of syntax rigorously observed. I read Russell and Whitehead's *Principia Mathematica* for the pleasure of it, Wittgenstein's works, Count Alfred Korzybski's *Science and Sanity,* as well as Einstein's early papers, all with enormous interest and relative ease, and mostly with the good feeling of knowing what was being discussed. The faculty deteriorated slowly, and finally disappeared some time after my text had been read and confirmed.[6] The energetic pitch would have been impossible to sustain for more than a time. But what I was able to contact in those years could take me lifetimes to digest. A breakthrough is not a definitive achievement; it is a long moment of lucidity. I further believe that there is generally only one major, life-directing breakthrough in a lifetime, and that such a one is amply sufficient.

Pondering my text's involuntary secrecy, I compared it to the two categories brought up by de Lubicz: the secret of the scientist, and the secret of the papyrus. The former struck me as a secrecy by default, seeing that the scientific disciplines were based on learnable methods that were actively taught; whatever knowledge was contained in that secret corresponded precisely and did not reach beyond a strict correspondence to that method. In fact, the very breakthrough that permitted my contact with de Lubicz also granted me access to the literature of physics, higher mathematics, and logic. The so-called secret of the scientific elite is merely based on public sloth. Ignorance does not displace knowledge in favor of secrecy; nor can it offer much security to "secrets."

The case of Pharaonic texts seemed somewhat different. The hidden component here was not tied to a public method that could be learned by intellectual effort. The laws governing symbols as "signs we must learn to read" have been studied since Champollion. In contrast, the symbolique, as carrier of the secret, functions according to laws that must be *known*, de Lubicz says, implying that no method of learning helps us here.

I found myself in an intermediate position: I shared with the scientific secret (which turns out to be no secret at all but only a qualified inaccessibility) a willingness, or better, a desire quite contrary to secrecy, a desire for communication; but the subject of my communication concerned a methodless approach to knowledge which apparently had much in common with a reading of the symbolique according to de Lubicz, who called it "secret." My stance between those two was logically untenable. It was a case of saying: "Unless the content of the text is already known, the text is unreadable, as the text is the key to reading the text. *Petitio Principii!* Or, in Louis Armstrong's words: "If you have to ask, you'll never get to know."

Although scientific and hieroglyphic "secrecy" seem to be quite different species, the limited accessibility of neither one nor the other results from dissimulated information. In both cases, the texts in question are generally available for public scrutiny, and the reading is merely a matter of the reader's capability. Having worked in communications for army intelligence in World War II, I remained interested in problems of coding and decipherment. I am well aware that every cipher has its breaking point. Furthermore, no secret can depend on physical concealment; the secrecy of a written message always depends on a cipher, never on a hidden manuscript. A secret survives because it can defy public scrutiny; only meaning *remains* hidden. Nothing is more public than the natural phenomenon, and yet all sides empathize with the notion of a "secret of nature."

Another conundrum I reflected upon was the "double reading" in de Lubicz and its relationship to my conviction that all texts had to be read *twice,* once for the terms, and then for the words. The obvious difference in conception here was that my readings were horizontal, so to speak, as the second had to follow the first in time; the reading of the symbolique on the other hand, although depending on the symbols, seemed to elicit a meaning independent of the reading of the symbols themselves. One reading in time seems sufficient. Either the symbols *per se* were read, in ignorance of any other kind of reading; or one read the symbolique by means of the same symbols, and one presumably did not return for a "lesser reading" (exoteric, historic). Here the two readings were stacked vertically, and there was a choice between high road and low: except that there was choice only for him who knew, and he would presumably read the symbolique and not the pretext. The reading of the symbolique somehow took place directly by gazing at the symbols; it bypassed the obvious exoteric use of the graphic symbols altogether. How was this possible?

Entirely motivated at the time by the breakthrough experi-

ence and its subsequent functional "encoding" to show an
incompatibility between knowledge and method, my interest
alighted quite naturally on this unmethodical reading experience de Lubicz called "the symbolique," which precluded any
and all learning, all theories, all models, in order to present
an absolutely pure knowledge, a knowledge necessarily *a
priori*. While my experience was limited to one and only one
way in which this could be achieved (the breakthrough into
the unknown which had been preoccupying me), I was aware
of speculations concerning an inborn consciousness, a raw
fabric with which the life experience weaves a tapestry of
knowledge.[7] This was the first time, however, that I encountered this "heredity" as an invaluable and complete gnosis,
sole object of the spiritual seeker. It based itself furthermore
on concrete physical ground through very convincing biological evidence in the genesis of natural form. Gone was the fear
of atavistic chains which other teachings might endeavor to
break, finding the freedom from slavery of the past in flight
from physical phenomena. The value of the extremes of concreteness and abstraction that manifested itself here would
become fully clear later. But I sensed already the totality of
the thought that marks it as philosophical cosmology.

⊖

I have given considerable time to this topic even before
introducing de Lubicz in person, nay, even before I finish his
book, in my Bruges living room, where I have just read the
foreword. More is said about the symbolique later in the book,
more is said about the "secret" in other books, and for that
matter, entire afternoons were spent on these subjects in tête-
à-tête. A thorough presentation thereof is not intended here.
Rather, I am preparing to relate a meeting soon to ensue with
the author, and am recalling my first contact with one of the
notions that were to prove so important in our dialogues. For
it is essential that I unravel the antecedents of my entry into
this esoteric sphere, as I was an unlikely candidate where

others either lacked interest or were rebuked. Intellectual curiosity would not easily be stirred by an offering such as the book I was presently reading. My own feelings concerning it were quite mixed. The discussion of contemporary science seemed naïve even in 1951, and I had encountered other and more successful applications of nuclear physics to esoterism and psycho-spirituality.[8] There were also overtones of the kind of mysticism which I usually avoid. But behind it all was the voice of authority I have mentioned, and as soon as I had read the five pages of the foreword, I picked up the telephone and called my newfound friend George Andrews to ask him: "Who is R.A. Schwaller de Lubicz?" He told me about d'Arschot's encounter in Cairo. De Lubicz was now living in Southern France. As I mentioned my interest in meeting the author, he told me that he himself was preparing just such a trip. He said that he intended to study with de Lubicz, that we could go together, and that he, George, was coming to Bruges to discuss the matter.

The idea of "studying with" had not come to my mind. What would one study with this man? Hieroglyphs? The "secret"? I wanted to talk to him about a "logical structure" that could communicate a breakthrough. As this breakthrough was obviously what it took to unseal the "secret," he should be most interested in my paper. The possibility never occurred to me that I, through my experience of breakthrough, would make an interesting sounding board for *his* ideas of symbolique. I wanted to meet him in order to communicate myself to him. I eventually stayed to have him communicate himself to me.

I now submitted de Lubicz's book to a thorough scrutiny, and by the time George arrived, my decision was firm. What hid behind the somewhat dubious prose[9] was important enough to warrant a careful approach, and this would be quite impossible if we went together. George is a visionary poet whose exalted ideas and bohemian demeanor would effectively block my access, I felt. It was decided that George was to go first and see what he could achieve. I would go at some later date.

George called me from Brussels soon afterward to announce his departure. Not having heard from him again for several weeks, Goldian and I left for Grasse in the Alpes-Maritimes, where we arrived on a sunny September afternoon.

At the Grasse post office, we were informed that Monsieur de Lubicz lived with Doctor Lamy in nearby Plan-de-Grasse, on the road to Cannes. I do not recall if we telephoned or simply drove to the residence. When we arrived at Lou-Mas-de-Coucagno, as the majestic country estate was named, and our car entered the tree-lined driveway, I had the fleeting impression that Doctor Lamy might be directing a sanatorium here. A uniformed servant ushered us into a small salon, and it was here, after a short wait, that we witnessed the appearance of Isha Schwaller de Lubicz from behind the heavy curtain that formed one side of the room. With her sleek black hair, her olive complexion and protruding eyes, she brought with her a distinct touch of the Middle East. She wore flowing white robes, heavy earrings, rings and necklaces, and about her there floated an air of gypsy fortune-teller.

After introducing myself, I explained that I had read Monsieur de Lubicz's book and had been struck by his ideas, and that I would be very honored to make his acquaintance.

"I must tell you," she said rather abruptly, "no one works with my husband except myself. I am his only disciple."

I hastened to make clear that such was not my intention and that I merely wanted to discuss with him some aspects of his book. I knew by her reaction that George had been there and gone, and thought it better to bring up his visit, but she saved me the trouble by doing so herself.

"Are you connected with a young American who came by here a few days ago?" she asked, her deep voice edged with suspicion.

"I met Mr. Andrews very recently and it is thanks to him that I became aware of your husband's writings," I replied. "For this I am grateful to him. I knew he was coming here, but preferred to make a separate visit by myself."

⊖

Only when I became familiar with the life of this household could I appreciate what an extraordinary occurrence these two visits by two Americans within two weeks or so must have represented. At the time, de Lubicz and his work were practically unknown. For the year and a half I was to spend here in close proximity, I recall only two occasions when he received visitors. Isha was more widely known through her book of psycho-spiritual guidance and two volumes of fiction on the Pharaonic theme. *L'Ouverture du Chemin* [10] is rather more successful than the run-of-the-mill psychic-aid genre. It is a psychologizing of abstract ideas, a technique Aor abhorred, as I was later relieved to discover. I myself have always had an aversion for this kind of interpretative endeavor. What saved Isha's venture was a strong organic consciousness that came mainly from Egypt. She had been studying Egypt even before Aor's interest developed in things Pharaonic, and she was an expert on the hieroglyphic alphabet. Her two *Her-Bak* [11] books are attractive; they fictionalize the childhood and adolescence of a peasant boy who became one of ancient Egypt's outstanding architects and sages. The relationship of Isha's work to Aor's, and the lack thereof in later years will occupy us further ahead. Isha played an important part in the Hermetic hierarchy of Aor's vision, though she played it practically unconsciously. They were far apart in their approach to Egypt, and Isha abandoned Egypt as a subject in her later work. She had returned to a contemporary psycho-spiritual context by the time we met her. Aor's scorn for the fictionalizing of the Hermetic Pharaonic subject matter (be it by Egyptologists or occultists) was too severe for her to face any longer. She tried, unsuccessfully to the end, to gain his support for the "witness" theory she had perfected in her later writings, using a fictional adaptation of the Ba and Ka theology to express herself. [12]

⊖

I do not recall what else was said at this our first meeting.
After a few minutes, she went to fetch her husband.

"*Cher Monsieur,*" I said when he entered the room, "I have
come to shake hands with the author of *Du Symbole et de la
Symbolique.*"

We settled down in some armchairs. We were all smoking
cigarettes.

"*Alors,*" he said, leaning forward and looking at me,
"*qu'est-ce donc qui vous occupe?*" *

I gave him a rapid sketch of the events that had brought me
to formulate the idea of nonmethodical knowledge and its
expression by means of the logic of functions.

"Forget about logic," was his reaction. "The answer is in
Pharaonic Egypt."

Then and there, I decided to do as bid, at least in his presence. From the very first, the atmosphere with him was cor-
dial. We were evidently making a good impression on both
Monsieur and Madame. Aor paid much attention to Goldian
whose French seemed to delight him. Isha, whom I instantly
had recognized as a fisher of souls, turned her full presence on
me and started to describe the book she had just finished, and
no, it was not about Egypt, but rather a sequel to the pre-
Pharaonic work. The book was titled *La Lumière du
Chemin.*[13] It did not matter that the conversation never returned to logic or to my structure of functions: I knew I had
not seen the last of this strange but pleasant couple.

When we got up to leave, there was a brief consultation
between our hosts, after which we were invited for lunch the
next day. Afterward, Monsieur added, we would have a look
at a book about Luxor which he had just published. Our entry
into the household had begun.

The next day, we were seated in the garden, at the edge of a
small park that had been established by Isha around a lotus
pond where papyrus grew. It was here that we met two other
members of the household, Isha's children from a former mar-

---

* "Well, then, what is it you are concerned with?"

riage: Doctor Jean Lamy, a respected obstetrician and inventor of Phonophoresis,[14] and Lucie Lamy, de Lubicz's devoted assistant. The servant who had answered the door that first day turned out to be Thérèse, the cook, and she now presented us with a superb meal. Later, Lucie brought down the three volumes of *Le Temple de l'Homme,* and I had a first and very cursory look at the book with which I would spend the next few years. De Lubicz tried to show us, by means of a volume of plates, why he had called Luxor "the Temple of Man." Such a demonstration is complex to begin with, and it sounded fairly disconnected, condensed into a half-hour exposé.

Though I had problems focusing on the Egyptological part of his discourse, ignorant as I was in that field, I followed him quite easily and with great interest whenever he broached philosophical or mythical domains. It was not the content of his ideas, but the workings of his mind that seemed to me so naturally straightforward and almost familiar in its simplicity. I had been prepared to meet an intellectual and scientist, but if he were one or the other, neither showed. He was a man of great authority and suitably opinionated, highly cultured yet delighting in the most superficial banter, and obviously hard at work on something he was keeping closely to himself. He was, furthermore, a typical bourgeois French gentleman. And he was a man of the right.

The European concept of "left and right" is based on a history of royalty and hereditary nobility. It cannot be understood in terms of American politics. It is as French as the Revolution, and while it is a metaphor to an American, it is reality to the French. The true right is monarchistic and theocratic; it desires authority, preferably divine, it believes in elites and in at least one absolute value, but sometimes in an entire pyramid of them. This standpoint could have much in its favor were it not for a propensity for demagogism, with fascism as its latest flowering. And while it is true that Stalin's communism is a similar blight on the left, I nevertheless have felt more sympathy with the latter side. Had fascism not intruded so brutally into my life, I would have been content to remain politically uninvolved. Only the left resisted fascism, however, and such resistance was a priority in my time. After the war and the illusion of a fascist defeat, I banned politics from my life as a dreadful waste of time. When saying therefore that I immediately sensed de Lubicz as *"un homme de droite,"* I should add that I merely registered the fact with indifference, as a minor identification tag. The French bourgeoisie is right wing and proud of it, and if other labels seemed risky, this one was certain: here was a nineteenth-century French bourgeois, with all the appealing qualities of that status, and with at least some of its inconveniences. My interest in him was in abstract realms, intellectual, philosophical, and logical, but the European "left and right" has the power to infiltrate them all.

I had little opportunity to speak to de Lubicz during the three or four meetings of our first contact. Isha was always present, and she monopolized me relentlessly. Aor furthermore seemed to prefer lighter conversation with Goldian, and they were getting on famously. I listened politely as Isha expounded on a variety of techniques of immortality with characteristic French facility. As my time with Andrew Da Passano had familiarized me with the vocabulary, I could have offered an opportunity for dialogue, but Isha was a teacher who wanted to teach from the bottom up. Not a shred of former knowledge was worthy of survival now that the disciple had tapped the true fount. She spoke openly and from the beginning of her spiritual vocation in the service of Aor's *oeuvre*, but she was also from the beginning a master of the incomplete pronouncement, trailing off in a whisper and a far-off gaze as if entering into contemplation. Much of her information was presented in allusion and innuendo, but always in a tone of such finality and self-confidence that one hardly dared to ask for further elucidation. The foreword to *Du Symbole et de la Symbolique* came to mind: Isha, with every move and expression, was playing the role of "keeper of a secret." And she had peremptorily cast me in the role of her disciple.

The few serious conversations I had with Aor at that time

put me entirely at ease. Although I knew little about Pharaonic myth or temples, and nothing at all about hieroglyphic writing, I felt a familiarity in his mode of thinking, a formal compatibility despite the strange context and vocabulary. So frustratingly absent in my exchanges with Paris intellectuals, the ease of communication here came as an exhilarating relief. At the same time I noted a reticence in him to expound his subject in depth, a frequent deflecting into lighter ground, and an evasive manner when faced with pertinent questions. I eventually overcame these hurdles by weeks of persistence, but in the social context of our first encounters, they effectively barred the possibility of an intellectual exchange such as I had hoped for.

So when we dropped by to say farewell on our way back to Bruges, and the possibility of another visit was discussed, it must have seemed to Isha that *she* was the magnet which might draw me back. In fact, as disappointing as this first encounter may have been from the point of view of my text and its communication, I already held the conviction that there was much to be discovered in this unusual household. We were at the time very mobile and unattached, and the switch from North Sea to Mediterranean presented obvious advantages. I believe my decision to make the move was firm then and there, although it was not until that evening that I could point to a single compelling reason.

We drove to Lyon and had a late lunch, after which I went to Derain's bookstore, depository for *Le Temple de l'Homme*, at that time generally unavailable elsewhere. The same evening at the hotel, I started to cut the pages and was amazed to find that out of the massive first volume's 750 pages, more than half had to do with geometry or geometric measure. The rest was in large part medical and anatomic, and there was an introductory section defining a number of philosophical terms and positions. All of it seemed of great import, but it was the geometric part that captivated me. To my recollection, geometry had not been mentioned the last few days. Or had it? Had I heard Isha mention something like:

"Vous savez, cher Monsieur, Aor est un grand géomètre!"

If so, this fragment had gone to join a vague conglomerate of data I had been bombarded with. My concern with mathematical language, to the extent that it existed at all, was functionally algebraic, and meant to be no more than a notation of basic logical relationships. What did it mean, for a man like de Lubicz, and in today's non-Euclidian climate, to be a great geometer? I was to find out.

Under the guise of an exposé of the foundations of Pharaonic mathematics, I was confronted with a cosmogonic theory of number of exceptional cohesion and expressiveness. And as I read into the night, it was a constant recognizing, like vistas onto a well-known but forgotten landscape. The feeling of simplicity and justice that emanated from this concept of number and figuration made it one of the great reading experiences of my life. It could have been a treatise on self-evidence. The text did not *teach* me what it said; I *knew* what it said, as any unencumbered, any *primitive* mind would know. We spoke the same language, and we were describing the same things.

$$\ominus$$

As soon as Goldian and I were back in Bruges, I informed the de Lubiczs of our decision to accept their suggestion that we move to Grasse in order to be in their proximity. Though I should perhaps already have known better, I also addressed a copy of *Knowledge and Implicit Functions* in a separate envelope to Monsieur. I received the following reply, which I translate:

Dear Sir,

This is the first time I have had the opportunity to see the search for Knowledge in its mathematical form. I thank you very much. Actually, there only remains for you to find the "form" in order to establish Knowledge Y-André according to the method X-André, with which I am evidently not acquainted. How can I assist you in this search? But perhaps you reject the teaching of the Sages of all times, Art and Nature, and prefer to opt for the form "f" of an algebraic equation?

In this case I would have much to learn from you and I regret that my old teachers, having come too early, never had the opportunity to acquaint themselves with this path, as well as with the new mathematical thinking of our atomists, by the way.

I would be grateful if you could define the term "Knowledge" [Connaissance] which you use! Are you not rather referring to "learning" [savoir] with that word?

Frankly, as far as I am concerned, I leave the "learning" [savoir] to encyclopedias in order not to burden myself, and I attribute to "Knowledge" [Connaissance] quite a different meaning than "learning" [savoir].

But if you mean by Y-Knowledge the same thing I do, then, pray continue your algebraic development, and perhaps you will find a series which, like Einstein's universe, will be an infinity closed upon itself.

Then we shall be going round and round together on the merry-go-round.

Meanwhile, please thank Madame Goldian for the beautiful postcard she sent Isha, and compliment her for her enormous progress in French. I believe Isha will write to you herself in the near future.

To both of you my best regards [the following handwritten] and take this letter as I would have *spoken* it to you, had you been here: with a smile.

I immediately tried to clear up the obvious imbroglio, cursing myself for my lack of judgment, my blind confidence in being understood. In a brief page I attempted to explain what was nowhere more precisely set down into language than in the very pages he must have been reading then. No other arrangement of words could ever be as precise. Communication along this line seemed out of the question: the best option was to make the incident disappear. It is difficult to evaluate the extent to which I succeeded. As I later proved my understanding of his position to be more accurate than that of anyone he was currently in contact with, he must have felt my text to have been a point of view superseded by his own. This was never the case, as I never felt any conflict between the two positions; the difference in my mind was a matter of terminology and theory of language. A difference of generation, also, close to two generations; almost a difference of century, by that fact.

For some time it appeared difficult to accept that a mind concerned with ordered sequences syntactically expressed by hieroglyphic or natural language, a mind well aware of the difficulties of meaning, heavily involved in hermeneutics, symbols, and signs, that such a mind would nevertheless sustain a position of alienation from a logical point of view. The necessity of a Pythagorean, let alone a Pharaonic logic did not strike him as evident, and he maintained Pythagorean theory of number (with which, to my mind, he worked constantly) to be a contradiction in terms. He put great stock in the spoken word (in spite of himself, he was influenced by the interest of his time in word-cabala), but none in terminology, none in structure. To me, the structure of signs by which we ultimately had to communicate (and what else was that monument of *Le Temple de l'Homme?*) was a major concern as a meeting ground of a common experience. If this were to stand in our way, the obstacle was minor. There is no better learning system than to adopt new terminologies. I changed my terms, but never had to modify the structure. And I never altered my conviction that language, if it held the power we credit it with when we entrust the best of our knowledge to syntactics—an order which includes all natural concatenations—deserves to be treated as the vehicle it is, and not as a thing in itself. To be avoided is the limiting of language so that it ends up speaking exclusively about itself. Although such subjects were not among our common concerns, I know that on this point he could not disagree.

The effort to retrace my *faux pas* failed entirely, as it had to. In return there came pleasant handwritten advice about leaving "algebraic expressions," and looking toward ancient Egypt, rather, with its arithmetic as example.

I had just pulled through a passionate involvement with non-Aristotelian logic and could not discount the stupendous letter-magic with which a nineteenth-century French occult-ist looks upon the term "Connaissance," as I was incapable of realizing that upper-case Knowledge implied more or higher knowledge than lower-case. Even had I had at my dis-posal a well-formed theory of language, it would yet have been impossible to entertain a dialogue along such lines. Here was not only a nineteenth-century man, but also one who would insist on having seen the light in Pharaonic Egypt. It was too early yet for me to appreciate fully the isolation of his position.

What could not come to the fore at that time, nor at any other as it turned out, was the instrumentality of my text to our meeting. Yet to me the events that were so irresistibly unrolling here were within the continuum of my text. The structure that had come to me was now offering me a physical proof of its validity. In my reply to his well-meant, but limit-ing sarcasm, I briefly tried to communicate to him my convic-tion that without the text which he rejected, contact with him would have been out of the question: it was the experi-ence of the text that made our contact possible. Barely two months earlier, before my text, I was a full-time painter and too occupied with my work to have allowed an involvement of this magnitude. The inevitability of the circumstances, the tempo with which events coalesced seemed to prove the power of the model. The very fact of my formulation taking a stance diametrically opposed to his expression, while sub-stantially and recognizably remaining of a very similar tone, seemed to confirm rather than invalidate the analogy of our experience.

Just as revelation is not found by reasoning in de Lubicz's terminology,[15] so knowledge is unattainable by method in my own argument. Only a man who writes from a position of breakthrough, furthermore, would structure his ideas in the particular way that had got to me so directly. As my text shows, it was gratis that I knew what I knew, without paying

the price of method, as a given something which he called
"Connaissance." I couldn't quarrel with the term, having
used it (though uncapitalized) in my paper, as the most concise description of my experience. Only through "implicit
functions" could this knowledge be achieved. And yet, although holding functional knowledge alone to yield a world
of causes, de Lubicz failed to recognize my language. The
reason for this lack of contact holds no mystery: he did not
believe in language. Yet it is through language, both his and
mine, that I discovered him. Had I not created a language for
my own experience, I would have been lacking a structure
which alone could consolidate the realization. Without language, I might have been a mystic, a seer, a prophet perhaps,
but also and most probably, an incoherent vagabond, a bohemian at best, and not even an artist. My vision superseded
art; it made the creative activity in the material medium
quite obsolete. From its position as a foremost instrument of
knowledge in the West during five centuries, art opened the
way to a broader vision. Art itself tries to prove this fact; it
attempts to transcend its medium in order to assert its vital-
ity. Circumstances which have caused the obsolescence of
this tool (circumstances we may have discussed and which
might surface in my notes, but do not bear directly on our
subject) have in our day reduced it to the natural instrument
of life's everyday occupations, be it manual labor, business,
commerce or medicine; true dedication elevates all of the
above to an art form in today's definition: art is a career like
any other, and knowledge usually a minor concern. There are
exceptions, of course, by definition not distinguished through
their visibility. The point is of some import, as the Hermetic
manipulation is itself an art, *Ars Magna,* and Aor considered
and felt it as such. In a time of commercialization of the
artistic temperament, only the Hermetic arts have remained
an instrument of knowledge. The adolescent false start in
Matisse's studio cannot be discounted in a man who felt himself an artist first, a symbolist second. From this frame of
mind steeped in art and philosophy, the cosmological inquiry
proceeds as from evidence.

2

We move to Grasse.—Metaphysical conjectures.
—Aor for the sixties.—"Vive la différence!"
—Le Plan des Anciens.—An alchemical
household.—Lucie.—Wagnerian soirées.
—First private interview.—Like the Fool from
the Tarot.—An absolutely concrete abstraction.

Isha put us in touch with realtors, and within a few weeks, we were settled in a two-room apartment outside of Grasse, on the steeply winding Route Napoléon. We were asked to lunch frequently, and were always welcome for tea. Aor was visible only at mealtime; he would appear a half hour before lunch and tea. During that half hour, he and I promenaded up and down an alley bordering the vegetable gardens, called "l'Allée des Philosophes." During the first two or three weeks, this was the only time at which I was able to talk to Aor alone. We mainly discussed questions raised by my reading of the *Temple*. My text came up briefly; I thought it best to treat it laughingly, as if it had been a childhood prank. He admitted he had taken one look and tossed it in the wastepaper basket. It was never mentioned again. I had decided to put my past concerns aside for the moment and learn what could be learned in my present situation.

It was in connection with this "Allée des Philosophes" that I first heard the name of Fulcanelli. The path, Isha explained, received its name because her husband had walked up and down it with Fulcanelli.

"Vous ne connaissez pas Fulcanelli, l'auteur du Mystère des Cathédrales?" [1] Aor asked with some surprise. I had never heard of the book, and he did not further comment on it; I asked no questions, being too absorbed in geometric concerns at that time to become deflected in other directions. I was also giving Aor's book a belated proofreading, having discovered a major error in the text. The error pertained to the basic laws of harmony: whereas a string vibrates twice as fast at half its length, the text maintained that the ratio was not 2:1, but 2^2 or 4:1. A string vibrating at 16 vibrations per second was said to vibrate at 64 at half its length, when in fact it vibrates at 32. [2]

My early involvement with music had familiarized me with the laws of harmony, and I had later done some work on musical intervals and the simple ratios of string length to which they correspond. I had in fact given a series of lectures on the constitution of the diatonic scale and the octave. [3] The error leaped at me from the page, and I mentioned it to Aor the next day. Lucie brought the book and opened it on the dining room table to the page I indicated. I recall Aor's first reaction. *"Ah, en effet, c'est une erreur de frappe."* A second look showed him that the error could not be typographical, but was rather an unfortunate piece of misinformation that had worked its way through the entire paragraph. Any serious reader would have picked up the error; it became obvious to me that this book (which had come out but a year and a half earlier) had only been scanned, never studied. It seemed difficult to believe that such a crass and fundamental error, prejudicing the comprehension of all subsequent text concerned with the laws of harmony, would not have been brought to the author or publisher's attention had it been previously noticed by a reader.

My discovery of this error (and of many to come) had a twofold effect: it definitely focused Aor's attention on me and on what I was doing; it also sharpened my critical reading of his book, now fallen from the pedestal of infallibility. The error had shocked me by the negligence it implied, and resulted in spurring my alertness toward the ideas as well. But it also made me realize the important function of error as a tool of awareness. The mere assimilation of what we accept to be truth in no way carries the impact of discovered fallacy. The detection of error is an awakening, an emotional experience that inscribes the correction with special significance and permanence. It moved me to include in my *Philosophical Geometry* a self-contained error without consequences on subsequent text.[4] It is in fact a demonstration of three modes of error I have learned to distinguish: error of context or reference; error of conduct; and error of language. At that time in my discipleship, torn between critical mind and surrendering spirit, I was deeply impressed by the ubiquitous existence of error and what it implied. My concern did help me maintain a part of myself I was intent on safeguarding, whatever I would be shown here, or told. As a practical result of this development I came to be sharply on the lookout for mistakes and misrepresentations, knowing that falsification would truly prove my understanding.

There also existed in de Lubicz's ideas a gray zone of speculation where true and false did not apply: the devolution of mankind in general, for example, from giants who once walked the earth to a near-animal state being rapidly approached in the modern world and vowed to cataclysmic annihilation, while an evolving elite gathers all of human experience for a resurrection in spirituality; and the belief that this cycle has happened many times before. Metaphysical reflections, I felt, where much is allowed, and truth or falsehood hardly the question. Or the more directly historical contention that the Nile was a man-made river, formed by several confluents by means of vast earth works and directed into the Nile valley for the purpose of evolving a civilization of the One. Such ideas presented no problem whatsoever to me. I sensed even then what now is becoming a commonplace, the certainty that an anarchistic practice of mind brings discovery, in art, philosophy, and science.[5] But it was concerning the interpretation of number and proportion in the monuments of ancient Egypt that I had severe misgivings. Here, obtained by several units of measurement such as a variety of cubits, a fathom, and even the meter, dimensions were converted into expressions of functions such as *phi* and square root of two, as well as multiples and powers of such functions, and the interaction of these elements was scrutinized for mythical meaning presumably injected by the master builders.[6] While the basic proportions of major monuments undoubtedly are influenced by such measuring devices as diagonals to square and rectangles, geometric, arithmetic, and harmonic proportions as well as the Golden Mean, the search for their occurrence in the slightest details of architecture and their interpretation in terms of myth pose considerable problems of credibility. Although I quickly came to perceive Aor's extreme sensitivity to critical comments along these lines, I did balk at the analysis of one figuration, the *Bes* of Philae and his harp of numbers.[7] In an otherwise most interesting study of arc-shaped structures occurring at Luxor as well as at Philae, the figuration of "*Bes* playing the harp, engraved on the arc at Philae, calls attention to the relation between music (harmony), and the arcs."[8] In order to prove that the concept of harmony is indeed expressed by this figuration, a most contrived analysis pretends to show harmonic numbers allegedly expressed by the sculptured harp. After spending a good deal of time trying to elucidate this demonstration, I eventually told Aor that I didn't believe it made sense. He immediately agreed that this demonstration was a failure, told me not to waste my time on it, and explained that it had been a project of Clément Robichon, an architect and archaeologist attached to the French Institute of Oriental Archaeology in Cairo who had become interested in symbolist ideas and who is cited as one of Aor's collaborators in the preface of *Le Temple de l'Homme*. I didn't pursue the matter further, but felt that the inclusion of such all-out fantasy hardly helped the already controversial topic of reading intent into architecture and figurations.

And yet, despite my guarded attitude, I assimilated beliefs that I clung to for many years before being disabused. I will proffer but one example, because it hinges on a dangerous rigidity of mind that will occupy us later: the overriding desire to see metaphysical ideas reflected in nature and society. Thus Aor maintained that the number five, being the number of vegetative life, could never occur in the crystal formations of the mineral world. Only recently was my attention drawn to pyrites from the Italian island of Elba, hunks of mineral in perfect pentagono-dodecahedral form.

Still, I must state in conclusion of this topic, that notwithstanding some farfetched hypotheses, entirely justifiable in view of the conjectural nature of the subject, notwithstanding the propensity for readily interpreting architectonic proportions to the glory of cosmic law, I generally felt de Lubicz's thinking guided by principles that evoked resonances of truth and reality. In the realm of metaphysics, no other proofs were known to me at the time.

Over seventy errors, practically all of them discovered as a result of my reading, were gathered in the 1961 errata list which was added to the unsold volumes of the edition and sent to its known recipients and purchasers. My labors showed the extent of my dedication to his work, and I felt Aor's skepticism melt. I believe I built up in him the confidence that his work was readable *now* for a general, albeit limited public, more readable, perhaps, for this public I envisioned (and whose existence he was unaware of) than for the denizens of a materialistic Egyptology where it was dropping anchor for the moment. The book was reviewed from the latter point of view by "Cahiers du Sud,"[9] but the perfunctory treatment given to the most ready applications in the study of ancient Egypt (not to mention an expected lack of awareness of the entire Hermetic infrastructure) must have afforded him little solace. He frequently declared that fifty years were needed for him and his work to be understood, against my expressed conviction that a bridge could be built here and now between his views and a currently budding spirit whose time had come. The year was 1960, and it didn't take a weath-

erman to tell. I was certainly correct about the relevance of
the work of R.A. Schwaller de Lubicz to the sixties generation, but he may have been right about the transmission of
the Hermetic Aor whose existence dawned on me only much
later.

However, I was still unable to insure myself a larger portion
of his time. It seemed to be generally accepted that I was
Isha's disciple, for what to me could only be construed as a
preparatory stage. I could not rush this process, and I felt I
could not escape paying my dues to Isha. I decided to take
advantage of her knowledge of hieroglyphs, and under her
guidance, I plowed my way through Gardiner's *Egyptian
Grammar.* Experiencing firsthand the incredible conceit of
Anglo-Saxon syntactics fitted to an unknown world of formal
intuition seemed to be the slim reward of this exercise. In
fact, I felt myself confined to a probation period, a trial possibly aggravated by the paper I had sent, which visually must
have conjured the hated pursuits of symbolic logicians,
whereas its substance in fact interdicted the entire domain of
knowledge to any logical conduct.

Our involvement, Goldian's and mine, with the de Lubicz
household, had very rapidly settled into a daily routine. We
would come for lunch, after which Aor retired, and we would
be left with Isha. The dining room table would be cleared and
we would settle around it, Isha, Goldian and I. Isha wanted to
read to us from her as yet unpublished book, *La Lumière du
Chemin.* I had understood that she meant to read excerpts, or
perhaps a chapter or two, but she ended up reading the entire
book to us. This must have taken two or even three weeks, as
there was much explanatory interjection from our deep-
voiced hostess. Halfway through, Goldian begged off, on the
pretext of her own work. Isha didn't mind, as I was her only
target. The relationship with the Mas-de-Coucagno had been
created by the needs of my breakthrough, and was riding on
the energy the latter had released. Perceptive as Isha was, she
could not have failed to notice my "illumination." Later, at
the time when I was working with him, Aor said to Goldian:
"Votre mari est un homme qui brûle." There was no doubt: *I*

and no one else had been chosen as disciple, almost without
having been aware of it. Totally unexpected was the fact that
Isha, not Aor, had taken over the teaching role.

There was no reason, then, for Goldian to interrupt her own
work. She came to lunch less frequently, and when she did,
would bring a book and sit in the garden, or spend some time
with Madame Robichon,[10] a member of the de Lubicz staff
among whose duties was the rebinding of books from Aor's
extensive library. And here we must let Goldian make her
bow and exit from the stage set by our title: her version of
these events will doubtless flesh out mine. Much could be
said about her relationship with Aor, one of respect and
friendship, but all of it must be said by her, and none of it
enters into the Hermetic, occult, political, or private aspects
of R.A. Schwaller de Lubicz. Her very gender barred her from
access, even if such had been her aim. For Aor firmly believed
in a constitutional impossibility of the female mind to handle
abstract concepts with the extreme rigor Hermetic philosophy demands. He made no excuses for this contention, nor
did he recognize exceptions. Isha, who had absolutely no contact with geometry, for instance, sustained him fully and sin-
cerely.[11] Male and female, from a functional point of view,
were as irrevocably different as sun and moon, and, cosmolog-
ically speaking: *"Vive la différence!"* The female function as
it relates to the Hermetic Aor has been treated only very
cursorily in any writings of his. Isha had expressed the female
point of view in her work ever since the early twenties. It may
be noteworthy that we have reached this Hermetic Aor
through his ideas on femininity.

Isha had finished reading her book to me and our daily
sessions were now spent in offering me an insight into her
and Aor's lives and accomplishments, *". . . afin que vous
sachiez qui nous sommes."* She told me about their meeting
which had been a mystic reunion. His call had come to her in
meditation, and although he was unknown to her at the time,
she was guided to him telepathically, as I understood it. Her
husband had raised no objections; with her children, she went

to live with Aor and eventually became his wife. Aor did not
speak to her of his work for the first seven years, but thereafter she became his sole disciple.

Several times during her narrative, she had spoken of
"*l'oeuvre* d'Aor." Now she was telling me about her children,
Jean, the doctor, and Lucie. I knew little of the doctor, save
that his office was situated on the second floor of the house.
He sometimes took a hasty lunch with the family; he would
come late and leave before dessert. "In and out like a draft,"
Isha would say. And now, speaking about his childhood: "Jean
as a child always wanted to contribute to Aor's *oeuvre*."

"You mean Egypt?" I interjected. I tended to refrain from
asking questions, as the rather intimate topic made me uncomfortable. We had but recently met, and she knew next to
nothing about me beyond my personal presence. Yet she was
treating me like a long lost family member who had to be
filled in on the state of affairs past and present. Now I wanted
to know more about Aor's work.

"Aor's *oeuvre* is broader than Egypt. He was already past
fifty when he first met Egypt. But he will speak to you about
this himself when the time has come."

I learned that Aor had encountered Pharaonic Egypt quite
inadvertently. During the 1930s, the family spent much time
on a yacht which was equipped for the convenience of Aor's
work. He was at that time, according to Isha, studying medieval texts.

"You should know that Aor is an authority on the symbolism of cathedrals."

Cathedrals! This brought Fulcanelli to mind and I mentioned his name.

"Fulcanelli was a great manipulator, but only Aor had the
doctrine."

Suddenly we were talking about it. It did not come entirely
unexpectedly. There had been many allusions to an alternative science. Aor stood in violent opposition to the developments of nuclear physics, a rape of matter, according to him.
He was undoubtedly concerned with aspects of epistemology;
this much was clear to me since reading his *Du Symbole et*

de la Symbolique. But the incursions of our conversations into this field were always brief; terminology would invariably slide from scientific to Egyptological, from a science to a sacred science, and end up with Thoth. Myth for him had replaced logic.

Yet there was more, and from time to time it had surfaced, tangentially, elided, or merely implied. It was in connection with Fulcanelli that I first heard of *manipulations*, of a *practice* paired to theory, and I heard it from Isha. Later every word Isha told me would be confirmed in depth and elaborated in detail by Aor. It was at this moment, though, that the notion of Aor's *oeuvre* fell into place along with other notions such as alternative and sacred sciences, medieval texts, and now *manipulation* to bring me to the one inevitable and baffling conclusion: I was frequenting the house of an Alchemist.

⊖

With Isha, I began the study of Pharaonic Egypt from a symbolist point of view. I read the two volumes of *Her-Bak.* Aor assured me of Isha's insight into the interpretation of Pharaonic texts, and her unique understanding of the hieroglyphic alphabet. Isha herself gave me the details of the quasimystical experience to which this knowledge was tied. It came to her in two stages, two Christmas days a year apart, and she referred to it as *"Le Plan des Anciens."* This plan, map, or blueprint, or model (I never was able to pin Isha down on the *form*, beyond French syntax, which this revelation took) offered, among others, the possibility of placing a certain number of hieroglyphs into a meaningful *order*, thus creating a natural alphabet. The question interested me from a logical point of view, as the concatenation of elements into a natural system. But the matter was one of Isha's guarded secrets, secrets I soon came to recognize as carrots on a stick: secrets, yes, but possibly available (after adequate trials, of course) to the true believer. It is plain enough, however, that only fools would draw attention to the existence of what they truly want kept for themselves, and I thought it best, whenever Isha would bolster my flagging interest with the perspective of the secret *"plan,"* to confess my unwillingness to shoulder this responsibility. I declared myself untrustworthy with "secrets," undoubtedly because of my concern with truth, and because of the potential for a conflict of interests I felt between the two terms. She assured me that inside the Temple, where she was sure I belonged, the problem would vanish, as would contact with the uninitiated.

My tongue-in-cheek attitude was caused in no small way by her literary production, in particular by *La Lumière du Chemin*, which she had just read to us. It seemed aberrant for an author to hold in her hand a hitherto unknown key not only to hieroglyphic literature, but to the organization of the entire Pharaonic civilization (as the *Plan des Anciens* had been represented to me), and yet write esoteric fiction of the kind represented in Isha's latest books, which had lost all relationship to de Lubicz's work on ancient Egypt. Why was she not giving us dazzling versions of the Pyramid Texts, for instance; why had she ceased to work on Egypt altogether? The contradiction was simply too stark for me to swallow whole. I felt a degree of ever-so-gentle imposture here, a feeling I have frequently noticed in myself when in contact with psycho-spiritual circles.

Yet the folly of superimposing grammatical concepts from Indo-European languages onto a prelogical picture script is too plain to warrant discussion, and can in no way be exonerated. The discipline of Egyptology is a nineteenth-century construction and will eventually have to be refounded on non-Aristotelian grounds. This line of inquiry seemed germane to my subject, which I held to be somewhere between logic, decipherment, and hermeneutics. Aor himself had carefully steered clear of any received ideas concerning the hieroglyphic writing. His decipherment remained immediate, as it had been in the first encounter of re-cognition.[12]

Although I had my share of tribulations with Isha's approach, I was rapidly breaking through Aor's defenses with my work in geometry. Here the qualitative energy which had propelled my breakthrough in Bruges had found its field of exercise on the same flat surface that had preoccupied the painter in me all along, and the continuity of the two-dimensional universe as foundation of both art and geometry was not lost on me. But what a difference! Two differences, to be precise: the difference first between the geometry I was now discovering and anything I had encountered under the name of "geometry" in the past. Secondly, the difference between geometry and art, which I now understood in practice. My long-standing rejection of "geometric art" (a semantic disturbance at best) now found full justification. Esthetic pretensions are as foreign to pure geometry as is absolute measure. Plane geometry, like the three-dimensional world we live in, develops by its own interior laws in a natural manner, thwarting therefore all attempts at personal creativity. Imagination is banned, contemplation of evolving structure the only concern. This axiom-free geometry, to which years later I attempted a modest contribution under the name of *Philosophical Geometry*, had much in common, therefore, not only with the reading of glyphs as practiced by Aor, but with cognition in the contemplation of structure as mentioned in my text.[13]

The discovery of Aor's work as an alchemical *Practica* offered a major clue to our contact. I realized that he too was attempting to situate me in what was slowly revealing itself as a strict hierarchical structure. Studying the organization of the Pharaonic temple, I recognized the model. At its head, the enlightened priesthood: the perfect identity of science and theology, its main duties *cognition of the present moment*. I now reread the page where Aor defines this "Absolute from which we constantly draw our power."[14] It is an *absolution* from time that is guaranteed in the innermost Temple, a constancy we trace through thousands of years in Pharaonic Egypt, or *Al-Kemi*, and which persists even in this age of progress, in the era of valorized change.

This atemporal presence needs identity; it needs name, form, function. To this end, it inscribes itself into time as Pharaoh, a cartouche identifying the cosmic moment. The priesthood determines Pharaoh by its science of divine things, and it notes its scientific determinations in hieroglyphs, *mdw-ntr*, "staffs for gods to lean upon." Everything is relevant to the determination of the moment, not only the position of planets and stars, but every observable event in nature, every phase of plant growth, every instinctual act in the animal world and every meditation of man.

In the Temple, the scientist-priest has scribes as intellectual servants. At the Mas-de-Coucagno, Lucie was scribe. She had a room in a second-floor section to the rear of the house where Aor had his library, his laboratory, and a small bedroom. These quarters were quite separate from the main house and were reached by a narrow winding staircase. Lucie was Aor's creation to an extraordinary degree; he had formed her for her function since she was a child.

"Anything I have in my head, Lucie can get on paper," he would say. Once or twice he commented on the fact that no ideas ever originated with her. He has carefully traced the parameter of her contribution to his work by having her share the dedication of his last book, published the year of his death:

> To my stepdaughter
> Lucie Lamy
> this work which owes so much to her conscientious efforts in the gathering of texts as well as in the diagrams and illustrations.[15]

Conscientious work is all that is asked of the scribe in the Pharaonic temple.

"I did the entire geometry without drawing a figure. Lucie did all the paperwork."

He had instilled in her all he could of the knowledge that can be learned, but she was innocent of knowledge "that must be known." Master of method, versed in syntax, in grammar, in the exoteric symbols that will guarantee basic communication, and, most of all, a superb draftsman and copyist of Pharaonic figurations, she yet was oblivious of, and as if blind to the symbolique which she served. This in no way caused her unhappiness, as physical blindness might. She fully ac-

cepted the limitations of her position and those he ascribed
to her sex, as long as she was allowed to work on the tasks
which he proposed. Faded and wizened from years of taking
measurements on temples in the desert sun, she lived in total
disregard of her physical appearance, a vivid contrast to her
mother who always presented herself berobed, bejewelled,
and mascaraed. For Lucie, the physical hardly existed; it had
been all but suppressed.

⊖

Being better informed with regard to the nature of Aor's
work made for a fuller grasp of the sense of our meeting. As a
pursuit to advance my inquiry, needless to say, Al-Kemi had
been even more distant from my mind than Pharaonic Egypt,
but now that the larger picture unfolded, I saw that I could
not have found a more appropriate source. What I had encountered here was a contemporary synthesis of a line of thinking
to which I was able to subscribe without hesitation. It is
known as Pythagorean, and until de Lubicz, it had been trun-
cated in Greece. The powerful taproot of Al-Kemi, reaching
thousands of years into a fertile past, had remained buried
until de Lubicz recognized its nature. It would permit me to
justify hitherto unclassifiable fragments of my intellectual
and psychic life, awakening aspects that had lain dormant or
even been suppressed since childhood. Suppressed by political
events, for example, as was the case of my involvement with
Germanic mythology, a haunting presence since my earliest
reading days. One of the first books I ever read was given me
by an unremembered friend of the family, who did not know
me and thought me much older. It was called *Deutsche Hel-
densagen* and it was to become my main reading for years. A
thick illustrated volume, it was a compilation of Nordic mythology presented for younger readers. I never quite believed
my brother's disparaging remarks concerning the fictitious
nature of the material, nor did his "kid stuff" remarks discourage me in the least. Although I never entirely believed in
the historic reality of the events depicted (despite full-page

color illustrations apt to stimulate any child's imagination),nothing seemed more natural than to find some distant
forefathers in those giants who once walked the earth, and to
feel the present as a decadent and feeble shadow of the past.
Some years later, the rise of Nazism turned everything German odious to me, and I abandoned my heroes. But I believe
that even then I had divined behind the mythological fact a
reality of a different nature, not entirely unlike what I was
discovering now through de Lubicz's symbolique. German
mythology was replaced by Pharaonic myth, but de Lubicz, to
whom I never spoke of my early preoccupations, reestablished
a link. After a few months of our sojourn, he invited us to a
performance of Wagner's *Ring* by the Bayreuth Company to
be given at the Nice opera house over three evenings. This
rare social occasion was memorable, not least for the scenario
Aor had devised, which translated Wagner's libretto into
Pharaonic terms, and which we discussed on days preceding
the performance. The vision also remains of his tall straight
figure, in full evening regalia, standing, or rather looming,
over the fashionable crowd.

Incomprehension of classical mathematics, of the notion of
zero, and of the differential calculus were other problems of
long standing allayed by my introduction to Pythagorean science. Distaste for this basic tool of modern technology was
rooted in its cavalier treatment of what in my eyes was brash
inexactitude. The notion of a continually diminishing variable approaching zero as its limit—without truly recognizing
this limit—left me with a feeling of insecurity, almost anxiety. It seemed to me that this limit was a nothingness from
which nothing could be learned and about which nothing
could be told, and this fruitless regression toward a void, the
imprecision of a situation "approaching zero as limit,"—all
this was incredibly discouraging to me. I had somehow acquired a sense for exactitude in the domain of number (perhaps conveyed to me by my father who worked in the
financial field), and now had to cope with infinitesimals be-

yond measure and hovering at the edge of zero, with quantities too small to make a difference. Difference, even infinitesimal, was difference still. It looked to me like nothing less than an inaccuracy, invalidating whatever procedure might follow.

As another example of my peculiar relationship to academic and practical numbers, I recall a misfit that caused me much anguish in my early years, and that I truly understood only after encountering de Lubicz's work. The problem is much the same; or better, it is complementary to the above. It involves the reading of music, a skill I developed almost simultaneously with the ability to read books. It is very possible that my first significant counting experience may have been the counting of musical time, where the measure starts with a downbeat of "one." Now when I later learned to measure distances with a graded centimeter, I could not understand why the measure failed to start with "one," like the musical downbeat. This incomprehension was enhanced by the fact that the stick never had a name for that beginning, and I recall staring at the end of the centimeter, where a copper tab took the place of . . . nothing, for zero was never marked. How could it be, indeed, as it was nothing! My question, had I been able to formulate it: why was here zero in the beginning, and not one? Both the problem of measure and of oneness in the beginning was slated to occupy me after I encountered the ideas of de Lubicz and philosophical geometry, where the geometric grid was to arbitrate the feud of absolute beginning in a world of time. It had been impossible for me to conceive inexactitude, however infinitesimal, as the basis for true results. I had as yet not perceived epistemologically the cleft between fact and reality which so intrigues both science and theology. Now, having experienced the liberation of the geometric from the fetters of the algebraic mind, the cosmos took on the extension needed to accommodate my intuitive as well as intellectual aspirations. I have never found value in an algebraic universe, even if, *faute de mieux*, I used a functional equation to express such convictions.

The two instances above are but poor examples of the reaches the enlarged cosmos allowed, but further elaboration would necessitate my pushing myself center stage, whereas I plan to remain peripheral. Yet the vision of Aor's Hermetic universe can only be *my* vision, although he would likely recognize it. Through it runs a golden thread which the philosopher walks as if a tightrope. And while he abstracts his mind into this minimal support, he guarantees his equilibrium with the heavy balancing pole of material results. Al-Kemi is a practical laboratory process, as I was told when we had progressed to talking of such matters.

"No one has been further from an understanding of Greek and medieval alchemy than Jung and the psychoanalytic school. Alchemy depends on laboratory results. It is a manipulation of matter which has always been known. It occurs everywhere in nature, all the time."

At the point he would speak as freely as this, I had already forced my way to him and past Isha. I recall that the turning point came right after the Christmas holidays, when Isha was visited by one of her disciples who also was very friendly with Lucie. She was a young lady from Switzerland who epitomized all I abhor in the psycho-spiritual milieu. She stayed in Grasse for a week during the holidays and came to lunch every day. The conversation was dull and I was intolerant of her presence and avoided contact with her. The episode depressed me, jarred my concentration, and after she left, I told Isha I was going to ask Aor for a private interview with the aim of establishing a closer working relationship. I saw Aor that very day after tea in his study, where I had been only once before, shortly after we arrived in Grasse. We had at that time been taken on a tour of the house, and shown every room except Aor's bedroom and the laboratory. On that occasion we visited Isha's room, situated next to the doctor's office on the first floor of the main house. The dominant element in Isha's room was a meditation chair, the seat, back, and armrests of which had been carved of a huge single block of cedar wood to fit her body. On her bed was the headed skin of a white bear, and a small table nearby held a sizable crystal ball.

⊖

Now as I climbed the back stairs, locked into an upward spiral by the whitewashed tunnel of the stairwell, I clearly knew what had to be achieved. I would have to underscore the sense of urgency that brought me here in the first place, and that I had hoped could here be satisfied. I would express my impatience with a social apparatus that seemed to smother all attempts at substantive exchange. I would have to admit that the involvement with Isha was instructive from many points of view; while certainly interesting, it brought no answers to the fundamental questions I was trying to formulate. While I flew to the second floor two steps at a time, the story to be told once again reeled through my head. Aor knew nothing about the Bruges breakthrough; having attempted to introduce the subject by showing him my text, and having failed, I had never brought it up again. It had hewn a wide window into my mental world through which I visioned a structure necessary and sufficient to encompass all that had to be known. Would we agree on what it was that had to be known? My confidence on this point was entire. Although our approaches had been as different as the centuries that claimed us, our object was unique. There could be no other than this unique act of total apprehension beyond words which is knowledge itself, where the particular disappears and only the greatest generality reigns, stark and devoid of content. In this utter silence words would form meanings in the most natural fashion, without our interference. Here the universe would speak, not the cerebral cortex. This is the act, the state of knowledge. There is no referent for knowledge. Knowledge is knowledge in itself, it is primitive and cannot refer to a previous self. It is the thing in itself, unless it be a mere representation.

There was no doubt in my mind that Aor had seen this and that he deemed it to be essential. This much I knew as soon as I had read a few pages of his book. The turns of mind which in my text I had symbolized by the appearance of an implicit function amidst a self-perpetuating string of explicit ones, this particularity could not be mistaken in him; it was present in his whole being. It showed itself in a multitude of operations where nature triumphs over rationality. In mathematics, for instance: the genesis of multiplicity through addition of units one by one[16] is to such a mind incomprehensibly misconceived. Nature, the naturally occurring act, undirected by a particular mind or will, multiplies by division. Only in this fashion, and not by ripping atoms apart, can knowledge concerning nature be gathered. This much was obvious to him, it was obvious to me, but it did not seem obvious to the scientific establishment of the day that mistook aggregates for the unity of being. Yet the intuition that knowledge of multitude must start with the knowledge of a oneness had somehow come alive for me, and Aor gave me the geometric tools to explore it.

Yet while this vision brought out in me an urgency for communication, it did nothing of the kind for Aor. My questions: was this not as important a topic as could be entertained? If so, why were we not examining this subject whenever we found time together? More importantly yet, why not attempt to present the idea of an alternative science to a milieu in dire need of it, namely to the circle of scientific epistemology?

Such questions had been on my mind since I had come to know Aor's true vocation as a practicing scientist. It seemed obvious that I could contribute to the logical foundations of such an effort. Whereas I had decided to suppress my own ideas as long as our topic was Pharaonic Egypt and its symbolique, such ideas certainly became relevant if our topic were to shift to an alternative science such as Al-Kemi promised to be.

By the time I had knocked, entered, and settled at the table where he sat, I knew that no prepared program would guide this conversation. I looked at him as if for the first time. He seemed more at ease than I had seen him before, partly no doubt because this room was obviously a favorite habitat. He seemed to have lost some constraint; a certain severity had disappeared, an ill-humor even, which I had often felt just below the surface of his mood. His head tilted a little, he was looking at me with a smile, a slightly mocking and perhaps somewhat mischievous smile.

"*Alors,*" he said, "*la chose hermétique, hein?*"

I had a slight hesitation.

"*Ce n'est pas pour cela que je suis venu,*" I replied.

"I am fully satisfied on that point. I know by now that you have not come for that. I do believe that you never gave a thought to this work, *l'Oeuvre,* before coming here. If you had, I would have found out and I would have asked you to leave. You encountered it gratuitously, which is the only way it can be truthfully encountered. This is the real meaning of *l'acte gratuit.* Not an arbitrary action of the personal will; that is modern nonsense. Gratuitous from God, not from the self. The self can't act, it doesn't know. But you stepped into this like . . ."

"Like the Fool from the Tarot," I ventured. We had recently talked about the possibility of a valid *symbolique* being transmitted by that deck of cards and entrusted to the gypsies or "Egyptians."

"Not quite. You don't even know enough to be a fool. You see, I have to be careful. There are people who would like to know what I do."

Expecting a reaction, perhaps, he looked at me, and then past me through the window that was softly shimmering in the Mediterranean winter sun.

"Governments," he added.

I remained silent. I chose to forego all questions on this mysterious statement, figuring that he would tell me what he wanted me to know. He would come back to this subject in the weeks and months to come, but for the moment, he broke the mood abruptly instead.

"Tell me, why don't you spend your time walking along the beach on a lovely afternoon like this. You can't possibly do any serious work before the age of forty-two anyway, and I don't believe you are that old. One thing is to encounter *l'Oeuvre,* another to understand it for what it is."

Here once again was the refusal to remain on serious ground, the sudden deviation of the conversation I had noted so many times; there was also the notion that I might be incapable of following his ideas. I took the prejudice of an "age threshold of comprehension" as a jest; admitting that I had just turned thirty-five, I assured him of my confidence nevertheless to follow him where he would lead.

"Perhaps you could," he said, his attention on the window again. All around him in the large and sunny room there were bookshelves and a variety of objects many of which he later had me handle: specimens of metals and rocks, fossils, magnets of different sizes and shapes, spectroscopes, scales.

And then he repeated, "Perhaps you could. You could begin. I meant what I said about the age of forty-two. It is a matter of cycles. Seven-year cycles."

Seven-year cycles therewith led us into the first of many afternoons of rambling exchanges, sometimes of lectures and at other times even of controversy, and always of delightful and satisfying insights.

"Cycles," he said, "are the only way to beat time and space. Yes, the only way to beat those two is on their own ground. And cyclical consciousness places it there. Time is not like a river that flows by and in which you cannot step twice. Time is a spiral, and space as well, a spherical spiral. Can you imagine a spherical spiral? Try!"

We both sat silent in deep concentration, staring straight ahead at space.

After a few long minutes, he broke away with a sigh.

"Ah," he went on, "the vision of the spherical spiral, the true vision of space! Very elusive, must be practiced. Important because it is the just representation of time-space, abstracted from the infinite flow and extension that pulls us into the facts. The spherical spiral is impossible to imagine, you must see it become in space . . . "

And he concluded with a convolution of hands and forearms that came closer than a thousand impossible words to evoking this double helix, no longer linear and gaining dimension in contrary motion by folding the edge of its space back onto itself. When after months of practice it seemed to me periodically that my vision of time-space was improving, it was always in the sense of this amazingly accurate gesture.

"The cycle is a functional rhythm, and cyclical thinking affords a concrete approach to the space-time problem. You can't make a move without that kind of concreteness. Without concrete foundation, abstraction turns into fantasy, into irrational numbers, infinite and transfinite universes, poly-dimensionality and . . . You have spent time looking at horizons, no doubt?"

I confirmed, adding that marine subjects had afforded me much opportunity for time on this ineffable frontier of blues.

"Indeed," he said, "we cannot deny the existence of horizons whenever distance reaches its limit. That goes for the horizon of reason as well as for the natural phenomenon. An absolutely concrete abstraction! The solar system is man's horizon. That does not mean that there is nothing beyond. Simply that what is beyond is not of his nature, not on the scale of his vision. Teleologically, the sun is the end of man. It is folly to think beyond. It will lead to nothing, and it might destroy what is."

I brought up the remarkable opportunities present in philosophical geometry for the bonding of abstraction and concreteness. This brought us back to space and time, as we admired geometry's independence from such tyranny.

"That is its value, of course, and because *it* is independent, it gives you a chance of applying the circuitry of the mind to that state of independence. Thus it forms the circuitry in its model, by *frayage*. Working on *its* abstraction helps your own abstraction. And for concreteness, the practice of pencil and paper is ever present. Yes, it is the great temple-school."

3

*Master and disciple.—A Pharaoh on the hypotenuse.
—Language games.—The obvious stone.—Perception
of the* Oeuvre.—*Diabolus in musica.—Duodecim
claves.—Definition by contraction.—Aor
approves our kitchen.—A musical tea.
—Biographical considerations.*

In this gentle and natural manner did I slip into discipleship
with Aor. After tea, I would now join him upstairs for the rest
of the afternoon. Later, when I read books which he did not
want removed from the library, I would spend the early afternoon between lunch and tea alone in the library, reading
while Aor took his siesta. At times, when there was geometry
to be done, there would be a session before lunch with Lucie.
Most of the geometric questions could have been resolved
with her alone, but he never, not one single time in over a
year, left me alone with her.

Aor's geometric activity was a thing of the past. Geometry
is like music, it must be practiced daily; he now was quite
removed from the level of practical geometric manipulations.
Lucie, having worked all those years on quadrilated paper in
his stead, was a mine of information concerning references,
work that had been done, or work that had been attempted

and had so far not found an issue. This was invaluable to me and saved me much time. Aor was willing to approach the domain of geometry only by two broad avenues, concretely on the one hand as indispensable propedeutics for the scientific vision, and abstractly on the other as creative contemplation of nature's most faithful handmaiden, number.

He had first written on number in 1914, and he considered number to be a prime form of perception. The explosive encounter with geometry in Pharaonic Egypt had come later. It should be noted that his creative contact with the Pharaonic mind was first accomplished on geometric, and not on Egyptological grounds.

"My experience in the tomb of Ramses IX[1] concerned the Pharaoh as hypotenuse, and the recognition was in the measure of the hypotenuse, not in the Pharaoh. Knowledge of the meaning of the hypotenuse furnished information as to the position of the king, and "king" is a concept that is very closely defined in the medieval world. We have here a triple connection: the geometry is the "schooling" that makes the reading of the symbolique possible. The symbolique gives us a clue through the hypotenuse, which is occupied by a crowned king with scepters. In this manner the hypotenuse is defined, and we now have an ithyphallic royal figure as hypotenuse of a sacred right triangle 3:4:5, whose sides are occupied by a serpent. A gesture of the figuration permits a correlation with number and measure. It was this particularly fortunate expression of the symbolique which drew my attention and gave me the key to Al-Kemi. But my perception was of number as *form*, and the only thing I saw at first in this figuration was the triangle 3:4:5 and the relation of 5 to 6 in the king with his raised arm."

As I mentioned, specific problems of geometric practice were rarely discussed in our private meetings, but abstract topics concerning philosophical geometry came up repeatedly. They seemed to me mostly related to a logical foundation underlying Pythagorean thinking. As broadly as I was willing to stretch definition of such a *logos* however, Aor

never admitted to a logical component in Pharaonic Pythago-
reanism.[2] We do not know at what moment the irrational was
discovered to inhabit the geometric universe, and how long
this knowledge was effectively suppressed after its discovery.
It does seem unlikely that a Greek mind of the caliber of
Pythagoras would have spent sixteen years at the study of
Pharaonic geometry without encountering incommensurabil-
ity, even if such a concept was theologically off-limits to the
Pharaonic geometer.

Several elements of controversy merged into this topic as
we explored it on various afternoons. There was the element
of the "sacred secret" which had drawn my attention from
the first contact with de Lubicz's writing. There was furthermore the matter of discerning and noting a logic even in the
most intuitive of behaviors, assuming that Pharaonic conduct
in the Twenty-sixth Dynasty could be qualified as such. And
then there was the subtle underlying attitude in which we
differed most of all, and which I have characterized as the
"left-right" dichotomy.

AVB: "Should we assume that the entire geometric structure of the Pharaonic establishment was set up in order to
cope with irrationality?"

Aor: "Why not? Does a theological dictum of this sort
bother you? But you know very well that no conscious decision was involved; Pharaonic geometry was never set up as a
discipline the way it was in Greece. The irrational is eliminated by absolution in the beginning. The absolute, that is
the only irrational, and it is put first, in the beginning, the
same beginning where the Greek John hears the Logos. Therefore it is absolved from any particular participation; the whole
without detail must be in the beginning, the homogeneous
whole: oneness, the ultimate irrationality. The beginning and
the end are the same; between them lies the passage from one
to two, with *two* being a new *one*. In the absolute, in principle, nothing can be told, not even its own irrationality. From
the beginning absolute to the ultimate irrationality: consciousness experiences this as a path. But it is an identity, an
identity by absolution. It's no use with words, better listen to

the language of the birds for notions such as these. That's why I hate to write."

AVB: "The language of the birds . . . ?"

Aor: "Also known as the language of the gods, *bien entendu.* The Hermetic cabal, not to be confused with the Hebrew Kabbala, which is a tradition. Tradition is a surrender, a betrayal. What is handed down in a traditional way is a betrayal of the recipient, not of the content of transmission. The tradition is presented as truth, and therefore is psychologically disabling to the inquiring mind. A collection of hand-me-down beliefs against the search for a metaphysical truth that proves its justice in practice, in the laboratory; such indeed is Osiris against Horus. Not a theory, mind you; theory has a different function, theory is the doctrine. I am speaking about a truth revealed by the grace of God. The cabal I am talking about has to do with *caballus*, the horse, the same root as in chivalry, chevalier, knights on horseback, like Bellerophon on Pegasus, *vous y êtes?* Pegasus, the volatile source. The phonetic cabal had quite a vogue around the turn of the century. After the First World War in Paris, Fulcanelli and his intellectual friends did a lot for it; it had been completely neglected for centuries, had practically disappeared although you find echoes in Swift, Bergerac and others. But it degenerated into language games and etymological fishing expeditions in the twenties. It became an end in itself, an intellectual end, when it should have been just an aspect of the symbolique. It has its place, though, and it is important all right if you want to read certain texts; all instruments of transmission are important. In my opinion though, the language games just aren't secure without a firm grounding in the symbolique, and they did lead a whole generation of adepts into a dreadful intellectual mess, Fulcanelli at their head.

"Well, what is it?" I couldn't help asking, though well aware of the question's naïveté.

"What is it? It is the use of the common idiom to say the unsayable. It is a cant, a jargon, God's 'argot' and his children's; the birds sing it and the rest of nature too. It is never spoken, but has been understood at all times and in all places.

Such is the original concept of the language of the birds, but as I said, it became intellectualized by Fulcanelli and his friends, it became over-etymologized. They interpreted the idea of a language matrix literally, an approach obviously quite contrary to what's needed for the language of the birds. The matrix is supposed to have been Pelasgian, and theories were evolved to root the French language directly in an Ionian idiom, so as to make it a privileged vehicle for the language of the birds. Right after the war and during the twenties in Paris, there was this tremendous linguistic renaissance in the Hermetic search. I stayed away from it; I felt it as a distraction from the basic symbolique. Of course we didn't know Egypt yet, none of us, and none of the others ever did get to know the Pharaonic. They remained Greek and worked on the language, but that never was my path. I remained silent, which prepared me for the Pharaonic temples. When I wrote it was about number, which is another perfect language. Published an essay on number in 1914. Actually, when you look at it right, the glyphs are the most accurate description of the language of the birds. Do you like the rebus idea? Saying with pictures of things, not with words? Not with *signs*, you follow me, not with signs, that is important. The only usable sign is a signature. That is the miracle of the hieroglyphs: the great collection of signatures. Ah, the Pharaonic mind knows how to read in nature, not only through the form, but through the abstraction, the mere signature. That's the level you have to feel. All you want to read are signatures. That doesn't mean the form is neglected. Just look at the formal perfection of those glyphs, nothing can budge them. The Chinese failed with their picture language and so did the Mayans. The form disintegrated, it became script. That is impossible with hieroglyphs. They are as readable today as ever, and they never evolved even then, hardly at all during several millennia of use. What a joke our languages are! Incomprehensible after a few hundred years! But the rebus, that is something else. And the hieroglyphs use its possibilities to the fullest. To read the glyphs takes the same mind as it does to read a text from the Middle Ages. Who says that the cabal, the language of the birds, is only phonetic? Yes, there has been valuable transmission of ideas by phonetic means, work done by some people around the Chacornacs.[3] One of the best things they did; intelligent, yes, and great research, but no doctrine!"

Aor had no use for rhetorical rigor; on the contrary, he felt that an intuitive and associative way of communication brought better results. I could empathize with such an attitude, as I had discovered this mental set to offer fine possibilities in geometric practice as well.

The conversation returned to the foundations of Pharaonic geometry. He was talking about the intuitive position of oneness at the beginning of any process, and I mentioned that such an act by the geometer had to be considered an operation of the mind, probably a postulation.

"It is obvious," he broke in, "and the effort to prove the obvious is the saddest waste of man's intellect. With the Pharaonic, the vision is so unencumbered that you can hardly speak of mental operations. That is the only way the symbolique can be seen clearly, with such simple intuition. How to make the step from there to a figuration, a representation, without losing the vision, that is the mark of the artist. Just the contrary of self-expression, by the way, and on the opposite pole of today's artistic ideals."

"And no compromise for the sake of transmission?"

"There is an essential aspect which cannot be transmitted. It turns out to be the most obvious, the most common, so generally accepted that it becomes invisible. It is ever present and constantly visible, all texts insist on that point. Go ahead, ask me: What is . . . *it*? I will sound foolish telling you that it is the *stone*, but if you knew stone, stoneness, its tremendous concentration, and its passivity, you would know that this is the material of the lode, the matrix of the mineral. It's the starting point, yes, you start with the stone to find the stone, where else? *Prima materia* and *materia prima* are not the same; one is a beginning and the other is an end. But it is always the same stone, the stone does not evolve. It is amazing that this fact of nature is not generally recognized, and that science still believes in an evolution of matter. Darwin's

theory has been exploded long ago; it never made sense from
the beginning. It was a disaster for subsequent work on evolution, and there is less truth in it than there was in early
fixist theories. Both sides are wrong, of course, because they
both miss the essential and central problem, the problem of
the fixed salt. It is hard to tell who did more damage to his
discipline, Darwin or that fool Lavoisier with his *rien ne se
crée, rien ne se perd.* We know now that everything is created
at every moment, and that everything is lost as well. But I see
no one drawing the consequences of this discovery. A discovery? A discovery of the obvious once again, a proof of the
obvious. I am telling you the truth about the stone; I am not
mystifying; pick up a rock and you have it in your hand. Now
you need the moment, the moment when everything appears
and disappears, the juncture of future and past. That is a moment of imbalance, and it is at such a moment of instability
that we can act. The *Oeuvre* is not the discovery of a technique, it is nothing of the sort, it is the perception of an
existing process. It is the *perception* that is the object of study
and prayer. That is the theoretical part, and after that comes
the practice, the proper gesture in matter and time. The perception of a process, the vision of an evolution, that is the
first aim of the scientist. *Prima materia* into *materia prima*
is a constant process of nature, it is mindless, and therefore
beyond the cerebral cortex. That is really the only difficulty.
There is no use addressing the analytic mind with Hermetic
language; it can do very little with it. Therefore the language
of the birds, not spoken, only heard."

"I was struck by what you said about the present moment
in *Symbole et Symbolique.* That moment of unbalance is
certainly such a passage from one to two."

"Yes, it's the absolute in the beginning, and the next thing
is two, the creation. When I say 'the next thing,' I am talking
about time. As the evolutionary process works in time, the
gesture, which is certainly a movement, adapts to that cosmic
time. That is the closest you can get to the present moment,
and it is close enough. If movement is the proper gesture,
there will be results. Mere presence will become the present

moment, and we shall be working on solid rock, and not in intellectual quicksand, *alors nous oeuvrons pour l'Eternité.* We shall have ceased to be mere symbols, we shall have taken our destiny in our own hands. That is a prime achievement of the *Oeuvre.*"

"Isn't there something like a scientific moment contained in that present moment, when we have a proper gesture having its effect in the natural evolutionary process?"

"I would rather say an artistic moment, *Ars Magna.* One that breaks the automatism between cause and effect. It is the characteristic of great art that the effect seems miraculous compared to the cause."

"It is quite true that surprise is a sure sign of good work . . . "

"Amazement, not surprise. But go ahead, call it a scientific moment, as long as we are speaking about sacred science. A scientific moment, then, is what you *do* with the present moment. And it is a gesture, it is the proper gesture for the occasion: *le geste juste.* You must know what the occasion is and therefore you read, or you pray, *c'est kif-kif,* you work: *Vous oeuvrez.* The present moment is the only moment out of time when you can operate. At that moment, at that present moment, you either have the gesture, *are* the gesture, or you are not, and you do not. *Vous oeuvrez dans le moment présent uniquement.*"

"Granted that there is a part of all this which cannot be transmitted, isn't there a line of transmission from Egypt through the Arabs and the Crusades in the Middle Ages?"

"It is theoretically possible. It is very tempting to think so, when one realizes that the Pharaonic hieroglyphs and the medieval texts say the same things. But there is no need for transmission, as both are speaking of an ever-present reality accessible at any time. Egypt and the Middle Ages are talking about the same thing, describing the same thing. The problem is to know what they are talking about. This takes study, and, they say, the help of a teacher, a good friend to show you *le truc de l'Oeuvre.* But I never had a teacher, and good reading will go a long way."

"So there is an element that can be called a *truc?* Could this be related to the thievery Hermes is accused of?"

I had been struck by the way he had pronounced the word "*truc*," a difficult word to situate in English. It evokes the English word "trick" by an associative process which exemplifies the theory of a language matrix, basis of a phonetic cabal. In fact, the French "*truc*" comes from the Provençal, whereas the English "trick" comes from a Norman root for "cheating." A *truc* is not a trick, nor does it carry any connotation of cheating. But it does imply a clever legerdemain.

"There is indeed at the inception of the Hermetic *Oeuvre* an insistence on a benign treachery that recalls the thieving god. I'll tell you the story some day about the theft at the origin of the alchemical renaissance that is known as Fulcanelli. The Promethean enterprise resides essentially in the theft of a fire, either the "seeds of fire" from the Sun Wheel, or else the fire from the forges of Hephaistos in the belly of the earth. The myth here is very complete; both fires are needed. But the creative fire cannot be bought or borrowed, it cannot be given or transmitted, so it must be 'stolen.' *Honestly* stolen, *bien entendu!* That's the *truc!* Let's go stretch our legs in the Allée des Philosophes."

I knew that he hadn't been quite candid with me concerning this topic. But when he was ready for a breather, there was no way of holding him back.

⊖

Although I arrived at Aor's doorstep a rank novice in the Hermetic arts generally, I held my own from the start in one specific field of inquiry: the laws of harmony. When Aor realized my practical familiarity with material whose access had been difficult for him, he encouraged me to assemble what I could on two main topics: the *diabolus in musica*, as the ill-famed interval of the diminished fifth became known in polyphonic writing, and the Pythagorean comma, a related phenomenon that lends rationality to an otherwise infinite cyclical tonal system. The relationship of the Pythagorean comma to the astronomical phenomenon of the precession of the equinoxes is quite clear.

"The zodiac of the twelve tonalities is an arrested moment in the endless spiral of sound, and the cog that arrests it is the Pythagorean comma. That much is plain to me. What is less so is the development that makes the *diabolus* rise out of this system. What else can this devil be but the destruction of a rational structure, incorporated into that very structure from the beginning, as a price of beginning, so to speak? He is the price paid for constraining an everchanging infinite, a cyclical infinity that is the very nature of the universe. Sound as an irrational infinity might be the perfect fuel for a mystic meditation, but the Pythagorean is a scientist, he must somehow find a rational representation of the irrational; he cannot be satisfied by the purely meditative sound, as the Oriental is with the drone; he needs the practical application, and therefore he needs an explicated harmonic structure, rationalized by the Pythagorean comma. He wants the ear to hear as knowingly as the eye sees. Therefore he needs a theory of form. Dangerous territory, but the only alternative to an untransmittable personal mysticism. Anyway, I feel in all this the not uncommon problem of understanding the theory, but not having the tools to grasp the practice. Those are God-given qualities."

"I see the danger of theoretical reductions, but I don't suppose the question ever arises as to whether the risk is worth taking; I would think there is no choice."

"No choice at all, the reflection comes *a posteriori*. If you want knowledge, you can go about it in a variety of ways, come to a variety of results which to yourself you might call knowledge. But when it comes to certainty in science, there is only one way to obtain it: through *proof*. And if you begin your work with the suspect evidence of a material universe that is but a support to a spiritual universe of superior reality, you must be prepared to prove it in no uncertain way: I mean in the laboratory. Otherwise you have no business around scientific ideas, be they the destructive ideas of academic science or the sacred science I have pursued all my life."

"What is proof in sacred science?"

"It is, like everywhere else, evidence that an initial assumption is valid. If you enter the laboratory with the assumption, the belief, the hypothesis, whatever you want, *enfin*, the frame of mind and heart that sees matter as a support for spirit, you must be prepared to stay until you have shown the two, matter and spirit, neatly separated. That will afford you the opportunity of paying undivided attention to the part you can handle, the material part, the earth part, the support. This part you can clean up and rearrange, and then rejoin with the other part, which is unaffected, unchangeable, always identical, the fire part, the spirit. Some day, when we understand each other on this subject of perception, I'll show you some things. They should be proof enough. The reds and blues of Chartres cathedral are byproducts of this search for proof; they have been the main preoccupation of my generation. But perception must make this adjustment into form, for without it, our sensorial constitution is inadequate, which is precisely why the event becomes a *diabolus*. I know of course that the contraction that is implied in the definition of tonality has its luciferous implications, but please, explain to me what made generations of popes, who were, if anything, theologians rather than musicians, what made them discover a devil in a musical interval, and how, according to you, is that entirely theoretical devil in fact tied to the Pythagorean cog that fixes the system into an instrument of knowledge. You should count yourself fortunate. Natural contact with form is inborn knowledge, but it has to be discovered, and not everyone is blessed with its revelation. But then, in times like these, it is usually squandered anyway."

I now explained how both topics, the devil in music as well as the Pythagorean comma, are dependent on a notion central to tonal structure: the enharmonic change, where extremes meet for a new oneness. Now the enharmonic change is particularly difficult to conceive for a nonmusician. Although the latter may be aware of the development of increasingly complex fractions, he lacks the frame of reference of the musical fact: the increasingly dissonant interval. He furthermore lacks the material representation of the musical fact, the keyboard, which is the most inclusive overview of the harmonic material. This aspect of an aural symbolique was closed to Aor. Its key, birthright of any musician, is *terra incognita* for the layman, whatever his talents in other domains.

I set up tables of fractional expressions for increasingly complex relationships between sounds, in other words, for increasingly dissonant intervals. The unfortunate deaf spot in Aor's perceptual makeup, his nonmusicianship, caused the intervals to remain fractions on paper, mere exoteric expression. The esoteric musical language and its effect, emotional inscription of the harmonic interval through the sound in the ear, did not enter into play for him. He was well aware of this, as I was always lamenting the absence of a keyboard on which to *sound* the abstractions we were discussing. Although not a performer, I have never lived without a musical instrument, and when we moved into our small apartment in Grasse, one of my first concerns was to rent an upright piano on which I could improvise and work out sound figures.

The only piece of music for which Aor had any particular feeling was Wagner's *Ring,* and this evidently more for reasons concerning the mythological libretto than for the harmonic complexities of the musical score.

We were speaking of the twelve tonalities; it was during the early days when I was still struggling unsuccessfully with a reading of Basil Valentine, and as the twelve tonalities came up in the conversation, he leaned forward in his characteristic gesture of emphasis: "Remember now: *Duodecim claves!"* Then, rather suddenly, and after a smile; "You do have a piano in your apartment? I would like to have a look at where you live, in any case. Why don't you have us over some afternoon, and you'll let me hear the details of this *diabolus."*

I was very surprised at this proposition; we had never thought in terms of inviting Aor and Isha, mainly because we could not imagine them in a context other than Lou-Mas-de-Coucagno. They never seemed to leave the property, which was, to us, most understandable. But I was delighted to find out they could be enticed into coming forth.

Ostensibly, the occasion was arranged to have me demonstrate *in vivo*, by the very sound, this *diabolus in musica* which remained so unknowable to him by the mere notation of numbers. We had talked about the development of the laws of harmony in Western music, the papal control in the beginnings of polyphony with respect to intervals allowed, the slowly growing permissiveness in the use of intervals, and then with the secularization of music, the rapid disintegration of tonality in the contemporary world. It was to him but another example of the need for "temple knowledge" accessible only to an elite, another demonstration of the "pearls before swine" metaphor. On points like this, the left-and-right differences between us showed strongly. We were once again discussing the domain of privilege, the secret. I did not as yet know that after the First World War he had represented an ultra right-wing sociopolitical movement whose rallying call replaced equality by hierarchy.

I had accepted his views on social organization as being primarily influenced by the Pharaonic model. They were complementary to the temple ideal that was viable only through a separation of a select minority from the many. It was a case of "when in Rome . . . ," the specific case of "when in the Pharaonic temple . . . "

But although my position with Aor made me a beneficiary, even an envied beneficiary of this organization, the latter never earned my sympathy. I am by no means a populist, nor even a defender of the masses. Karmic destiny has placed me apart from them this time around, and I accept the position gratefully, as a privilege. Like everything else, it has advantages and drawbacks, a topic upon which I could expand, were it within our context. Still, everything that might tend to autocracy was suspect in my mind, and this suspicion was even here to be borne out. For the moment, though, none of this entered into my considerations, and legitimate queries were smothered by the creativity of the encounter.

I told him how in fact the *diabolus* had been the mainspring in the disintegration; how, once the flatted fifth is accepted, an ambiguity is introduced which the system is unable to withstand. He was struck by the possibility that the restraint imposed by the popes since Gregory could have actually been motivated by a knowing foresight. In any case, he approved of the sense of the sacred with which this approach imbued the laws of harmony. A sense that certainly seemed to reflect traces of a God-given gnosis.

"The vibrating string must have been one of the earliest instruments of knowledge, along with the flat, inscribable surface, and of course, those primeval instruments: volume, color, and number. These are the modes of creating *form*, the only ways we have in the struggle with perceptual definition. Always the same fight against objectification, the same struggle against the contraction!"

"Definition by contraction," I ventured, "obtained by the senses alone, but still preferable to syntactical or nominal definitions."

"Quite true, as long as you remain ever-present to the fact that your perception is a contraction of an infinitely larger context. Such presence, not of mind, but of spirit, is hard work in the long run. As long as you are *obliged* to deal with the irrational, acknowledge it, don't brush it aside; it is bound to show up sooner or later and you will have accomplished no more and no less than just another loop on the cyclical merry-go-round. You'd be better off saying: here is the irrational, the infinite. All roads lead to it, so it must be the one reality, the One, always the same, everpresent, *Dieu, enfin,* and as it is the end of all our paths, it must also be the beginning. We'll put oneness first, we'll start with the irrational. And do you know what will happen?" With a twinkle in his eye, "We'll never hear from it again!"

"But you believe that *number* is the very first expression of form?"

"Of course, one becoming two is a first consciousness, and before anything else, it is an event of number."

I had been studying his concept of form; along with function, it seemed to provide the two main pillars of his epistemology.

"I don't know," I said. "I don't know if I see this matter of form quite clearly. For example, we can propose that nature manifests itself in a profusion of discrete entities. Although we know these entities to be involved in a complex interrelationship with their environment, there is a separateness which we perceive immediately. Can we consider this edge of separation to be *form?*"

I had been preparing this speech for some time.

"Yes, to an extent, and as long as you do not call it the *object's* form. By the time we objectify, we are lost. Form is precisely the net that will catch reality before it sinks into the object. This obviously takes a total reeducation of our means of perception. That's really where everything must start. An empty, uncommitted perception of the concrete fact, received by a knowledge of abstract reality. We must remain in touch with the facts, they are really all we have; remember, this is a matter of science, not of extasis."

"Blessed be the facts," I said.

"Yes," he concluded, "they are the bedrock of reality."

⊖

We had invited Isha and Aor for tea. It was the first time we had seen Isha *à la ville.* She had traded her flowing white robes for an elegant tight-fitting black cocktail dress. As always, she was magnificently overdressed for the occasion. On the introductory tour through our two bedrooms and living room, I was surprised to see Aor lag behind and enter our kitchen. I joined him and observed him checking the kitchen stove, opening the oven door, checking the aeration flue with considerable attention. He turned to me and nodded his head in assent, disregarding the fact I had never expressed any intention of engaging in alchemical practice.

"This is all right," he said, "you can work here."

Over tea, we settled around the little upright. I had unearthed a piano score of Wagner's *Tristan,* and I intended to analyze for him the modulations in the *Tristan* theme. I had previously explained the necessary resolution of the dominant to the tonic, with the dominant third turning into the leading tone and finding its resolution in the root of the tonic, and the dominant seventh settling into the tonic third. I had shown the dominant third and seventh as the "movers" of the modulation, with their powerful drive toward resolution in the tonic's root and third respectively. I could now give him an aural content for these theoretical concepts, enhancing it with the visual experience of the keyboard intervals. I sounded a four-voiced G major chord, with doubled root, to make him appreciate the relative steadiness and constancy of the vibrational communion of the simplest string ratios: 1:2 for the octave, 2:3 for the fifth, 3:4 for the fourth, 4:5 for the major third.

Then I introduced the dominant seventh into the tonality of G and sounded it against the third. I let the tension of the dissonance build for a moment before resolving it into the tonic C's root and major third. I then completed the four-voiced C major chord with the fifth and the octave to reestablish the repose of the simple ratios.

Now in the dominant chord, the interval between third and seventh is precisely the flatted fifth, the tritone, the renowned *diabolus.* And the keyboard showed him graphically that this interval splits an octave exactly in two. In the series of complementary intervals to form the octave, the third complements the sixth and vice versa, the fourth complements the fifth and vice versa, but the flatted fifth is complemented by a sharped fourth (inversion of a flatted fifth), as it is the interval that divides the chromatic octave into two even parts.

"Natural division is always into *uneven* parts," he broke in. "I can already feel the cardinal sin that will call for the devil. The product of an even division will never be stable in its duality. It makes sense that this interval would tend toward resolution with all its might."

I agreed that the division of the octave into two equal parts through the flatted fifth indeed leads to an ambiguity in the resolution of this dissonance. Whereas the pairs of intervals mentioned earlier, the fourth and the fifth, and the third and the sixth, both proclaim the essential character of their tonality, the first by indicating tonic, dominant, and subdominant, the second by indicating major and relative minor, the interval of the flatted fifth wants only to resolve, that is, to modulate toward another tonality.

"Unfortunately," I concluded, "the flatted fifth is no longer certain what its tonic is."

"Yes," he said. "I get the idea, but I certainly would like the experience."

"Easily done. It has occurred to me that it is the interchangeability of the two elements of the interval, the third and the seventh, that undermines the certitude of the tonality."

"Yes, it is a perfect paradigm for duality within unity, that state of constant becoming. Now let's hear what it sounds like."

"You've heard it a million times," I said, striking the bare bones of a classical resolution from dominant to tonic in four-part harmony.

I took as example the dominant chord on G, where B is the third and F is the seventh. The interval between dominant third and seventh is a flatted fifth, the *diabolus in musica*. B and F, in their relationship of flatted fifth, are reciprocal centerpoints of their two systems: B is the center of the duodecimal system that lies between F and its octave, F', while F is the center of the analogous system that lies between B and its octave, B'. Together, they strive in opposite directions. When B is the center of F, it will act as leading tone to resolve the dissonance into C. F in that case is irresistibly drawn into the tonality of C where it becomes the third. Without moving, G had turned from root of its own tonality into the fifth of C. The modulation of the tonality of G into the tonality of C is completed.

But when F is the center of the B scale, the context will enharmonically change it to $E^{\#}$ and therefore into the leading tone of an $F^{\#}$ tonality that is as far removed as it can be from the tonality of C, the result of the previous resolution. B in this case plays the role of dominant seventh and forces the modulation into $F^{\#}$ tonality, where, as $A^{\#}$, it becomes the third.

It is the equality of the complementary segments of the

octave that makes their terms interchangeable: in a flatted fifth each term can belong, as third or as seventh, to two different tonalities as remote from each other as tonality can be. Hence two resolutions are possible, both occurring with equal ease, each as compelling as the other to the ear. One single dissonance leads to two different resolutions, none favored over the other unless it be further characterized by context. But these tonalities are not merely different; they stand at opposite poles, namely the two poles of the flatted fifth interval: between C and F#, the interval is a sharped fourth, once again representing extreme instability. A dissonance which finds with equal ease resolution in two extremes! The ambiguity this fact introduces into the relationships of the twelve tonalities—such is the seed of destruction bound to bring down the entire system of tonality.

We had talked for a good while, and I was satisfied that I had been able to present the matter with reasonable clarity. I know my lecture was appreciated; Aor suggested that I prepare some material along these lines of harmonic theory, number, and tonality for inclusion in an eventual second edition of the *Temple*. This was the first of three times he talked of including some work of mine in his book; he specified that I was to be given credit. The proposition was most speculative, as the first edition was barely two years old, and not moving at all. The other two occasions concerned geometry: a method of addition and subtraction of angles, and a two-dimensional demonstration of the function *phi*.[4]

Our conversation about theft and trickery in connection with the Hermetic work brought to mind a little essay by Norman O. Brown called *Hermes the Thief*,[5] and in a subsequent get-together, I mentioned the work with some approbation as an interesting study in the mythology of the Greek god. It was an unfortunate move, and he looked at me as if I had taken leave of my senses.

"Do you really feel that this author of yours, whoever he may be, can contribute anything at all to the subject of Hermetism in the sense in which I use the word?"

He had asked a similar question on a previous occasion when I had mentioned Bachelard's studies of the four elements, which seemed to me to contain some remarkable intuitions. I was indeed not yet aware of how rigorously he avoided reading or referring to anything contemporary. In the case of Gaston Bachelard, my *faux pas* was far more pardonable, as de Lubicz himself had quoted a work published in 1934 by this exact contemporary and compatriot of his: in *Du Symbole et de la Symbolique,* the book that had motivated my initial visit, his feelings toward contemporary epistemology had not been uncomplimentary in the least. In the 1951 *Notes sur la Pensée Moderne,*[6] the attempt at communication through a purely scientific link still dominates. It is addressed to an academic approach through the implications of non-Newtonian physics. Not only does de Lubicz acknowledge the work of a naysayer such as Bachelard,[7] but he puts stock in the latter's opinion that there has been a "mutation of the Spirit." It must have taken some complacency even then for Aor to venture that M. Bachelard's *"esprit"*—capitalization of which was strictly de Lubicz's—had much in common with his own idea thereof.[8] Furthermore, he credits rational science, which he considers as having reached a surrational stage, with clearing the path toward a suprarational esoterism. He goes as far as endorsing today's scientific working method for its "extreme precision," and lauds the "absolute loyalty of our scientists in their experimentation." This from a man who less than a decade later contemplates drawing the line between a sacred science he represents and present-day technology by subtitling his book on *Le Roi: La Science Inhumaine et la Science Sacrée.*[9] But most revealing perhaps of our author's mental set at a time when the basic work for *Le Temple de l'Homme* was already completed, is the attempt of communicating the esoteric notion of the "present moment" in terms of Werner Heisenberg's uncertainty principle.[10]

A considerable change must have taken place in de Lubicz's

point of view between the time he left Egypt and the time I met him. *Du Symbole et de la Symbolique* does not yet explicitly lean upon the Pharaonic image as a tool of transmission. Not yet committed to communication of and through Al-Kemi, it is a last attempt for contact with the "new scientific spirit" of non-Aristotelian logic and non-Newtonian physics, a spirit that seemed to many thinkers of the time a radical departure from naïve *fin-de-siècle* materialism. Only now was I able to appreciate the extent to which I had been misled (albeit most fortunately so, as it turned out) by this small volume which was the only work of de Lubicz known to me before our encounter.

I mentioned this aspect of the work which had arrested my attention so forcefully, and wondered if a later text such as *Le Roi* would have been able to reach me at that time.

"Whatever the answer to such communication questions, I disown the book. Never mind that it was efficient in your case, it was a flawed undertaking. There is no possibility of influencing the rationalistic progress of science; it is too profitable, too useful. Utility in a material world is not what a sacred science offers, despite all the hunting after gold. Certainly, it is possible to influence the evolution of lead into silver and gold, speed up the mineral process that takes place naturally in the mine, but such an endeavor has never been achieved for material gain, or for power in a material context. Anyhow, that book might as well not have been published, as there are only a few copies around, thanks to those good *fellahin* who put the torch to Schindler's print shop. Such events are significant; they should never be overlooked. It is just as significant, by the way, that you were able to put your hands on one of the few surviving copies. But I disavow the approach of speaking *their* language; it is not the way to say what has to be said."

I asked whether there were copies extant, and what my chances would be of obtaining one. I had sent back the copy I had been lent by George Andrews.

"Yes, I have some copies. I'll give you one. It's a worthless book now, everything in it that had some value has been said, and said better, in the *Temple,* and the rest is best forgotten."

"Yet it would have been very unlikely for me to run across
a copy of the *Temple,* and even more unlikely for me at that
time to recognize the ideas in a Pharaonic approach."

"I agree, but that can hardly be a concern for the author. It
took me a long time to find the language for what I had to
say, and only with Pharaonic Egypt did I find *my* cipher, *my*
symbolique. A symbolique must show itself, it cannot be invented, and it cannot be conventional, like the artificial languages of symbolic logic. Can the Christic revelation be
"invented?" It cannot; it must flower on the bedrock of perennial myth, as a symbolique, and then it will in time lend its
cipher to a few great authors, as it did in the Middle Ages. I
would have used a Christic symbolique to say some things,
had Fulcanelli not tricked me out of the idea. *Il m'a eu, il m'a
eu pour mes idées. Enfin,* once again the infinite wisdom of
destiny. *Maktub, c'était écrit,* it was written"

He had lowered his voice toward the last, as if he were
talking to himself, but I nevertheless caught the shade of resentment. Had he forgotten my presence for a moment, and
what exactly did he mean by saying that Fulcanelli had taken
him for his ideas? My surprise was tempered by various inti-
mations I had had from Isha, but I had interpreted them to
mean that Aor had influenced Fulcanelli, or perhaps taught
him some things.

"He *tricked* you?"

I was about to mention the layered Trismegistos whom
Norman O. Brown had recognized in the oldest stratum of
Greek mythology: behind Hermes the Thief is Hermes the
Trickster, and behind Hermes the Trickster is Hermes the
Magician.[11] But he barely gave me time to think better of it.

"Yes, he appropriated my work on the cathedrals."

"How did that happen?"

My impulsive question did not conform to my usual reticence, but I needn't have worried. Willingly, almost eagerly,
he told me the story.

4

*Fulcanelli introduced.—Texts, techniques, and secrecy.
—Reading Basil Valentine.—L'expérience.—The
disappearing Hermetist.—A burdensome legacy.—A cosmic
inside joke.—Understanding Basil Valentine.—The
perceptual gesture.—The odor of the god.—Affinity
and order.—The Perception Construct.—Sacred science.*

By the time Aor became active in Paris during the First World
War, he had accumulated a considerable documentation on
the Hermetic symbolism of cathedrals. These were the years
of the Hermetic revival which had stirred in Paris since before
the turn of the century. At the time of our story, a dedicated
group of searchers was working in traditional ways, with Flamel and Basil Valentine as principal texts. Among them, the
name Fulcanelli circulated as the real mainspring to the entire movement.[1]

I noted then, and it should be brought out now, that in
telling me the story, Aor spoke about Fulcanelli as if his identity and his name had never been in question, whereas earlier
he had insisted several times that "Fulcanelli" had to be
taken as a generic name for a many-sided effort extending
over close to half a century.

"I came in touch with the man quite naturally, as we were frequenting the same café, the Closerie des Lilas, in Montparnasse. This was before the First World War. I was doing many things then, studying scientific theories on the constitution of matter, reading all the Hermetic texts I could lay my hands on, studying painting with Matisse, frequenting the Theosophical Society, and also studying the symbolism of Gothic cathedrals. Yes, I already knew then that cathedrals were one more expression of the symbolique. They were alchemical texts carved in stone, just as I later found them in Egypt, many years later. Yes, I started that kind of work by myself as soon as I arrived in Paris; I was barely twenty years old. Kept all this information to myself, of course. But I did meet some people, Milosz for one, with whom I shared many things, and then Fulcanelli, although I generally managed to stay away from his coterie. I never took a liking to Fulcanelli, but he was the only one in Paris I could talk to about the *Oeuvre*. He had a few disciples of sorts, a fellow named Boucher, I remember, and Eugène Canseliet, of course, who never left his side. They had formed a society, a club for promoting Fulcanelli. 'Brothers of Heliopolis' they called themselves. I had nothing to do with any of this, of course, but I came in touch with it through Fulcanelli. He was the only one who knew anything, and I got together with him. Talking to him, I realized that he was no ordinary amateur, no 'puffer,' and certainly no fake. He knew what he was doing, from a practical point of view. He was about ten years older than I, and rather well connected in the publishing world, or so he told me. But there were aspects he did not understand, theoretical aspects, what I call doctrine. He had been very influenced early in his studies by Arab scientific philosophy, particularly Jābir. Well, you have read some of those things, you know how materialistic they can be. But that was very much his line, and that was the contrast between us. The complementation, too. He had made a *technique* of the proper gesture needed in the work, instead of leaving it to being divinely inspired. But what a technique! An unbelievable manipulator! That is valuable, of course, it is what makes the artist, but it does not make the philosopher. I guess he himself realized to what degree we complemented each other. He was a very strange fellow, a prankster, and he lived the Fulcanelli intrigue in all its details. His entire life revolved around building up the Fulcanelli image. Of course, until he came out with his book, there was very little to it, to that whole Fulcanelli business, just talk. Only with the *Mystère des Cathédrales* did it gain any substance. As the Fulcanelli legend developed, everyone in that milieu turned to the work Fulcanelli was doing; information about what Fulcanelli was doing was obtained from the 'Brothers of Heliopolis,' particularly from Canseliet, Champagne, or Sauvage and Boucher. Dujols was also involved, but all this is unimportant. What matters is that Fulcanelli organized this activity from behind the scenes, but he didn't have a voice. He did not have the symbolique to express himself. He was still speaking in terms of Basil Valentine and Flamel or Jābir, but he himself had no specific form. And that was what I was able to give him. Or what he stole from me, although one doesn't seem to feel robbed of what one doesn't miss."

He fell silent for a moment, and I let the silence be. When he began to speak again, he reminisced about the powerful atmosphere at that time among Parisian Hermetists, the feeling of excitement created almost entirely by these innuendoes and veiled statements that could always be traced to the "Brothers." Fulcanelli was working on the glass, it seemed. That was not unusual in itself, as the search for the Chartres reds and blues has directed Western alchemy since the Templars brought the stained glass idea back from the Crusades.

"It has become the favorite detail for study, and rightly so, for the tincture in the mass definitely indicates the right track. I was also working in that direction, of course, but not with much success until I started to work on that manuscript of his. He couldn't make heads or tails of it, that's why he brought it to me. Well, no use talking about that, I doubt if it would make sense to you right now. When we started to work

together, he made me take an oath not to reveal his double
life, never to identify his name with Fulcanelli. You may feel
that after all this time, and with all the speculations, some of
which are bound to be correct, it would no longer make any
difference, but that is not how I feel. I made the vow and I'll
keep it. He also made me swear that our relationship should
remain unknown to the other 'Brothers,' and we always met
alone, in hiding almost. Not that I saw him that often. But he
revealed himself as Fulcanelli to very few people, and from
that point of view, I really knew him better than anyone else,
I practically made him, once the *Mystère* came out. And I
certainly knew better than anyone how far he had gone in his
work, and I can tell you that he went no further than I did,
not one step further. *Mais je dois taire son nom.* I must keep
his true name to myself."

I felt, I assured him, that to make its point, the story hardly
needed this identification.

"Of course not," he agreed, "and the fellow himself was an
uninteresting lout. But Fulcanelli, he was the incarnation of
a great classical artist. Anyway, he was extremely circum-
spect with his double identity. He knew small groups of people, I found out, but they didn't know each other. He
approached me in the Closerie, one day when none of his
friends were present; he sat down briefly, introduced himself,
and told me he had heard of me, and would I come to see him.
And he slipped me an address in Montmartre, where I agreed
to meet him a few days later. A terrible garret he lived in. And
the first thing he did was to ask me to take an oath that I
would never reveal our relationship nor what he was going to
tell me. Then he told me that all the ideas that had circulated
under the name of Fulcanelli had come from him and his
experiments. And I swore never to reveal his name. I didn't
like him any better in those dismal surroundings, but somehow I felt we had some work to do together. And I was not
disappointed. That is when he showed me a very strange
manuscript, and told me how he had stolen it."

It seemed that Fulcanelli, expert in Hermetic lore, had

worked for the Chacornac brothers who had a bookshop on the quays in Paris. He had evaluated and catalogued incoming books. The Chacornac brothers purchased libraries that had been mouldering away in provincial estates, and they came up with some astonishing finds. Aor had accumulated most of his library at that time.

"A good part of it was eighteenth-century nonsense, speculative natural science, absolutely worthless, but in interesting bindings; that stuff sold well. This particular manuscript, a mere six pages, was very different, though. They were handwritten notes, evidently taken by a practicing adept and made during an experiment. There were oil spots on the paper. It was written on stiff drawing paper, roughly cut *in octavo* and yellowing at the edges, and the ink was *bistre* and fading. Fulcanelli thought it came out of the 1830s, around the time Cyliani was being published. He thought he recognized a similarity in approach.[2] I myself am convinced that it was influenced by Goethe's *Farbenlehre*. He had found it in a rare tome of Newton's alchemical writings. He told me that as soon as he looked at it, he felt it was 'good.' So he stole it. Through this manuscript, we became partners in some work. But there is no sense talking about that. They are laboratory procedures based on symbolique. What I was talking about was my association with him and the fact that he got to know about my work on the cathedrals; it came up, inevitably. He brought out a manuscript and put it on the table. Eventually we did some work along lines I had laid out; I let him do the trickier manipulations, and we were far more successful than I had been on my own. It is a gift, the gift of the artist, the ability to manipulate. But of course he had squandered this on insignificant experiments, because he couldn't situate the texts on which he depended, writers like Flamel and Valentine, at the level where they belong. Anyway, I showed him the documentation I had gathered of cathedral symbolism. He got very excited and assured me he would give me a hand in publishing it. I was at the time thinking about moving away from Paris; the whole social affair was taking too much of my time. But I had been working on a book that would show with detailed proof, through the structural elements of the cathedrals, and through the sculpture and ornaments, that they were a Christic expression of the Hermetic *Oeuvre*. I had been running a group with Isha and Milosz, and I had kept my work on the *Oeuvre* quite apart. It's best that way. I had shared my technical laboratory concepts only with Fulcanelli, and my Hermetic philosophy only with Milosz, the poet, you know."

"Yes, Isha has told me about the de Lubicz name."

I knew he had been born René Schwaller of Alsacian ancestry, and that the French poet O.V. de Lubicz Milosz, a prince of Lithuanian nobility, had adopted him. I recall distinctly that "adoption" was the term used by Isha.

"I would suppose so," he said with an air of mock resignation, "but that's another topic. Milosz was neither an adept nor a Hermetist, but Fulcanelli was a little of both. He obviously knew a lot about alchemical manipulations. There is a natural bond between people who have done this work with any degree of seriousness, and I did talk to him about all the material I had gathered concerning the symbolism of cathedrals. At the time I intended to publish something on the subject, and he made me believe he could help me; he had connections. He really was most interested when I showed him the manuscript, and asked to borrow it for a few days, to look at it a little more closely in view of presenting it to a publisher. It took me a long time to get the manuscript back, and when he did return it, his opinion was that this material should not get published, that it revealed too much, and publication was bound to lead to adverse consequences. A regular confidence man he was, that one! But I admit I had had thoughts in that direction myself, and he merely confirmed them. Well, I had other things on my mind. I was at that time preparing the move up to Suhalia,[3] and that was an enormous undertaking. We left shortly thereafter and I gave no further thought to the matter. I didn't stay in touch with the Paris people, wanted to get away from all that social involvement. Then in 1926 I find out about the publication of *Le Mystère des Cathédrales!* It was entirely based on my work."

I recall that this session ended abruptly about this point. And while we were to return to the subject of the mysterious manuscript in the near future, he never again mentioned the twofold theft and trickery at the heart of Fulcanelli.

⊖

Aor insisted on my reading certain "good texts." Every *good* text was said to carry the entire *Oeuvre*, but was written and had to be studied from a particular point of view to yield its full meaning. There is a vision pertinent to each particular cosmic moment, and it is the cosmic moment that preoccupies the good author.

"Don't misunderstand the moment. Moments can last a long time. The present moment, such as I define it in my book, is in fact eternity. The Hermetic problem of our particular moment is Salt, but we have no good and complete texts from that point of view; we have good texts from the point of view of Sulphur and Mercury, but the shift in emphasis on the problem of Salt is recent, since around the turn of the century, and in direct relationship with post-Newtonian physics and the crisis in Darwinism. This was the concern of the Chacornac group, although they never quite had the right vision of things. The texts closest to the point are undoubtedly Basil Valentine and Nicolas Flamel. But first you must know the Emerald Tablet, with the Commentary, of course. I have it in my room; I'll bring it out next time."

Beyond compare as pure philosophy, the Emerald Tablet had been traced by Aor through its forerunner, the glyptic Narmer Tablet, all the way to the edge of prehistory. While the Emerald Tablet is well known, a commentary by a sixteenth century adept, Joannes Grasseus, whose identity hides behind the professional paradigm of *Hortulanus*, the Gardener, is but rarely seen in print. This was the first text Aor discussed with me in some detail.

But it was from the Benedictine Basil Valentine that I

learned most about the mind of the alchemist.

"You don't read Hermetic texts to obtain information on alchemical procedures, you read them to form a mentality and a perception. Just keep in mind what is involved here. All through the history of Western thinking there is this split between the Pythagorean and the Aristotelian, only the split goes back further, to Kemi versus Babylon. Contemporary society is the inheritor of Babel. But right along with it runs the line that starts with the Pharaohs, and the mentality is opposite. It shows most clearly in the mathematics. You know, *rien ne marque tant l'esprit que les nombres.* It makes a fundamental difference in the entire scientific structure whether you conceive of two as one plus one or as the dividing of one into two."

By far the most influential text for the practical work of Aor's time was Basil Valentine's *Twelve Keys of Philosophy.* Very pagan in its reliance on astrology, mythology and mineral relationships, this text contains its share of pitfalls for the "puffer," the despised *"souffleur"* devoid of philosophy, who reads his texts as a cook would recipes. The first hurdle concerns the order of the twelve chapters. The adept, a slow and thorough reader, realizes that they are not meant to be studied in their sequential presentation. In his edition, where he prefaces each key with a few descriptive paragraphs, Canseliet points to this fact in his discussion of the first key:

> As concerns the symbolism of these twelve images, the attentive reader as well as the sagacious experimenter will not fail to notice the deliberate dispersion of Basil Valentine's development, who felt the obligation to abide by the usual ways and manners of the Masters.[4]

Forewarned, I did my best to solve the riddle, all the while remaining very conscious of the fact that I did not know precisely what I was looking for. Aor had me read the text over and over again, and I scrutinized the twelve figurations until I knew each one in great detail. But I continued to be aware of reading a jumbled-up text. Finally Aor relented.

"This text is remarkably clear when put into the right order, and quite obscure in the order it presents itself. But note that the order itself is clearly indicated in the text. That is part of what makes it a masterpiece of esoteric writing."

I was by that time fairly exasperated from the countless hours I had spent on this seemingly futile project.

"But what is the sense of communicating something by putting it into the most obtuse form possible!"

"But you don't understand, the only usefulness of the text is its obscurity."

I admitted that I did not understand.

"To penetrate a good alchemical text takes the same kind of effort needed to penetrate the natural phenomenon. The text is set up for that purpose. I will gladly give you a hand, but what I tell you must not go any further, *il ne faut pas que ça aille plus loin.*"

I wasn't sure I had understood correctly.

"You mean you do not want me to repeat what you will tell me?"

He gave me a long, hard look.

"Yes," he said after a while, "I know this goes against the grain for you, because you don't understand the value of the text. Its obscurity, if we must qualify it in that manner, can evaporate in an instant, the instant the reader makes the discovery of the author's mentality, his bias, his angle of vision. With a good author, the discovery can be akin to a revelation, an opening of perception, and that is the value of the text. And the possibility of such a revelation is destroyed if light is shed on these pseudo-obscurities. Explanation will effectively destroy the power of the text. I could give you a version of this text that explains every image, every analogy, every mythological or astrological reference and correspondence, and you would have learned nothing. It is not a learning you are after, it is a God-given revelation which is hindered by any rational interference. I would be destroying the text if I wrote a glossary."

This is how the hurdle of the "secret" first came up. In the "God-given revelation" which, according to Aor, the text might afford, I incontrovertibly recognized my experience of breakthrough. Added to it now was the notion of "secret," presenting itself in an unexpected guise, however. The secret in this case was not being kept to prevent others from knowing, but on the contrary to preserve the possibility of knowing. The text was to be considered as a precious "tool for breakthrough," an instrument of knowledge. In order to make contact with the author's reality, a specific mental and emotional effort was to be made, and if that effort was assisted or eliminated, the experience of breakthrough could no longer occur. In other words, as long as the text remained irrational, a possibility of knowledge existed. Made rational, the text merely reduced to a network of analogies which could provide interesting intellectual research perhaps, but would prove without value for the adept's progress.

I had kept silent for a time. He leaned forward and looked at me with utmost seriousness.

"Have you any idea how much time I have spent over the *Twelve Keys*? The months, the years I have spent over these few pages? I have been reading this book since the age of nineteen and I'm still reading it. Always in the hope that one more reading, under the right conditions, in the right frame of mind, in the right meditation I should say, would make one or another as yet obscure proposition shine with the splendor of evidence, open up the vision, make me *see* the man at work, make me feel the gesture, not contemplate the object, but sense the color, the number, the volume. *La forme, vous y êtes!* The *form* is the only passport to heaven. And to read a good author time and time again is the second best way to get to know the form."

He leaned back; I was fascinated. He was smoking his pipe, which he did in an effort to cut down on his cherished Turkish cigarettes.

"The best way is *l'expérience*," he added with a smile.

As the French term covers the English meaning of both

"experience" and "experiment," I felt entitled to ask; "Do you mean this in a pragmatic sense, or as laboratory work?"

"Pragmatic! *que diable!* None of that! Forget the *pragma.* Nothing practical or useful in a materialistic way enters into this work. The *Oeuvre* is useless except as *proof.* The aim is not to make gold or medicines. Once a result is attained, there are unexpected byproducts, of course. If you recognize them, you can use them. But you will get nowhere at all looking for them. Perception of form, that's all that can be worked on. And inscription of *l'expérience,* a technique of the emotional complex, the prayer at the athanor."

I explained the language problem.

"*Aha, en effet,* that is a difficulty. It must be significant that the Anglo-Saxons separated the abstract general sense from the concrete and technical one, *non?* Never mind, here is what we are talking about: the external experience of perception coordinated with the internal experience of consciousness. No memory, no creative imagination, no elaboration whatsoever. The perception is form, form, and only form. We know our instruments, don't we? Or do we? Do we know how to use our five senses for what they are? *Eh bien, Monsieur, non!* Emphatically no! We no longer know. But we can have contact with a few people who trained themselves to see, hear, touch, smell, and taste and who have written about what it is like when the senses are tuned to their element and stop seeing, hearing, touching, smelling, and tasting *things,* an objective world. It has *become* this way; we know from Pharaonic Egypt and from the *practicing,* the *manipulating* investigators of the natural world, that the perception of the primitive, in his natural inborn spirituality, is always identical, whatever culture or century. It is this perception that a good text is meant to induce."

He then recommended that I should read the text once more.

"Remember what you are reading. Look at the title: *Duodecim Claves Philosophiae.*"

And he put such an insistent accent on the "duodecim"

that I could not help thinking he was giving me a clue.

Until then, I had done my reading of Basil Valentine in Aor's study, between lunch and tea time, while he was taking a siesta in his room. The book which he would bring me before retiring to his quarters was a very old edition, part of a collection of Hermetic texts. I believe it must have been a copy of the 1741 edition by Guillaume Salmon, although I cannot be certain. On this day, however, after the discussion I just related, he excused himself for a moment and returned with an edition of the *Twelve Keys* edited by Canseliet and published by *Éditions de Minuit* in Paris in 1956.

"Here," he said, handing me the book, "you have deserved your own copy. Consider it a present."

I have kept this book with me all these years in silence. It has brought me more than an understanding of the Benedictine's *Keys*, more even than a fair insight into the work in general (from Basil's point of view, of course!); it brought to my hand the most palpable proof of a determining conjunction for the course of Hermetic science. I am speaking of the collaboration of Aor and Fulcanelli.

$$\ominus$$

Life seldom abides by the dictates of strict chronology. It spins its becoming in cycles of time, with all the repetitions that cycles imply, with analogy at identical moments of different loops on this spiral that winds and unwinds not in space, but in orientation. There is a sense to nature because there is a *direction* to the living phenomenon. And only with direction do we truly know where we are going.

I therefore do not apologize for temporal leaps in my story whenever they serve to bring out more clearly the subject, the Hermetic, occult, political, and private Aor, into the brightest light we can muster. I pray for floodlights in this search, but must be satisfied with the glow of a candle. The life of the alchemist is notoriously hidden, a contradiction in terms which he carries over into his acts: he always builds a chink into his armor through which memory can flow lightly and steadily. Then he prepares the discovery of the issue. This is called discipleship, a correspondence full of subtleties and mystery. It transcends all other ties which could bind the two participants. Personal considerations are set aside, for as soon as they intrude, the discipleship ceases. Not so the effects of the discipleship, however. In Hermetic transmission, furthermore, there is no school, only master and disciple.

The "disappearance" of the Hermetist is a carefully orchestrated progression, witness Flamel, Fulcanelli, . . . and Aor. Usually, the hiding place is behind another work of importance: *St. Jacques de la Boucherie* for Flamel, *Le Temple de l'Homme* for Aor. I believe it is a game played with circumstance, design, and intuition. *Homo ludens* within the adept bears closer scrutiny. Play, trickery, deceit, and genius all live here in uncomfortable proximity.

Be that as it may, in this particular case, there were forces consciously created by Aor himself for their effectiveness in making the Hermetic Aor disappear, save for these pages, after my generation. Hidden within Schwaller de Lubicz, he left the Hermetic synthesis from the point of view of our cosmic time; by tradition, he also left the voice to proclaim it. The monument constructed to Schwaller de Lubicz, in its lumbering exoteric manifestation, has liberated the Hermetic Aor, and I know that he knows: *L'Oeuvre vit.*

The extent to which I became the repository of the Hermetic Aor surfaced years after his death, and it is this jump in time that brings these necessary digressions.

When a first attempt at publication of the works of Schwaller de Lubicz was organized in 1973, I contacted the author's estate, represented by Lucie Lamy. She responded with friendly letters and we corresponded tentatively on matters of editing, among them the possibility of an introductory biographical sketch of the author. An attempt at biography, unsatisfactory to my mind because of omissions, distortions, and misplaced emphasis, did exist in the form of Isha's *"Aor," R.A. Schwaller de Lubicz. Sa Vie—Son Oeuvre.*[5] We shall have occasion to return to this memoir. At the time I am placing the reader now (1973–74), the time of a first discussion concerning eventual publication of de Lubicz in English, I felt that any biographical note that would certainly preface the work should take into consideration the Aor-Fulcanelli relationship about which he had talked so much and so freely to me. Not a word of this appeared in Isha's book. I therefore approached Lucie with the thought that on this occasion, some clarity should be shed on the events which had seemed so important to Aor. To my amazement, she denied any knowledge of them.[6]

From that moment on, details began to gather into one large fresco of the events. I recognized in a flash that this matter would remain entirely in my own hands. I started to remember incidents that had not struck me in their time, but now took on special meaning. There was the oft-repeated caveat concerning the female mind, constitutionally incapable of abstract thought and therefore unable to participate in the *active* pursuit of the Hermetic *Oeuvre,* although entrusted with an important *passive* role. I had known that Aor never spoke to Lucie about the *Oeuvre,* but I hadn't realized to what extent he had kept her apart from this, his principal concern, and to what extent he had confined her to the role of scribe in the Temple of R.A. Schwaller de Lubicz.

Although I was and remain convinced that this was the true state of affairs, another possibility existed which I could not afford to neglect: that she knew all I knew, and perhaps more, but that she had her reasons for wanting to suppress all evidence of Aor as an alchemical manipulator, destroying the Hermetic adept in order to keep alive only the front of the Egyptologist. This was the aspect of him in which she was the outstanding authority, whereas no contact existed for her with his occult side, which must have struck her as a mysterious, even unsavory component. Perhaps she felt it as an incomprehensible quirk in an otherwise brilliant personality, and her duty to eliminate.

Having thus discovered the possible uniqueness of my information, I began to feel the full burden of the Aor-Fulcanelli legacy.

A memory that comes to mind: after using a rare edition of Bernard de Trévise as the basis of a discussion, Aor left the book on the table as we broke up our session.

"You see," he said, pointing to the book, "Lucie will come in here and bring the book back to my room, to the spot where it belongs, and she will never, never open it, because I have told her that it is not for her."

While the above arguments may explain the existence within his intimate environment of a mysterious silence concerning this episode, they offer no explanation whatever for the silence maintained around the Fulcanelli succession. Dujols, Champagne, Canseliet, the Chacornacs—these men were well aware of Aor's existence, and he of theirs. Aor made comments about these men that indicated at least an acquaintance. His position in Paris at the time having been what it was, things could hardly have stood otherwise in such a restricted milieu. Yet I have never found his name in any published work.[7] Fulcanelli is full of Aor, but not vice versa. I am not obsessively bookish and have defined my task in such a manner as to contain all my research within my study. Fulcanelli, I am well aware, is surrounded by a great deal of published speculation, and I have glanced at much of it. None of it, however, concerns the persona Aor so diligently built into my mind. Aor is my subject, and objectivity not my main concern. Fulcanelli enters this story only because he preoccupied Aor to the last in a very private way, a Hermetic way in harmony with our title. In no way does my approach suffer from the certainty of having been told the truth.

Nor can I seriously dwell on a scenario that I have devised in extremis, when the mystery of it intruded too insistently into my life. Maybe . . .

Maybe this cultured gentleman, whose contribution to

Egyptology attracted the attention and support of the likes of
the Aga Khan and Jean Cocteau, who had published savant
tomes and whose work had been the object of study in a well-
known French literary review,[8] this gentleman, now quite out
of touch and totally immersed in a personal work, spends the
best part of every afternoon with a young man about whom
he knows only what is revealed by his immediate presence;
he speaks to him about the Hermetic arts, of which he has a
practical grasp sufficient to warrant a large-size professionally
equipped laboratory in his home; he also tells in great detail
a story that his wife has previously sketched out, a story that
is possibly a piece of fiction through and through. Did Aor
invent all this? Under the circumstances, I couldn't help giving the matter some thought, although the idea of this syn-
chronized imposture is utterly incredible.

Not that he would have lacked the sense of humor for such
an elaborate imposture. He possessed his share of the prankster associated with this work ever since Hermes. We need
not limit ourselves to a literary genius like François Rabelais
when looking for humor in alchemical writing. All cabals, all
argots, develop their private jokes. It must be remembered
that everything surrounding the Hermetic text is itself a
cabal. The discovery of the manuscript, as in the case of the
great Benedictine, is itself a part of the manuscript discovered.
When Flamel describes his quest and the travels it entailed,
when he speaks of the mysterious manuscript that fell into
his hands, his various encounters and the sites thereof, all
these events must be read as part of the description of the
work that brought the public *scribe*, master of the calligraphic
gesture, fame and fortune. No cabal, no slang functions without humor, and there is a prank in the very idea of a language
misleading to all but a few. It is the cosmic inside joke that
turns the master into a fool, bent in laughter.

In de Lubicz, the humor is deadly serious. Is it humorous to
introduce a treatise on a Pharaonic temple by hundreds of
pages of geometry and theory of number, without which, as is

well-known, no one enters this temple? It may be amusing subsequently to watch from the inside while a church is being built without the help of compass and ruler! As if that wasn't precisely the mode of construction which gave us the tower of Babel . . .

Galgenhumor, the humor of the gallows, is what the Germans call this kind of pleasantry. It reflects a thorough lack of confidence in present-day intellect.

"There is no way to escape it, we shall have to go back to chipping flint," was his earnest evaluation. "The mentality must be changed from the bottom up, and this is best done through number and geometry. Number is the purest and most perfect expression of esoteric knowledge, and we must return to those bare bones; we have gone too far astray in the imagination. Imagination can be a valuable aid to perception as long as it remains an imaginative imitation through which the perception can be *lived*.[9] It has no place in the workings of the scientific mind that searches for an understanding of those perceptions. The mind must remain passive in the act of cognition, and it can do this in number and geometry, because number and geometry appear absolutely defined in their form, as defined as volume or color. There is one image, though, that can become a matrix of form and thereby arrest perception before it gets lost in the limits of objectivity. Not the image of imagination, mind you, which is an easy three-dimensional substitute for the *volume* of perception. I'm speaking of the image on the flat surface, on the wall, the two-dimensional image. Have we spoken of the rebus yet?"

We had, as I have reported. So we spoke again of picture-writing, and its advantage over syntax and vocabulary.

"The etymologists," by which I knew he meant Fulcanelli, "are children of our time, but the glyph is the sign of tomorrow. Not one of those grammarians practiced geometry, not one of them realized the problem of perception, of decipherment. Number and geometry show the structure of that decipherment, since they present themselves as perfectly knowable. Do you realize the advantage of natural phenomena making their appearance named in perfectly defined form, instead of objectified into a substance that we cannot come to terms with, and therefore burden with conventional nomenclature? You do, I know, that's why we are talking. But how can this become generally understood, without people disqualifying themselves either because they 'know nothing about mathematics,' or else because they know too much and are thoroughly spoiled by irrational numbers and differential equations. It takes vision to realize the perfect formal definitions of one or two, and therefore the perfect comprehension they allow: a comprehension of the irrational in one, and of the poles of our universe in two. The same goes for the square and the diagonal: total presence in the perception, including name and relation. The same, again, with glyph. Totally present in the flat, two-dimensional image."

"And totally absent in the image-volume of imagination?"

"Indeed, but totally present again in the volume that is space."

$$\ominus$$

Armed with my new insight, I had taken up Basil Valentine again, and found my level of reading much improved. I systematically combed the text for all possible references to the number twelve, explicated or implied, and had gathered little that seemed of consequence when I reached the Ninth Key. Here, in a review of a colorful planetary system, the author presents the idea of weighing the zodiac upon the two arms of Libra, the scale. Naming the keys from one through twelve according to the zodiacal signs, from Aries through Pisces, I began to dispose them on the scale as indicated. This gave me a quite different arrangement of the chapters, as well as indications concerning relationships between chapters. I began reading once again from the beginning, and this time I seemed to be reading a different book. I had made a step in understanding, a step somehow transcending the particular case at hand. I could no longer deny the validity of Aor's argument:

the discovery of this detail did comprise an experience of suddenly broadened horizons which I hope, by this minimal presentation, not to have defused for the eventual reader of the Benedictine.

We were in those days spending considerable time on questions of perception and form. I was being somewhat successful with my spherical spiral exercise, which I had come to consider a welcome relief from the thought problems these new experiences inevitably brought with them. I mentioned that our increasing involvement with a definition of form seemed to displace an emphasis on function I had noticed in my reading of *Le Temple de l'Homme.*

"In theory, I mean in communicating from writer to reader, it is a lot easier to be concerned with the principial level of function than with perception of form. The one is an abstract, causal level, usually degraded to a concept of law, while the other can be the shared presence of an evolutionary moment. But you have to realize that function can achieve the immediacy of formal perception only through the living moment of the bodily organs, on the foundation of animal reaction. There lies the domain of the perfect gesture at the correct moment, there lies the art of life. It is a neglected field of study, unfortunately; witness the sorry state of our medicine. Any other approach on a typically human level of perceptual intelligence will take formal perception to mean an objective evidence. In that case, when all you perceive are objects, it becomes useless to speak of function and functional consciousness because with that kind of perception, psychological consciousness falsifies everything. I am teaching a functional consciousness that necessitates a momentary cut, *une coupure,* an elimination of the cerebral cortex so successful that not only the machinations of the brain disappear, but all formal representation as well. But very few people possess the meditational mastery to perform the proper gesture in that abstracted state, and the practical training cannot be conveyed in theory. So we can do no more than talk about it, hoping we communicate. But formal perception is immeasurably more accessible; in fact, it rushes at us with great force. We have to hold it back from its universal propensity of making us identify form with object. So perhaps one should advocate a therapy of formal perception before proposing a functional consciousness? What do you think?"

I thought that there was certainly ample opportunity in the arts, Hermetic and otherwise, to practice the proper gesture of functional consciousness, and he agreed. I also concurred with the difficulty he had brought out of eliminating all formal representations in a meditational state. I had learned with Da Passano that thinking of nothing was still thinking, and I agreed that it would be more creative, at least from the artist's point of view, to revalorize form instead of eliminating it at the crucial moment of cognition.

We concurred that for the average perception, function reduces to formal relationships and he conceded that in itself, function remains as abstract as the axis of the wheel, the irrational though unquestioningly accepted immobility at the center of rotation. Function thus is an immediate perception only in its organic expression, in the living body. Anywhere else, it becomes an act of reason, it acquires a name, by information, so to speak.

I was at the time unaware of the pages in which Aor had spoken with such intensity about functional consciousness. They belong to the *Reflections,* a collection of brief pieces, seldom more than a page or two in length, that were grouped with *Nature Word* as belonging to the same time, and had therefore been published posthumously. These paragraphs are the overflow of the clever scenario set up by *Nature Word,* Nature's sixty-five answers to questions unstated, capped by one singly explicit question, alone to be left unanswered by her. *Nature Word* is an eloquent call for a functional consciousness. But the one question that receives no answer from Nature is a question concerning not function, but *form.*[10] A tangible form as intermediary, as mean-term in the process of knowledge, such is the quest that has left Nature speechless.

And such also was the intellectual pursuit that engaged him most readily at the time I knew him, seven or eight years after he had formulated the question.

"Note that as soon as functions stop being identified through their bodily existence, they cease being subject to immediate perception; they become logical subjects in an act of reason, and we can tie them down with a name, without harming them. Form, on the other hand, as I've said many times, form must never be burdened with a conventional name in our process of perception, a perception which in this case *is* immediate, because we inevitably would contract it to a particular object.[11] The 'name' must appear as part of the form, not as part of a man-made language,[12] unless it remain useless for determining any functions beyond the most mechanical ones, and we end up with a Newtonian cosmos we thought we had put behind us along with Piscian realism. If you want to know function, study the function *phi*, the dichotomizing function manifested as form in *number*, or the vegetative function in the *color* green, or again the harmonizing function in its *sound*, and the styptic function determining *volume* as form. That is what I call creative perception, the perceptual *gesture* which can never be written on a page, never be revealed in a text, only in the living moment. Here lies the teacher's importance. The master of science does not teach words, he shows a gesture. Why else the laboratory? Research is nonsense unless perception is considered a part of it. Because perception is a gesture, the written word can teach very little about form. But you are a painter, you must know what I mean; the painter investigates the possibilities of form. His canvas is doomed to failure, but the practitioner can make giant steps in his concept of form."

"Yes, he can even be catapulted right beyond his discipline," I interjected; I knew this to have been what happened in my breakthrough.

"So much the better, he is now ready for a more inclusive discipline. *Il faut toucher à tout!* We must never specialize; the more general our view, the clearer our perception. You can see where everything in the modern world works to pervert perception, but if we want to work out our destinies we will have to find a cure. We must speak abstractly, in terms of functions, but we must perceive the concrete gesture by living the cosmic fact. The gesture as it relates to form cannot be replaced by the word: the formal level is too fragile and fugitive for names. The form is only *perceived* through the gesture, never named. Remember, all we are saying pertains to formal perception and not to functional consciousness, which is pure identification. The difficulty with functional abstraction is the same as with all ecstasies: they remain personal, they lose contact with the concrete, they are useless to science. Yet everything must start with such experiences; they furnish the necessary background, they show the possibilities of abstraction. But then must come a realization, at least if you are a scientist. And here we need a link between that functional abstraction and the tangible world, we need the intermediary, *mediety, le moyen terme.* That will have to be form, and there will have to be a tangible aspect to that form.[13] A step beyond nature! But at least it points to where the work lies: in the reform of perception."

I still remained uncertain of having situated his notion of perception and form correctly. Generally speaking, it seemed to me that what we perceive naturally, as nature, is a multiplicity of units, interacting only feebly, and mostly not at all. The symbiosis of nature, the vast complex of associations and unions that we *know* as a universal involvement of everything with everything, that world is not perceived, it is a functional and abstract world.[14] We perceive a separateness immediately; we cannot perceive the oneness: perception details the phenomenon. Does the effort lie in softening the strict definition, and permitting more inclusiveness, more general interaction? And would it be at this edge of separation that we have to contact the object's form before we contact the object's materiality? I used to prepare questions of this sort, statements of the best of my understanding, but it was useless, as Aor avoided all attempts at further definition for fear of narrowing the idea of form or estranging it from function and from function's representative: gesture.

"Just as I call functional consciousness a gesture of identification, so I could say that formal perception is a gesture of relation. We have already talked about imitative imagination as a tool for functional identification, where no formal perception is needed.[15] But now to find the polarity to this abstraction, in order to obtain tangible scientific results, we need a means, and that can only be form. It is the form of the object that must become the subject of *immediate* perception, not the object itself."

"How is that immediacy to be understood?"

"That immediacy of form is a direct presence to the mind; it is a spiritual vision. All senses perceive, but obviously the immediacy of their perception differs. It is a nice measure of contemporary spiritual blindness to attempt immediacy, so-called, through instrumentation, microscopes, and telescopes, as if that could avoid the ultimate reduction of perception which inevitably occurs at eye level, when the cerebral cortex sends instructions to reduce form, macro or microscopic, to an object for which the brain has invented a name. *Une fiction d'un bout à l'autre!*"

"Doesn't that limit perception to the visual event?"

"Because of the immediacy which the definition of form demands, we are indeed favoring visual perception. Yet the auditory aspect has the same immediacy and is superior in precision, furthermore. Trouble is, it is limited to the degree of being practically useless. Tone, which relates to sound the way form relates to object, carries the ready-named, ready-numbered laws of harmony, one of the most fundamental cosmic forms. I defy you to divide a volume into a ratio of 4:5, for example, or 3:2, or even 2:1 visually, and with any kind of accuracy, and yet the ear does it naturally. It even has some kind of built-in vernier when the difference becomes critical: the smaller the difference between two tones, the more pronounced the dissonance. This kind of accuracy is absolutely unknown to the visual, but it is innate knowledge for the audible. This should be a clue for the correct use of eye and ear, but we continue seeing *things*, and we listen to noise, mainly, and sound, and specifically, we listen to *words*. Never do we hear *tone* in that process, but we pretend to *see* tone in color. This is a good example of how the senses overlap, and what direction a sensorial synthesis has to go."

"I suppose that such auditive formal perception takes the ear of a very special kind of musician, not just of a music-maker. More like a Pythagorean hearing the music of the spheres . . . "

"The important concept is the *hearing*, indeed, and not the listening. For the eye, it is perceiving, not looking; for the ear, it is hearing, not listening. There is a passivity involved, because the senses present a resistance to the invisible, the inaudible, the untouchable, untasteable . . . Did I get them all?"

"You left out the unsmellable, but I get the point."

"Ah, the unsmellable. We have descriptions in Egypt of that psychogamous moment when the unsmellable becomes smellable, and it is said that 'the odor of the god pervades the palace.' All good authors mention the olfactory events in the work. But this is even more specialized than sound, and it takes quite some practice to forego the immediate reaction: 'It smells like . . . ' followed by a noun that corresponds to a visual concept. Such a nose is useless, although its memory can be trained to a very fine intelligence. But let's return to the ear and to the *tone*, the knowledge form that corresponds to it. For audible form, communication is even more difficult than for the visual, as the ear bypasses the higher centers of the brain. But there is no doubt that events such as vibrating strings offer relatively incomprehensible visual forms, whereas absolute precision prevails in their auditory form."

"Can I assume that from an informational point of view such audible forms are restricted to harmonic material?"

"The ear is the organ of harmony, and exists for the perception of harmony; it cannot do otherwise. The crass rationalization of tone through its degradation into sound-concepts is our limitation. Don't just study string length when you study harmony, study the ear as well, otherwise your understanding might remain strictly intellectual."[16]

"The other senses must then be fairly useless in the perception of form?"

"Their information must be translated into a visual and spatial image which not only lacks immediacy altogether, but remains, by and large, imprecise and quite general. The feel and the taste of an apple, for example, may give you the concept 'apple,' but cannot be construed as the perception of an individual within its environment."

I readily visualized perception of form as a first and quite unspoiled synthesis of the natural phenomenon, but I couldn't help wondering about the role of *structure* in this perception, about the material or substantial constitution which yet is manifestly at one with the form and inseparable from it.

"Substance, matter, or structure have no part in the perception of form. They need an analysis, an examination of detail unknown to form. Form is never reached by measure or reflection. Form is always and only *perceived*."

"And form can therefore make no immediate statement about function?"

"But don't forget that the intuition of perception is only a first step. If it remains but a flitter such as it usually is, then no work is accomplished, and evolution is furthered only by the gravity of time, the time of mechanical functions, deductions whose premises are objects observed through instrumentation, *enfin*, that whole edifice which is ready to come down and remains standing only because a better construction is inconceivable, irrational. Very well then, let's dispense with it by making it our very first principle, a oneness in the beginning, always the same geometric conduct of the mind. If the irrationality is faced and admitted from the beginning, subsequent conduct will be concrete; if this commitment is skirted, all conduct falls into a chasm of materiality, with the observer tied hand and foot to a rhythm designed by a great god, tied so securely that all consciousness of that rhythm disappears. Academic sciences have discovered this dilemma only recently, but they cannot conceive an alternative, they don't understand Prometheus, the Hermetic gesture that "steals" the fire. Only his personality, seated in the liver, according to natural medicine, is punished for the theft. He himself, Prometheus, remains the creative hero. There are crimes for which only the crime itself is sufficient punishment. Foremost among them is the crime of lèse-majesté. But its expiation also carries the highest rewards."

I understood that the mere perception of form could not convey a knowledge of the entity's function among other forms. On the other hand, everything points to the universe of natural phenomena as a web of functional interrelationships. I wondered if we did not deprive the natural phenomenon of all meaning by rending this functional net and isolating form within a context.

"Unless we want form to remain a purely esthetic concern, we cannot consider it apart from the entity's function. Form and function are the two basic general principles through which we grasp the natural event. The first tends to answer a question of "what," the other of "why." Yet both lack the substantive materiality that could answer a "how." This third member of the defining ternary of the natural entity, this "how" is the domain of measure and analysis, the field of substance and materiality as well as of structure. Contemporary views tend to identify form with structure, yet form is what makes the oneness of entity, while structure is its full detail."

I now conceived the natural entity as the conjunction of form and function with a third and variable term (I called it "the third term") lending concreteness to the event and ranging from metaphysical substance through atomistic structure to the palpable physical material. We discussed the order of variability of this triad within the natural phenomenon.

"Function is a model of invariance throughout the realms

of nature. Gravity, polarization, attraction and repulsion—these functions express themselves at all stages of objectivity. Functions such as digestion and respiration are by no means 'later' in a so-called functional order, they merely appear to span only the later vegetal and animal realms, the realms that indeed are chronologically later than the mineral. The functions, however, those of digestion and respiration for instance, these functions are present at polarization, make no mistake. A function does not necessarily have to manifest itself in matter at all times: the cause is not compelled to show an effect, it can remain in a homogeneous causal state until its time of heterogeneity has come.[17] This can be shown under laboratory conditions. I would advise you to remain quite open also to the idea of such functions as these exerting themselves in the mineral realm as well, although they would not be obvious to a structured perception. Preconceptions, whatever their origin, rarely make trusty companions for this kind of investigation."

"As compared to function, form would then seem like the essence of variability, wouldn't it?"

"Invariant function produces variety of form. Still, all these many aspects can be categorized as forms; they are the individuals of a species. But this third term, as you have come to call it, indispensable for the grounding of the structure, that third term loses even specific definition, which is precisely why we categorize it merely as a 'third term', by default, *si vous voulez*, a third term necessary and sufficient to afford the function-form event. If a collective noun were to be found as third term, it would have to be as general as the fact that there is something rather than nothing; it would have to be the collective noun for sheer existence."

"Then the third term is conditioned by a point of view?"

"You could say that the third term indicates a level of abstraction at which the entity is perceived: the level of substance, or the material level where substance is informed, or the structural level where substance is ordered. And all manner of shades, variations, and combinations of the above as

there are thinking minds. This is why metaphysical disagreement dwells in the third term, while by and large, there is
little difference of opinion as to the perception of form: detail
never enters the formal argument. Generally speaking, it is
the power of concreteness that gives third terms the most
solid common ground."

"Did I hear you speaking of *order* as a third term?"

"Structural order, of course, what better place than structure to find order? We must be very careful with the notion of
order, particularly when speaking of functional order. It
seems evident to us that there should be an order in functions,
but actually, the functional order is simultaneity. I might
refer myself to a functional order, but when we stop to think,
we create a temporal and spatial milieu by language, a volume
that is a form and not a function. Nothing controversial about
formal order, of course, it is obviously chronological, it is
genesis. Will you tell me that the same is true for functions,
that the respiratory function, for instance, is manifestly of a
later order than the primordial polarizing function? You'd be
absolutely wrong, and I could make an excellent case for the
immediate flux and reflux of respiration in the dualizing polarity. There is a breath in the earliest creation! And doesn't
polarization, separation, division already contain the essence
of digestion or elimination? I tell you, keeping and rejecting
is as old as duality. There is no early and late here, as there is
with form; there is simultaneity, an event that does not fit
into language. As we cannot express simultaneity in language, we cannot help speaking of functional order. Let's take
it for what it is: grammatical language."

"A convenient and somewhat negligent way of expressing
ourselves?"

"Convenient sometimes, as when we contrast functional
order with spatial, chronological, numerical, or social order.
Actually what we mean to indicate by functional order is not
the ordering of a number of separate functions; it is rather
that function in itself is the essence of order, that order is
inherent to function. Thus it is not *order* we find at primor-

dial functional levels, but affinity and harmony. Between creative oneness and multiplicity, is there order? I almost said: is there *time* for order? Contrary to form where a chronological order is obvious, namely the order that is the genesis of form in time, functional order is pure instantaneity. The instant cannot be ordered; order is absent at the beginning, and between unity and multiplicity there does not exist an order such as we can geometrically prove to exist between oneness and duality. Between unity and multiplicity there exists a milieu of harmony and affinity that already implies a multiplicity. Before you have order, you'll have pervasive harmony and omnipresent affinity. *Vous y êtes!*"

I wondered if the dual number that exists in Egyptian hieroglyphs was significant in view of the differentiation he was proposing between duality and multiplicity. He brought out that this distinction is found in Sanskrit and many older Indo-European languages, and that in primitive perception, the distinction was certain between "the pair" and oneness as well as multiplicity. This led to a lengthy discussion of grammatical language versus picture script, and of the impossibility of the inflected word to capture the perception of two identical objects that can only be illustrated in the temporal and spatial vacuum of the flat surface, the two-dimensional abstraction of the plane.

"An excellent example of two-dimensional image, of plane image as a form of perception!"

At a later time, while working on some notes from those days, it occurred to me to gather in his published works the references to the term "order," and it turned out to be a relatively meager harvest. "Affinity," on the other hand, is a much more frequent reference. In *Nature Word* there is an admonition against thinking in terms of chronological order instead of functional order, the comparative use of the word he had mentioned.[18] In *Sacred Science,* we find a cosmic order in obligation to a "natural chemical affinity," order bound by necessity, order as a second generation, a progeny of harmony and affinity.[19] What I understood was that while formal order is necessarily chronological, being dependent on a genesis that in itself is time, functional order could only be instantaneous. In *Nature Word* there is a page examining the question of "unity or multiplicity of causes" where we are shown multiplicity in disorder, a definition of chaos.[20] This creative oneness in the beginning generates by its primordial activity *not order, but harmony by affinity*, through attraction and repulsion, through polarity, and only "then" does order come to the worlds. Harmony effaces multiplicity, says de Lubicz, which means that becoming is negation. It also means that in *creative* oneness, there is a total multiplicity in absolute absence of order, the perfectly homogeneous milieu, Chaos. A sole-singular generative function negates that multiplicity by harmonization, re-creating a new multiplicity: dialectics of being and non-being, extreme affinity.[21] Again in *Nature Word*, he speaks of an "invariable functional order" directing what is essentially analogous to the formal order, namely "phenomena engendered one after the other."[22] While the multiplicity of forms is clearly indicated in this serialization, a succession of change that can only lead to change, the invariance within the functional order contradicts a functional becoming and implies functional simultaneity: if an ordered sequence of functions had ever existed, invariability could never have been regained. Invariability, the identity and simultaneity of all possible changes, is given all at once, *en bloc*, "in the beginning," because it can never be regained where change has established order. Such is the ambiguity of "functional order."

"Of course, you can always say that there is a 'first' primordial function, the scission of origin, the function *phi*. But it is just a convenience, or better, an inconvenience of language, because immediately and simultaneously with it, there is a whole net of functional activity. Immediately, simultaneously, all those words say already too much and they give me the uncomfortable feeling that a notion of time creeps into your mind, a chronology of events. So everything is distorted, and you end up doing no more than cogitating, triturating ideas. The best manner in which to conceive principial functions is as a harmonic milieu of affinities. By the way, are you still practicing perception of the spherical spiral?"

Although the idea of a perceptual reeducation had come up several times, the contemplation of the spherical spiral was the only practical training he had ever presented me with. I was used to early morning meditations since my time with Da Passano, and had included the spherical spiral exercise in this hygiene. As far as the theoretical background for this perceptual therapeutics was concerned, two relations of the sensorium were fundamental: the relation to the *elements* of perception, and the relation to the *forms* thereof. The mechanics of the relation of the senses to the elements has been variously described in his work.[23] They show the most primitive functional contiguity of man and his milieu, a communication system of five mediums that inform perception. It was the second relation that preoccupied him at the time I knew him. I later diagrammed the sensorium-form relationships into a Perception Construct which might be helpful in these discussions (Plate I).

"It is interesting to study the senses from the point of view of form-perception, to become aware of their functions as formative instruments. Realize how prejudiced we have become in favor of sight, because it seems to give us the volume so immediately and, we think, so surely, so certainly. But that isn't even the eye's primary function; this perception of volume is entirely secondary, it is color that is the primary sight-form, because sight has as medium the element Fire. In the same way, volume is secondary form for the hearing function; it is sound that is primary. But volume is the material presence and all the senses partake of it. What is seductive is the directness of sight, it being the only exposed nerve of our body, and going straight into the brain! The immediacy of it is what attracts us, but it is a solution of facility, and without perceptual education, it results in a universe of objects, of things. Actually, for the proportional perception that gives us so many profound hints as to the cosmic constitution, the ear is a far better tool. The laws of harmony are just that, perception of ratios and proportionality, and here the sound-form is without equal. And look at the extension of the ear as formative instrument, look at the field it covers! Sound belongs to it entirely, and it shares number with the eye through its perception of the laws of harmony. And it participates in volume, as we have seen, as all senses do, through the vibratory phenomenon. So actually, ear and eye hold equal dominion over the universe of form."

"Being the organ of harmony must give the ear some privileged contacts."

"Contact with the general disposition of affinity. Undoubtedly the reason for its being the seat of orientation. Harmony is the foundation of all sensorial possibilities, the basis of differentiation that makes the sensorial phenomenon. What is manifest is differentiated from what is not."

"I presume that for practical purposes, in perceptual education, we need consider only sight and hearing."

"Well, a qualitative education of touch, smell, and taste is possible, although perceptual excellence of these three minor senses is most often a gift of nature. Take touch, for example. A qualitatively educated sense of touch might manifest itself by an intimate "feeling" for an entity, such as detecting the therapeutic attributes of plants by touching them and crushing their leaves with the fingertips. You can speak to Isha on this topic; she knows a lot about it."

I had already heard from Isha herself that this exceptional faculty of hers was a great help in their developing the Suhalia Homeopathic medicines, one of the products of the de Lubicz's establishment in Switzerland.

We spoke more about the way the three lower senses, touch, taste, and smell, had furnished their experiential groundwork for aeons, when evolution was still entirely determined by endless repetition in time, before the emotional filter had allowed inscription of experience. Beginning with the higher mammals in the Tertiary, there is an evolutionary acceleration as the ternary of lower senses, entirely concerned with *volume* as knowledge form, relinquishes the reins of evolution to the two higher senses, ear and eye.

"That trinity of lower senses can in fact be summed up under the sense of touch," he continued, "as both smell and taste are a matter of contact: taste is a touching by papilla specialized for contact with liquids in a specific minienvironment. It is a differentiation from touch proper, the touch that is specialized in the fingertips, but that exists to various degrees in all parts of the body. That is the touch of solid, and to its apperception, liquid is merely a lesser solidity."

"And that lesser solidity has in time imposed itself as a separate contact with the milieu, the sense of taste?"

"Exactly, and the same process with a state of even lesser solidity: air. For that element, touch is even more elusive, yet we still perceive the touch of air as we flail our arms."

"So that olfactory organization is a very refined and specialized touch?"

"Yes, specialized to the degree of detecting an essential scent to this elusive state of matter. Note the close relationship between smell and taste. Note also that the sense of touch diminished in importance as the phenomenon loses consistency. For the ear, touch has become vibration, and for the eye, vibration has become light."

"We still *feel* sound, but we no longer feel light."

"And touch, I mean the three modes of touch, touch proper, taste, and smell—touch has contact with *volume* only. The overwhelming importance of volume as a form of perception, what makes it concrete form *par excellence,* is the fact that it is the only form that contacts the full pentagon of senses. It is extreme concretion in form."

"And number must be extreme abstraction?"

"Yes, you can say that the universe of form, pervaded by affinity, spans between number and volume. Volume and number are the forms of origin, whereas color and sound are later forms of more advanced evolution. Number exists inside and out of the least mineral structure as surely as does volume. Polarity is already number, in the same way that space is already volume."

I questioned Aor concerning the form of perception he calls "plane-image." In the plane—the two-dimensional abstraction—differentiation perceived as image can only be obtained through color. On the homogeneous chaos represented by a blank "white" sheet of paper, only a "lesser blank" can create a heterogeneity, and this differentiation is perceptible as color. Nothing but color can register on the plane, and only the eye can touch it.

"You must understand that the functions that rule color in *fact*, such as the greenness of the chlorophyl function or the blackness of putrefaction, are quite distinct from those that rule color in *image*. Between three-dimensional volume and the puncticular intuition of "dimension one," perception finds a mean term, a mediety, a judicious proportionality between material fact and irrational reality."

This middle ground of two-dimensionality becomes the field for a form of perception called "plane-image" by de Lubicz. In this world, color has become agent of a form, just as light, in the three-dimensional world of facts, is agent of the color-form. The very closest relationship exists between the form and its agent, such as between volume and space, or sound and vibration.

"With plane-image, the two-dimensional picture, we have a sort of color to the second power, because color has in turn become agent, and through this "color squared" we gain the level of abstraction that is expressed by the notion of image: the level of intuitive intellect needed for this imagery."

"So color straddles the two levels of abstraction: the three-dimensional level of fact, and the two dimensional level of image?"

"Indeed, the basic color-form depends on the universe of facts, as do sound and volume-forms. The perception of plane-image-form is an evolutionary step on the scale of abstraction, and will become agent of the number-form: *thought*, and when in harmony with the ear, will become the intuitive intellect of *Entendement*, the synthesis of hearing and seeing in order to know."

"I suppose the plane-image-form encompasses geometry as well as written language."

"Of course, and all that appears in two dimensions is necessarily symbolic."

I am certain that at the time, I did not as yet fully grasp the central role of perception as intermediary between concrete elements and abstract form. I therefore repeat my warning of the beginning: we cannot suppress the writer's inevitable subjectivity; the subjectivity of what he heard, what he saw, what he contacted a quarter of a century ago, and the subjectivity of his telling it today. It would not further our purpose to undo our understanding of today in order to be faithful to a past situation. Today I fully comprehend the importance of his preoccupation and give it the central role it deserves: the subject was perception, the object was form. Back then, I may well have understood the correlation of the senses to the material world through the harmonious four elements, and the abstraction of this information through the human instrument into a functional, a spiritual symbolique. Yet the implications of this state of affairs have only gradually gained clarity over twenty-five years of contact with the works, and by the natural maturation of the ideas.

This subjectivity of the particular moment also colored my perception of the notions discussed, a perception unaware as yet of being itself the subject. Who was perceiving, in those days? I had for some time been discovering a vision closer to myself, and Aor named it for me: the sacred science of Pythagoras. It was the method of this science, or the impossibility of method, that had captivated my interest. I could never forget that he was presenting me with proof for the experience that had meant the breakthrough of my vision, and that this breakthrough had formulated itself in terms of knowledge, of function, and of method. I had therefore not expected to spend this much time and effort on a matter such as "perception" (a subject I had hitherto relegated to the speculations of psychology), and he must at times have noted an impatience.

"It will do no good to show you something if you are unable to perceive it. You understand that no scientific work is possible if the scientific facts are incorrectly *perceived* to begin with. That takes a bit of training. But you are working hard, and you must have noticed, as I have, that you see the world quite differently now than when we began. But if you look around, you will see some unbelievable interpretations. Take the perception of the evolutionary urge to rise toward the subtle, for example, away from gravitational contraction: that urge is fulfilled in our day by spaceships, as if the physical body were a part of the move. All their scientific answers are machines!"

"But hasn't there been a change in this kind of thinking since Heisenberg's work in 1928?"

"I've acknowledged an intellectual, if not yet a spiritual change by saying that the temple has grown larger. But it's a matter of all or nothing. As long as you begin your investigation with the idea of reality as a multitude of material objects surrounding you, instead of with an irrational metaphysical entity, you will continue to perceive only objects. And what I want to show you is not an object, it is a form, a metallic form, although that is an expression that doesn't make much sense, does it?"

"Well . . .

"The form is obtained from the manipulation of a metal, that is what I mean. It is as if the soul of the metal had been separated from its body. Just a manner of speaking, of course, but it is one of the manipulations that has occupied the adepts of our time, and it lies on the path toward the reds and blues of Chartres."

5

The reds and blues of Chartres cathedral.—Plea to the reader.—An antediluvian Sphinx?—The genesis of number.—Divine thievery.—The levels of the diagram. —Sacred secrets.—Good pages missing.—The circle of my masters.—The stone.—A purloined manuscript. —Indigo is indigo.—Live gold!

The reds and blues of Chartres! We have spoken all along of a Pythagorean science, a different mentality whose inexplicable accomplishments taunt us from the depths of time; so far, however, this notion has remained abstract. Now we shall call as witnesses the blues and reds of Chartres, typically undervalued, neglected, and obscured in today's environment. Although by all rights entitled deeply to affect our outlook onto the history of science and civilization, these precious jewels of light shine almost unnoticed in our drab synthetic world.

Whenever the subject of the blues and reds of certain medieval stained glass windows (typified by the Chartres reds and blues) came up, Aor marveled at the lack of impact borne by facts that do not fit our scientific rationality. Undone by neglect rather than actively suppressed, these facts are curiosities allowed to coexist with the tenets of a logic that purports abhorrence of such contradictions. For the manufacture of this glass has remained a mystery to scientific analysis. No chemical pigmentation is to be found, and yet the glass seems tinted throughout its mass.

"I have retrieved fragments of this kind of manufacture in crucibles of early Pharaonic sites. It is a nontechnical *truc*, the most readily available proof of alchemical manipulation, at least in our time. This is what I worked on with Fulcanelli. Once you can infuse reds and blues into glass in this manner, you have proved the gesture of *'separatio,'* you have 'separated the earth from fire, the subtle from the dense;' remember your Emerald Tablet. It takes great agility to separate while keeping *both* parts. Yet this is essential, for there must be body from which the spirit can rise, as there must be earth for the descent of the fire. The glass is colored by the spirit of metal, by the color-form. Being form, color combines a sensorial materiality with a spiritual perception. I can show you this, but that will not make you believe it any more than you do now. You are right, it is not to be believed, it is to be experienced. Only the gesture will give you knowledge; without the gesture, you can only conceptualize. Only correct perception will teach you the gesture, it cannot be shown from man to man. That is why in the Middle Ages, the making of these blues and reds was not transmitted from father to son in a workshop. At times the production would cease all throughout Europe for several generations, and then reappear in new *ateliers.* The gesture must be *found*, and only perception of form can invite the gesture. The color-form of metals is the spiritual imprint on those metals, the imprint of the metallic soul, its link to spirit. Separation into above and below, for a metallic entity, is separation of the colored spirit from the basic gray lead body, without destruction of the latter, as I've said."

When speaking of laboratory procedures, Aor used traditional terms as being the most precise expression in the matter at hand. When relating these discussions, I must therefore yield to a terminology I know to be in disrepute, albeit, to my mind, unjustly so. The notion of Salt is the result of an al-chemical perception, and there is no way, here, of speaking about salt without speaking in alchemical terms. I can only assure the reader that I am on the side of clarity and truth in these matters, with no intent or reason further to obscure a development I am fated to transmit, in spite of its persistent obscurities. As for my own involvement, it remains from many points of view mysterious to this day. Perhaps when all the details have been gathered in the manner of these pages, they will form stepping stones across events I would myself scarcely believe, had I not lived as close to them as I did. It would not be gracious, therefore, to blame a discouraged reader. I can only hope he would heed my plea, so that we may make our way together through this labyrinth.

Sulphur, Mercury, Salt, what can this language mean to us today, when despite a "new-age" penchant that has us mouth-ing vibrations, higher states of consciousness, eternal returns, and celestial influence, our day-to-day commitment remains to the visible, practical world of common cause and evident effect, devoid of mystery and miracle. In the depth of our minds, despite our deprecation of today's institutionalized science, despite conclusions legitimately drawn by this very science (Heisenberg, 1928), indeed, despite our honest and traditional conviction that there is more to life and matter than meets the thinking eye, our reasoning refuses to con-ceive a radically different approach that would give us radi-cally different results. Could any physical or chemical operation possibly have eluded the intelligence and superb instrumentation of our scientific establishment?

This, to begin with, is the worst way to envision the ques-tion. It reminds one of the inebriated gentleman who, having lost his keys in a dark alley, persists in looking for them under a far-off streetlight. There is no sense searching in matter, admittedly well illuminated by our cerebral cortex and its extensions from microscope to telescope, to search for what cannot be found in matter as such, in the matter our science and common sense define.

Before attempting a closer look at these two different approaches that have alternated their predominance over our civilization and can aptly be contrasted as Pythagorean science versus Archimedean technology, it should be said that the current scientific establishment is less than honest when confronted with surviving results of an obviously different mentality. We can start our examples fittingly at the very dawn of Western history, with the Sphinx sculptured into rock at Gizeh, proving by its water-eroded base that it spent a lengthy time submerged up to its head, the latter exhibiting the very different traces of wind erosion. Sustained by geological inquiries that reveal mollusks and other sea organisms in upper strata covering a petrified forest below, do these facts influence our current concept of prehistory even one iota? Or could a pre-Pharaonic monument of great sophistication and a civilization whose antiquity makes our heads spin possibly find room within current historical thinking? An antediluvian Sphinx, fable or reality? The facts point to reality, but science prefers a fable.

These blinders against all evidence incompatible with contemporary theory mark an obscurantism nowhere more devious than in the official hypotheses we are proffered concerning the ancient civilization of the Nile Valley. How do we explain the feat of pyramid building where forty-ton blocks are lifted into place side by side with a precision denying sufficient space to fit a blade? We don't, unless by theories far more miraculous than the event. Nor do we explain cores of granite drilled without high-speed rotary machines, or the hollowing of thin-necked alabaster vases. Again, what lighting was used in certain rock-temples, walls faultlessly carved with glyphs, where no natural light, direct or reflected, can possibly reach the chamber, and yet not a trace of carbon has been found on walls or ceiling? These results undoubtedly stem from a radically different approach, a different vision, a different aim. As de Lubicz put it: "Matter was no obstacle for Pharaonic science." But today's mentality questions why this natural power over matter and phenomenon would not have been used to some *practical* purpose, why it would have failed to lead to *progress!* How difficult it is to abdicate a point of view!

Yet as the word and its syntax can alone give substance to thought, is it not plain that this different mentality would express itself in a different language even while using familiar words? Alchemical terminology is obscure as long as the mentality of the adept remains obscure. The point is that despite appearances to *our* mentality, Sulphur, Mercury, and Salt, trinity of alchemical principles, are accurate terms within a language to be used less for conceptual definition into syntactics than for pictorial arrangements of the nature of the rebus. This use of language is arduous for the intellectual and categorical mind, wherefore again and again, each in his fashion, good authors admonish the student to look for images rather than words. So Bernard de Trévise, in his epistle to an unsuccessful practitioner: "The sound of words has fooled you," he diagnoses in a critique of his correspondent's procedures. He specifies that the puffer failed to understand the quality of this elusive Sulphur which needs to be known "according to the essence of its matter and to its alterations."

I will be asked whether I seriously opine that meaning has been furthered by such syntax, and I shall confess that I do. To search for quantity in a principial substance is evidently the height of naïveté. The qualities of Sulphur, on the other hand, are traditional and well-known. It is said to be composed of two of the four elements, namely Fire and Air, and as each element in turn is a conjunction of two of the four qualities, a qualitative analysis in alchemical terms is readily available. Thus Fire is hot and dry, while Air is hot and humid. Sulphur grips Fire and Air in a strong bond through their common heat, while the dryness of Fire and the humidity of Air set up a conflict, a tension which has reached its equilibrium in Sulphur: within an atmosphere of heat, there exists an equilibrium of dryness and humidity.

$$\text{SULPHUR} = \text{dry} \xrightleftharpoons[\text{hot}]{\text{hot}} \text{humid}$$

This could be considered a species of alchemical formula

for Sulphur, and it certainly is "the essence of its matter," as Bernard says. As for its "alteration," it can occur only through the instability of the dry-humid tension. In this conflict, it is always humidity which takes the upper hand, for reasons that should become evident in this development.

As humidity increases, it tends to take over the ambient atmosphere held by the heat of Sulphur. The heat provokes humidity, and increasing humidity invariably will form a watery element whose qualities are humid and cold. Now just as Sulphur is the conjunction of Fire with Air, so Mercury is the conjunction of Air with Water. The aerial element of Sulphur combines with the element Water called forth by increased humidity, while the coldness of Water enters into conflict with the sulphurous heat now displaced from its atmospheric function.

$$\text{MERCURY} = \text{hot} \underset{\substack{\longrightarrow \\ \text{humid}}}{\overset{\substack{\text{humid} \\ \longleftarrow}}{\rule{2cm}{0pt}}} \text{cold}$$

Mercury is a qualitative mean term between Sulphur and Salt. The latter's "formula":

$$\text{SALT} = \text{humid} \underset{\substack{\longrightarrow \\ \text{cold}}}{\overset{\substack{\text{cold} \\ \longleftarrow}}{\rule{2cm}{0pt}}} \text{dry}$$

shows its becoming out of Mercury by prevalence of cold provoked by mercurial humidity, which cold in turn "freezes" humidity into dryness. This evokes the element Earth, qualitatively characterized as dry and cold. The ambient atmosphere of Salt replaces Mercury's humidity by a coldness within which a humid-dry balance is found.

A complete schedule of this qualitative concatenation which knits the quaternary elemental level with the ternary principial level would look as follows:

⊖

This development will certainly not see even the most speculative enthusiast flying to his athanor, nor was it meant to. The aim is a better conception of a different scientific mentality, of a different approach to the constitution of matter. Not much longer, I fear, will I be able to detain those whose hopes are receding of gleaning here some useful information; be it then that I insist on my own experience, which knows all diagrammatic alchemical expressions, when solidly founded in form, to warrant lengthy meditation rather than cursory judgment. They share this requirement with primitive geometric figurations, square and diagonal, circle and diameter, inscribable polygons, angles, and the like, the implications of which a lifetime scarcely suffices to investigate. Such constructs are contained within numerically well-defined systems and we can see at every turn that for both mentalities, Pythagorean as well as Archimedean, number is the basic tool of science. Each has its particular approach, and if elsewhere we might have drawn a differentiation between the two in terms of quantity and quality, better yet can we characterize them in terms of number. For nothing stamps the mind more indelibly than the nature of its concern with number. And it is in conceiving the genesis of number that the most incisive and irreconcilable rift in mentality occurs: one side would have two become through the addition of one to one, while the other, aware of an all-inclusive oneness at the beginning, cannot conceive a second *one* excluded from the first, by dint of which to perform this operation. Rather than in *addition*, the genesis of number here finds its operator in a *division*, a scission of oneness into duality and a geometric multiplication once this duality is established. Later operators will add and subtract, but not before a dualization by division has been accomplished. "All science lies between the numbers one and two." This is where de Lubicz starts his philosophy of number, and the statement is Pythagorean to the core, with its implications for the octave in musical theory. It mustn't be forgotten that alchemy is Pythagorean physics, and that Pythagoras studied in the temples of Al-Kemi. Such concepts are of number, but not of mathematics, and number has the same glorious validity for both imagery and logic. Pythagorean number will never build Archimedean machines, but it will surely guide the mind in the image of natural phenomena. For division is the root of multiplication in cellular nature, a fact that has never preoccupied symbolic logic.

⊖

Based on the information I had gathered from Aor, I worked up a construct (see Plate II) to show as clearly as possible the qualities which characterize the predominance of each of the three alchemical principles: heat for Sulphur, humidity for Mercury, coldness for Salt. This structure shows principles and elements held in a network of relations between trinity and quaternary, and ruled by the permutations of two pairs. Completed to show polarized duality manifesting a vertex of puncticular and irrational oneness, this pyramid of Pythagorean number forms the renowned *Tetractys*. An exaltation of the four elements reveals quintessence as basis of the *Pentactys*, emblem of manifestation traditionally associated with the five senses. De Lubicz better than anyone has dwelt on the significance of this philosophy of figured number; the topic needs no further comment, unless it be to emphasize the distance separating this cabalistic concept from the usual numerological speculation.[1]

The construct meant to underline the absence of a *dry* milieu in which heat and cold would set up the equilibrium of qualities. It also showed substance first as humidity, and then expanding in opposite directions through the activity of heat and cold. The gamut encompassed in the beginning oneness, its qualitative analysis, and the harmonic unity of the human sensorium appears encased, hemmed in by a limiting dryness. Within the range of the alchemical ternary, the center of gravity is held by humidity, and the poles by dryness.[2]

I readily admit that this structure offered satisfactions

rarely provided by academic physical theory, and I could fathom its significance for an alert and non-instrumented mind, the primitive, natural mind I was coming to associate with the adept, the non-academic alternative scientist.

Arid Fire, so inimical to life, is known to Pharaonic myth as *Seth*, master of the desert land. Yet as we gaze upon our construct, we cannot help but feel that the cold dryness of Earth yearns for the dry Fire which would close the cycle of our diagram into a new principial entity.

The construct also shows clearly why the "alteration" in Sulphur, "according to the essence of its matter," must always be directed toward Mercury, and why, therefore, the equilibrium of dry and humid is always broken in favor of the latter. Within nature, within the Osirian cyclical event, Sulphur transmutes into Mercury by excess of humidity, having nowhere else to go once its inner stability is unbalanced. As the sole quality unfitted for principial ambiance, dryness, producing aridity, is a dead end in nature, as nature cannot recombine the dryness of fire with the dryness of earth. The very impasse implies an opportunity for a step nature is unable to take, a step beyond nature. It is the Promethean act, the intelligent manipulation of "divine thievery," the godly flight into the sun, and successful return. It is Horus, Osiris' lawful successor whose neverending struggle with his brother Seth we are now able to understand. It is also the alchemical *Grand Oeuvre* in one of its aspects, the dry way of the crucible whose sign is the Cross.

Lest the reader suspect being taken on haphazard rambles through symbolic thickets, I must reassure him that we are following a carefully mapped path that will rejoin our point of departure: the problem of salt, a grasp of which would be impossible without a modicum of comprehension of the varied motifs here presented.

The next time I took up this subject, I began by reviewing the levels of the diagram: oneness and polarization, as metaphysical absolute and mirror image, were absolved from scrutiny. On the ternary level, three principles could be the end result of a gigantic scientific effort . . . or of a simple act of faith. In our day, we are experimentally and experientially aware of the fundamental cohesion of three as number, be it in logic, in physics, in nature, and even in society. Triune Sulphur, Mercury, and Salt antedates most of this erudition, however, and trinity on a principial level antedates it all. Is intuitive perception less valuable because it scorns the proof of its own evidence, and is scientific faith conditioned only by material proof? Questions whose innumerable variants must have crowded the brains of sincere manipulators of all times.

Next, four as number, square in the second dimension, becomes, in the third, four pillars of materiality: the four elements. The interaction between principles and elements is manifest even in language: Salt and Earth, Mercury and Water, Sulphur and Fire. The septenary made of three and four, prominent in symbolique, is an object of study in de Lubicz's work.[3]

As indicated above, *five* is not achieved on a qualitative level. Three active qualities alone—heat, humidity, and coldness—occupy this band of the spectrum. Dryness appears double, at each end of the scale. It is inactive limitation, and the principial ternary, through the heat of Sulphur, the humidity of Mercury and the coldness of Salt, is still the effective component here; what prefigures quintessence is as yet but an arrangement of three and two. Quality is an impasse until the appearance of psyche which bypasses qualities through a sensorium anchored directly in the elements: the fiery sight, the aerial smell, the watery taste, the earthy touch, essence of the elements, pulled together by the quintessential ear into the harmony of a "hearing" intellect through *five* senses (*entendement*).

My diagram showed the connection to the theory of perception by naming trinity in its terms. The active *function* of Sulphur contracts the passive *substance* of Mercury into a salt-*form* (a vermillion cinnabar in the laboratory reaction of sulphur and mercury), and I had gathered it was this latter salt-form that had been the particular object of attention at the beginning of the century among Parisian Hermetists.

I now began to examine a hypothetical breakthrough that would vanquish the dryness and expand this trinitary level *before* the sensorial synthesis. As we had already discussed the theory of perception at some length, it seemed clear that any rerouting would have to be effectuated at the qualitative state and before objectivation. While there is much to be gleaned from the qualitative arrangement of the pairs of *twos* in their adaptation to the state of *five,* the completion of the *Pentactys* is not achieved on the basis of quality alone.

Breaking through the "natural" diagram on the "cold" side of the Earth element (Plate III), the chain is continued by linking the quality of dryness, now solely related to Earth, with the other element in whose constitution it enters: Fire. With the parallelogram completed according to this hypothesis, we see, on the principial level, that an entity unknown to the natural constitution of matter would be called for, a principle composed of Fire and Earth which I simply marked with an X. Beyond this irregularity, the series of principles resumes with Sulphur and continues normally for another series of Sulphur, Mercury, and Salt.

I thought at first that a similar development could be undertaken on the "hot" side of the qualitative row, where dryness this time would be committed only to Fire and would have to be connected to the Earth element in order to effect the breach. This was a mistaken assumption, however, as we shall see later.

My construct did little more than gather and develop graphically information I had been fed in discrete fragments over the weeks. Yet when I casually brought these pages to one of our meetings, I was surprised by the sequence of reactions they provoked in Aor. I recall the slight initial jocosity backed by a hint of scepticism which dates the occasion as a fairly early episode. Indeed, it may well have been the first nongeometric topic in which I became actively involved. It should be remembered that at the time (1959–60), the only published work in print was *Le Temple de l'Homme,* an overwhelmingly *geometric* opus. I had so far refused to let other topics interfere with my total concentration on the geometric and harmonic components of the work, but the physical aspect now had intruded forcefully. Was it Aor's thinking of me primarily in terms of geometry and logic that caused this look of surprise once he had taken cognizance of the gist of the presentation; the sketch of a smile, followed by the stare which showed that his mind had wandered? All this in a matter of seconds, but long enough for me to notice. Then, still not having said a word, he walked to the table (we had been standing close to the door, by a drawing board where I had spread out these papers among others). He sat down, started to scrape around in his pipe, and spoke without looking at me.

"I hadn't realized the extent of your interest in Pythagorean physics. This is quite a nice little *schéma* you put together here. To tell the truth, there seems to be more in those diagrams of yours than I had thought I told you. But now that you've gone this far, you practically force me, morally speaking, to help you go further. You see, I have led you into error, or rather, you have done so yourself by taking bits of information, connecting them very cleverly, I must say . . . "

"I used to work for army intelligence in communications." This irresistible irrelevance got its chance due to his hesitation at this point, and he took it kindly, still poking at the carbon in his pipe.

"I believe it," he deadpanned. "Seriously, though, if I didn't know for certain that you fell into all this blindly, like the Tarot Fool so close to your heart, poised on the cliff, blessedly ignorant and innocent, I would swear that you have come here to find out things just like these!"

After a silence, I recall wondering whether perhaps he had meant to tell me not quite so much.

"Well, yes and no. I mention elements, principles, qualities, and whatnot in my conversations, because I know that this type of information doesn't stick with most people; they have no framework for it. I have certainly told you nothing that can't be found in a great number of texts all the way back to Greece and even Egypt, all forgotten by today's academies.

But I never had things come back at me in this way, like this physical speculation of yours. And when I notice that you have gone astray, as was inevitable, in all good conscience, I have to straighten you out, seeing that I am in a sense responsible. This correction, however, brings us to matters which . . . to matters that . . . ''

"To secret matters, perhaps?" It fairly slipped out; I hadn't meant to be so direct.

"Well, I know how you feel about that word, simply because you do not understand the meaning of secret; the saving thing is that at least you know the meaning of the *sacred*, and that is rare enough in our day."

"Yes, if it is a *sacred* secret, I will treat it as qualified."

I had meant to make him smile, and I succeeded.

"*Bien, bien,* it's all right, and there is nothing here that I wouldn't have told you in due time. But you are quite correct, I might have asked you to keep it to yourself. *Ceci, guardez-le pour vous,* have I never said this in our conversations? I cannot recall a particular occasion, but perhaps I have, once or twice, and if I hadn't, I might have said it when speaking about what we are now bound to discuss. But the point of the present situation is that I didn't bring up the subject, *you* did, with your diagrams. Perhaps I would have *never* brought the topic up, and it would never have existed for you, just as it never did for the others who have heard me speak, and some have heard me for a lot longer than you. I'm referring to the past, *évidemment;* here I see very few people now. *Guardez-le pour vous,* I could still ask you this now, but it is not the same now, the opportunity to decline receiving the information no longer exists. One is not obliged to participate in a secret; there is choice. It is a responsibility that must be accepted blindly, or not at all. You have circumvented this choice, but I must assume that your strategy was no more than honest interest in the matter at hand, which I certainly don't intend to discourage. Anyway, it is your own work that makes the information come your way, with me as intermediary. Already the setting up of the diagrams has shown you what a splendid picture it offers and how far it goes. So I'm saying, having in mind the pearls and swine of the Bible: *guardez-le pour vous*, keep it to yourself, or keep it *for* yourself, no more, no less."

Guardez-le pour vous! Of course I had heard this! Once, twice? I didn't know. We had talked about not diffusing certain particularities of Hermetic texts, such as the order of chapters in the *Twelve Keys* of Basil Valentine. A special instance of discretion seemed to be involved in that case, however, motivated not by possessiveness, but rather by a concern for the integrity of the text. What else had he told me to keep to myself? Offhand, I was unable to recall a specific occasion. The French expression slips into conversation so easily, so innocuously; it is accepted thoughtlessly, the more readily so when no future confidant appears within reach of consciousness. But what did he mean by that expression? Was it a sophisticated code for swearing the other to silence for the rest of his natural life?

"But as I said," he continued, "your knowledge is faulty, and I do not want to carry the blame of having led you astray. I have seen it before, perfectly intelligent men wasting their lives on trivia because of a misconception. This search is indeed like the search for gold in one way only, and that is the way in which it tends to derange even the most reasonable of men. I used to know a very capable physicist who spent his time intermittently boiling a piece of copper in water according to a rigid schedule which never allowed him an uninterrupted night's sleep. I was able to help him, but he had been at it for years before I met him. There is no limit to the madness of a misguided puffer; not that I accuse you of such, of course; to the contrary, it is a pity that a mind with such a theological bent as yours has so much difficulty believing in God. In all the times you have drawn the square and its diagonal, didn't it become evident to you that God exists? If it had, you would understand the secret. It is personal, very private, it is a glimpse of the divine and the workings of His power of genesis. And it is bound to be misused by rationalists, positivists, empiricists, or whatever else they call themselves; every insight gets debased into usefulness or entertainment, distractions from what really counts. Well, you know all this, but it should make you understand that I am not anxious to contribute valuable information about the nature of things to governments that make bombs out of such insights. That's not all of what accounts for secrecy here, but it is a part of it, and a part you should understand, at least if you believe in the Hermetic opus. There is that word again: belief. Once you believe, there will be at the very center of your being a tiny private thought that is a secret, that must not be known by others under penalty of becoming lost and thereby endangering the entire position. An inadmissible hypothesis, perhaps, an undeclared postulate? Who knows? Only one's self knows. If you do not want the secret, you must not believe, you must only *know.* And you might find this very difficult. But that is another part of the secret, the part, precisely, which we cannot speak about. The secret of the governments, or the Jesuits, or the entrepreneurs, that secret you will have to grant me, the rest is beyond your ken for the moment. But miracles happen! Anyway, I have chosen to write very little concerning the topic you are studying, and the little I have written is in my drawer and will stay there a good long time. You have no idea of the length to which some people will go! At the time I worked in Paris before World War I, when I was first in touch with Fulcanelli and this alchemical activity was under way, at that same time we began noticing that all the good passages in the old books at the Bibliothèque Nationale and in public libraries all through the country were systematically being cut out. By good passages I mean those that were needed, those that pertained to salt. It turned out to be the Jesuits, not surprisingly. They are more dangerous than even big governments. And it is well-known that both the USA and the USSR are running experiments with dabblers in all kinds of occult stuff, from psychics to pseudo-alchemists and who knows what not. It has always been a good policy not to attract attention, to be unknown, particularly in times like ours. Now let's put an end to this discussion. Here's my final word: the secret can only be for believers, for faith. Reason will encompass the sacred, but not the secret."

"Isn't it sufficient that reason knows about pearls and swine?"

"It helps. But enough of this, let's get to work."

And he pointed to some other diagrams I had drawn up and which concerned harmonic theory, tonality, and the cycle of fifths.

⊖

This was the beginning of those full winter months when Aor, apparently satisfied on my account, tacitly indicated my acceptance as his disciple. There are infinite subtleties to such a relationship, particularly when the aggressive and inventive novice is allowed to pursue his ideas freely instead of being constrained by intellectual submission. Yet it did not take long to realize the difficulties I would encounter in remaining true to my own purpose. I kept representing in my mind the things that remained clearly myself, those I meant to keep intact; I let the others fade away as new ideas took over. There were a good number of angles from which my experience could be envisioned; my favorite perspective, because truest to myself, is also the least communicable.

What I sensed was that I was "in the circle of my masters." I had first come to know that peculiar energetic environment with Da Passano, when states of reverence were called upon before beginning the work. The nomenclature was his own and most fitting. In the circle of one's masters, a very specific type of work is done, and one leaves the circle significantly changed, vitally transformed.

When I returned from the war, I painted subjects such as "Le Grand Mal," a creation whose flailing arms and legs made its convulsing body espouse the angles of the swastika ever so slightly in an image perceptible only to the most obsessed. I was also plagued by nightmares from which I would awake with blood-curdling screams, their nightly regularity for years making it impossible to accept invitations as a houseguest. I

worked myself out of that morass by encountering the circle
of my masters for the first time through the reverential work
with Da Passano. He was a true instructor, which in fact is
all he claimed to be. He worked the bottom, being familiar
with those strata. I seize this opportunity to pay him the
tribute I have withheld in person. He is well trained as an
alarm clock, but only for those who are sleeping soundly; the
others will not hear. He was a man after my own heart, the
kind society calls a failure. I know little about the origins of
his school, Castellani in Milano, but I believe it is closest to
a Western Zen. He referred himself to the Knights Templar
and offered a very effective meditation.

My second encounter with the circle of my masters now
had come through the circuitry of the mind, through geometry, through science. Aor introduced me to a scientific circle
of masters, taking his place among them. This afforded me a
better contact than I had had before. This time the encounter
also was broader and of longer duration. Contact has remained to this day, albeit somewhat irregularly. At the time
of recognizing the event, however, I was vividly in that ener-
gized space where the faculties stretch their limits into the
unknown and return with results. Such is the contact with
the masters.

What was here proposed could not be taken lightly. It was
bound to change my life as radically as had the first episode.
This time, however, the circle of my masters was encountered
not at the bottom, but rather at the top of my own life. That,
I believe, is what made this encounter a breakthrough,
whereas the other was a type of convalescence. I was at the
time beginning to feel that I had my craft in hand; I had been
selling well for several years and had been capable of living
very comfortably on my art. I had just sold a good part of my
production in New York and was off to a winter in Flanders
in order to paint in the luminous dark light of my childhood.
Then had come the breakthrough, and as a result I was now
working in the circle of my masters. By now I felt that compared to what was happening to me, painting was a minor art.
The true art was *Ars Magna*, an instrument of knowledge,

and I was learning its logic in geometry while in touch with its practice, a manipulation in space, the Opus, the *Oeuvre d'Aor*. I stopped painting entirely, giving up without regrets a budding career. I broadened my horizons considerably, however, and never doubted that I would survive. I talked about my actions with Aor, who had himself made such a decision in Paris in the early twenties, and who held that it was better to starve rather than to give up one's own personal time. He considered working for money to be tantamount to slavery, and he felt entitled to a livelihood simply because he lived the life he lived, because of the quality of time he generated. Let those whose ambition it is to work for a living own the goods of the world: such is the bargain struck on this path. Winning the game makes you master of your time, at once the most elusive and pervasive of commodities.

My situation was hardly desperate. I would always manage. Since I had never thought of art for a career in the first place, I had no trouble dismissing it as such. My fling with commercial success had taught me that when money is valorized, the work is degraded.

$\ominus$

The turn taken by the discussion on qualitative analysis of alchemical matter hastened the inception of my discipleship beyond all expectations. My lucky and as yet uncorrected "error" seemed inadvertently to have forced Aor's hand. This new level of our relationship was not further discussed between the two of us, but Isha must have been informed, for I noticed an abrupt change in her attitude. Her possessiveness vanished from one day to the next, and she became distant. I still consulted her on some hieroglyphic details, but mainly in order to smooth the transition. A certain hostility, which was to grow in the coming months, can be traced to this event. Perhaps the seed of my eventual departure was sown at that moment. I had entered a territory where she as well as Lucie were out of bounds, a lofty region where Aor had housed alone and where the female sex was unwelcome. This

ILLUSTRATIONS

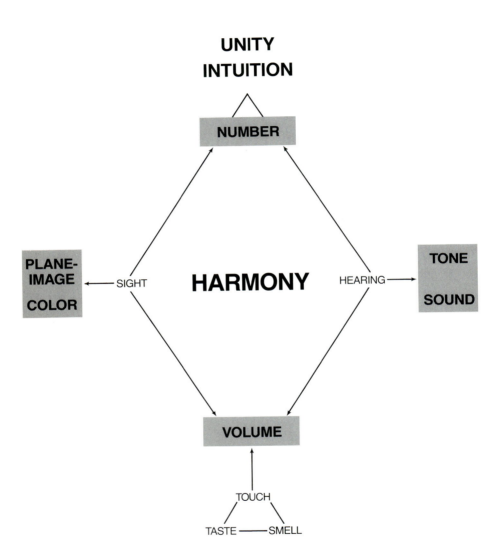

PLATE I

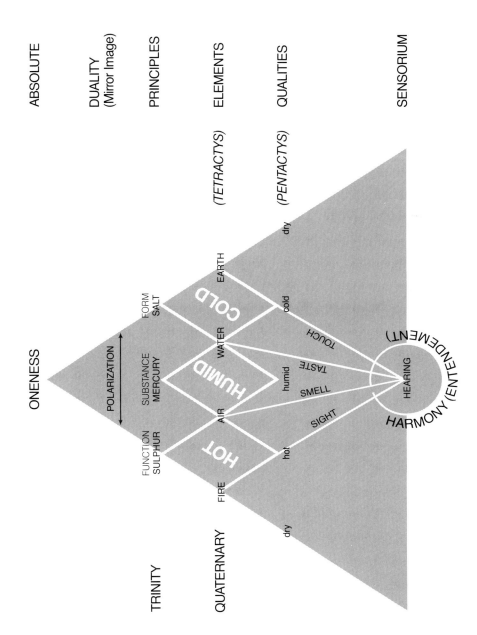

ABSOLUTE

DUALITY
(Mirror Image)

PRINCIPLES

ELEMENTS   *(TETRACTYS)*

QUALITIES   *(PENTACTYS)*

SENSORIUM

ONENESS

TRINITY

QUATERNARY

POLARIZATION

FORM
SALT

SUBSTANCE
MERCURY

FUNCTION
SULPHUR

EARTH

WATER

AIR

FIRE

COLD

HUMID

HOT

dry

cold

humid

hot

dry

TOUCH

TASTE

SMELL

SIGHT

HEARING

HARMONY (ENTENDEMENT)

PLATE II

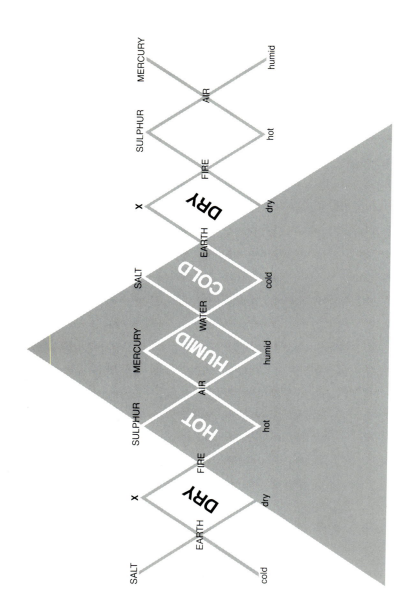

PLATE III

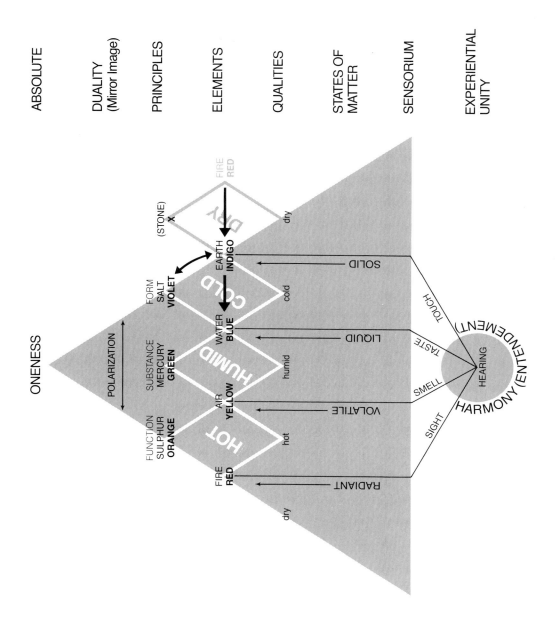

ABSOLUTE

DUALITY
(Mirror Image)

PRINCIPLES

ELEMENTS

QUALITIES

STATES OF
MATTER

SENSORIUM

EXPERIENTIAL
UNITY

ONENESS

POLARIZATION

FIRE RED

(STONE) X

DRY

dry

EARTH INDIGO

FORM SALT VIOLET

COLD

cold

WATER BLUE

SUBSTANCE MERCURY GREEN

HUMID

humid

AIR YELLOW

FUNCTION SULPHUR ORANGE

HOT

hot

FIRE RED

dry

SOLID

LIQUID

VOLATILE

RADIANT

TOUCH

TASTE

SMELL

SIGHT

HEARING

HARMONY (ENTENDEMENT)

PLATE IV

ensemble avec le véritable vinaigre puissent beaucoup. Car l'esprit du vinaigre est froid et l'esprit de la chaux vive extrêmement brûlant, et c'est pourquoi ils sont estimés de natures contraires et recherchés comme tels. J'ai déjà p⟨…⟩rdinaire et philosophiqu⟨…⟩r quoi que ce soit, d'ex⟨…⟩portes sont verrouillées ⟨…⟩

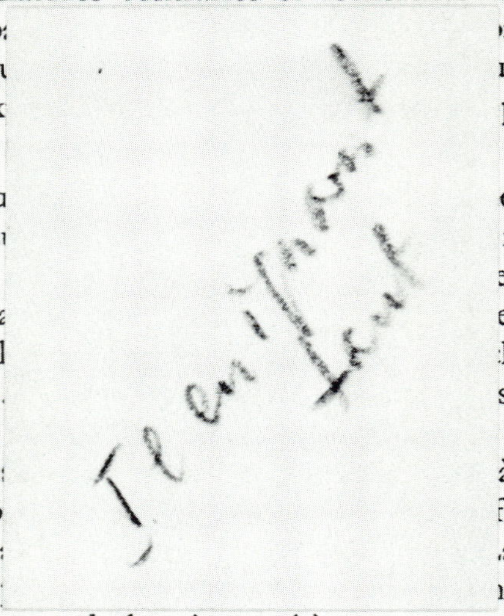

En adieu⟨…⟩e ta matière dans une s⟨…⟩mercure et fermente-le ⟨…⟩e tu mettes en fermenta⟨…⟩et mets en ordre avec l⟨…⟩hoses selon leurs poids⟨…⟩si né d'un auparavant⟨…⟩continuelle chaleur. En⟨…⟩à trois fois, suivant la p⟨…⟩⟨…⟩s ; tu auras la fin et tu ⟨…⟩a douzième clef, sans ⟨…⟩ent précis, enseigne l'usage de la teinture (1).

(1) Que pourrions-nous dire du sel, après notre Maître qui en a tant disserté ailleurs avec tout le détail possible, quoique souvent d'une manière cabalistique, afin de n'être compris que des " Fils de Science " ? (*Demeures Philosophales*, op. cit., passim.)

Nous répéterons seulement, avec lui, que notre sel est véritablement un feu ; qu'il est composé par l'artiste à l'aide de produits indépendants de ceux qui sont réservés à l'Œuvre ; qu'il est, suivant encore l'indication sincère de Limojon de Saint-Didier, de la nature de la chaux. (*Le Triomphe Hermétique*. Amsterdam, 1699, 1re édition, p. 43.)

Le sel n'est feu qu'en puissance ; c'est lui ce *feu-eau* ou cette *eau ignée,* sèche, qui ne mouille pas les mains et de laquelle nombre

PLATE V

R. A. Schwaller de Lubicz, Plan de Grasse, c. 1960

was more than just a quirk of his, it was a well-established, researched, and experimented way of life, and an approach to sexuality which can be traced to his earliest writings.[4] There was jealousy abroad, yet I had done no more than knock, and he had answered.

The subject matter that had been agent to my new situation was especially productive in bringing with it further details of the Fulcanelli affair.

"The sequence of the combined principles and elements forms the seven steps of the octave,"[5] he started the next day, pointing to one of my diagrams (Plate III) which I had left with him overnight, "and you are certainly on the right track with the idea of breaking through the Sethian desert and making a dry milieu the basis for a transition to a new octave. This idea is as old as our science, it is the essence of the dry way, *la voie sèche,* but work on this had been quite unsuccessful in our day. First of all, let me point out that such a transition is impossible on the Fire side, where dryness participates in a *radiant* state as part of the creative function. Before the sensorium, before the eye has been formed by radiance, this state is pure energy. There is no substance yet to get hold of here, nothing to work with. We must go to the dryness on the formal end of the spectrum, to the solid state; in other words, we must work on salt. But your diagram shows the problem very clearly: the next octave would have to have Sulphur again to start the sequence of principles, but that is impossible, as in this position, one of its components would have to be Earth, the Earth that would link it to Salt in the previous octave. In fact, our first principle in the next octave would not be Sulphur at all, which is a combination of Fire and Air, but a principle whose nature combines Fire and Earth. Well, there is no such principle in nature, according to this physics; there is no principle X, as you put it in your diagram. Note that I said: in nature! Would it help you to know that your X principle could be considered a fair description of what adepts call: the stone?"

He was looking at me intently, watching my reaction. But

I was to disappoint him on two occasions that afternoon, and this was the first. "The stone" remained a term for me, and substituting it for my unknown X did not further my comprehension. For a moment, I had no reaction at all. Then I caught myself and attempted some comment.

"No," he interrupted me, "there is no way for you to appreciate this information. It will take you many years to evaluate the power of such a definition. And until you have done so, I could well say: *guardez-le pour vous!*"

I protested that I was quite aware of the power of the *position* occupied by the X principle in my diagram and henceforth to be called "the stone," if such be the convention, but that "stone" did not shed more light on the significance of this position than had an unknown X.

"Of course, you haven't read enough. I hope you don't visualize the philosopher's stone as a rock or other mineral body to be locked up in a cupboard when not in use. The stone includes the gesture that handles it, that makes it happen; its identity as stone exists only in the manipulation; at other times it is that most common and valueless substance the books always talk about as being found anywhere. I call your X principle 'stone' because the dryness, the milieu of dryness comes into being and the stone *is* dryness, as Salt is cold, Mercury humidity, Sulphur heat. And that dryness which is new to the natural octave, will now act on the natural salt with the power of that X principle, and the work it must accomplish is precisely the work one would ask of the stone, which has a dryness never attained by natural salt: the stone is going to dry the salt in order to effect the next octave. Am I going too fast, *vous vous y perdez?*"

I had taken the paper and filled in the elements that had come up in the discussion, the states of matter, radiant, volatile, liquid, and solid (Plate IV).

"You will have to look at all this for a long time; no sense attempting to get it down all at once, it must sink in. Look here at your diagram. You can see the problem lies in the fact that the last step of the natural octave, namely Earth, would have to coincide with the first step of the new octave, namely

Fire. That makes perfect Hermetic sense of course, it is Ptah-Hephaistos, Fire fallen into Earth, an animated presence in the mineral bed, in the mine. Obviously there is a metallic manipulation involved here, and it was generally agreed that it had to be approached from its formal aspect, from the principial salt. The details don't make much sense to you now, of course, they are laboratory matters. Anyhow, not much progress was being made, that I knew of, until Fulcanelli came up with that manuscript I have talked to you about, and you might appreciate its content now. A strange document it was, indeed. The text seemed quite coherent, it had a definite beginning and a *Finis* as signature, complete as Fulcanelli found it in that valuable edition of Newton's Hermetic writings. He told me he had worked on it for some time, but couldn't make head or tail of it. He wanted me to have a look at it. Well, I did, and I realized that it was a manipulation of salt in the direction I had been looking for. But the remarkable feature of this manuscript was that it spoke almost exclusively in terms of *color.*"

He now developed for me the theory of color which underlies the published posthumous text.[6] This text had not been revised by the author to reflect the state of his knowledge on this topic such as it stood when I worked with him at the end of his life. These were certainly some of the pages he meant to keep in his drawer for a long time, as he did. Yet less than two years after they surfaced in the estate, they found their way into print unedited, in an obsolete version which still shows ambivalence concerning indigo, the prismatic entity central to the entire color-language. As he now launched into a subject clearly close to his heart, he first reviewed for me, in his personal manner of envisioning natural law, the prismatic spectrum according to Newton. He spoke of a triangular form decomposing unitary white light by its dispersion into the seven primary prismatic colors: red, orange, yellow, green, blue, indigo, and violet. Of these, three are fundamental, namely red, yellow, and blue, and another three are the three possible results of one-to-one combinations of the first three: red and yellow, red and blue, yellow and blue, namely orange, violet, and green respectively. This leaves the vexing presence of indigo, usually not considered among the fundamental colors.

Although I had spent the best part of my adult life in daily contact with color problems in art, I had given little thought to examining the colors of the rainbow and even less to the peculiar position of indigo.

"I always thought of indigo as a dark shade of blue, or perhaps a deep violet-blue."

"No, no." He was smiling. "You must not look at it in that manner. You can intensify blue all you want; it'll never give you indigo, which has a somber luminosity unlike any blue. And it has no violet at all, because violet is the result of a red and blue mixture. Indigo is indigo, you cannot obtain it by any mixture. How would red occur at that place in the spectrum? But we are already in the midst of this mysterious circumstance which in fact had been the preoccupation of the adept whose papers I had come in contact with through these strange circumstances with Fulcanelli."

And he showed me how the scientist had identified the trinity of principles with the three composed colors, and the four elements with fundamentals, thereby including indigo in this group (Plate IV).

"At least that is what I read into these notes. They were mere abbreviations into a personal shorthand and not easy to read; I don't wonder that Fulcanelli had no luck with it. Perhaps the text just stimulated some thoughts that had been in my head ever since I worked with Matisse. Anyhow, by the time I had arranged the prismatic colors along the lines of principles and elements, the text fell together, and I was ready for the laboratory. This man had worked on an alteration of form through salt, and he noted it down in terms of the blue-indigo-violet imbroglio I am trying to point out to you. You can see the inevitable irregularity that occurs at the end of one octave and the beginning of the next. The same irregularity occurs in the musical octave and in the planetary system. That of course was where the effort had to play, where the violet turns to ultraviolet and disappears for our vision. This is where the adept attempts to join the end to the beginning —have the beast bite its tail. Here is where a new red can be born, the red beyond violet, the one that is felt in violet and that disappears into ultraviolet. The idea may sound strange, yet when applied to the Water-Salt-Earth complex, it makes marvelous sense. Just as indigo and blue do not give violet, so Earth and Water alone do not possess the qualities to form the salt we are looking for, the fixed salt of permanence, which is an effect of spirit, of perception; *c'est l'entendement*, it is the understanding through the organ of harmony. With this instrumentation we are capable of acting on the salt of nature. The formal element can be and must be manipulated. Fire and Water must be made to join, and this can only be effectuated through the Fire of the Earth. The Fire of the Earth must be bound to Water. The important lesson here is the use of the Earth-Fire to accomplish the Fire-Water combination, the Seal of Sal-Amon.[7] Indigo must be shifted to blue and become one of the components of violet. We are merely preparing a milieu for the new redness to become visible. We are working on metallic forms, of course, substances we know in their relation to color, not only by their lines in spectroscopy, but by other more intuitive ways. Anyway, the result of the experiment is captured in glass, and here comes the difficult manipulation of the decantations which the letter in Canseliet's foreword talks about. The end result will be a glass that is red in the mass without being pigmented. We have merely prepared the milieu for the phenomenon to happen, but the new octave will be attracted to the prepared milieu. Spirit has to be caught in the net, as the Pharaonics say. You have read the letter I am referring to, have you not? It came from Fulcanelli's master, supposedly. You remember what Canseliet wrote in his introduction to the *Mystère des Cathédrales*? You don't remember? Well, read it again; now you'll know what he is talking about. Talking, mind you, nothing else! Fulcanelli manipulated, although he never understood salt at all. As for the others, it was just a literary métier, even if they built themselves laboratories. But the possibilities were discussed, so Canseliet certainly knows what he is talking about.

Look it up, the description of the successful experiment is worthwhile."

I promised to do so that very night, in the 1957 edition he had lent me. But for the moment I marveled at the complex logical existence led by the spectrum's indigo. Until this moment, I had only heard of red, yellow, and blue as fundamental primaries, from which all other hues were composed, including the composed primaries: orange, green, and violet. But what about indigo? If it is not a fundamental primary, then it must be composed. But what fundamental colors entered into its composition, if we consider that the mixture of red and blue yields the violets? If indigo was merely a dark shade of blue or blue-violet, why did it rate a place among the seven primaries? We differentiate a shade of dark and luminous red by calling it purple, but we do not assign it a post among the primary colors. Similarly, indigo cannot be called a dark and luminous blue, as such nomenclature defeats the purpose of having singled out indigo as a primary color. Such confusion in nomenclature nevertheless persists in the posthumous fragment that was certainly meant to remain in the author's drawer.

"What is remarkable about this manuscript is that it changed the well-established trinity of red, yellow, blue, to a quartet which now included indigo. Or so it seemed to me when I first started to decipher the very personal language of that fascinating experiment. It is quite true, whatever its intensity, blue never reaches indigo. And indigo can never be obtained by any mixture whatsoever. So the hypothesis was well founded. But you see where it leads us. The *composed* colors have become principial trinity, whereas the *fundamental* colors have become four elements."

By using color as a guide to an alchemical operation which readies salt for a sulphurous fire, the mysterious text seemed to have made a much needed contribution to the symbolic language of the contemporary adept. Symboliques are a function of the cosmic moment. Christic redemption was an efficient symbolique within the cosmic moment of a medieval author such as Nicolas Flamel. Sidereal or mineral symboliques, so prevalent in pagan texts, also arise in intellectual times. The greatness of a text lies in the adequacy of its symbolique. The basic alchemical structure presented here and in the pages of *The Egyptian Miracle* can be unequivocally declared to be an outstanding contribution to the definition problem of salt. In these few pages, the culmination of Aor's contribution to the contemporary alchemical renaissance lies buried; and this crucial juncture is tied to events, as we have seen, that had brought us back to the Fulcanelli Saga.

It had been a long afternoon, and Aor was tiring.

"Have you ever seen gold?" he suddenly asked me, quite out of context, it seemed to me.

I told him I had.

"In what form?"

"In coins."

"That is nothing, that's a dead body in the coin. I mean the metal in the mine, live gold. Come with me."

And to my surprise he got up and walked toward the door. I followed him. We went to the laboratory.

The large rectangular room had two rows of elongated tables with sinks and water faucets. Several Bunsen burners on the table, a few flasks, glass jars, other paraphernalia. The room was light, clean, and white, and it looked fairly unused. On the far end there were some chairs and he asked me to sit down. Then he went to one of several glass bookcases that stood against the wall and opened it. The shelves were lined with bottles of all sizes and colors. He came back to the table with a small vial.

"Here is red gold," he said, and took one of the glass saucers that were piled nearby, pulled an old cork from the vial, and shook out a powder that didn't look like gold at all. It was red, at first glance.

"Go ahead, touch it!"

It was softer than graphite. My finger seemed to float over its substance. And then I noticed that it was red in the mass only. A thin layer on my finger did look quite golden.

"Rub it on your fingernails," he said, "*allez-y!*"

I did as I was told, and now the fineness of the yellow hue appeared. This was undoubtedly a noble substance.

"Do you recognize it?"

I nodded my head in assent.

We both stared at my fingernail.

And then, in a sudden move, he practically jumped out of his chair.

"Put it on all your fingernails and we'll go downstairs and have tea," he said in an unusually jocose tone. His mood had turned almost exuberant and he seemed much younger. I felt as if I were with a college buddy about to play a prank on someone.

The situation embarrassed me. I looked at him, and back at the little heap of red powder on the table, got up, sat down, and realized that this was something I had no intention of doing, that it went entirely against my grain. I recall that Goldian had accompanied me for lunch that day, as she was binding a copy of Radiguet's *Count d'Orgel* in the workshop. I knew I would feel foolish and quite out of character arriving downstairs, where she was certainly already waiting with Isha for our descent, with my fingernails painted in gold.

"No," I said, "I don't think I want to do that."

It was the second time that afternoon I disappointed him.

"You don't have the passion for gold, and that is all right, it will make your life easier. But you won't have the drive that comes with it. Therefore you'll do less."

That made perfect sense to me then, as it does now.

6

*Quoting myself critically.—The staircase
portrait.—The gift of God.—A congratulatory
epistle.—Epistemological musings.—A glass genealogy.
—Intriguing marginalia.—Midsummer plans.—Unsolicited
details.—The salty pearls of experience.—Breakthrough
to Egypt.—Transformations of Aor.*

As soon as I got home that evening, I reread the 1957 preface to *Mystère des Cathédrales*, where Canseliet published a letter purported to originate from Fulcanelli's true initiator. Today, at this moment, I again have Fulcanelli's book before me, opened at Canseliet's preface, and I am once more partaking in the heroic events referred to by the writer; the writer of the *letter*, we must assume, not the writer of the *preface!* Asked for his opinion on the authenticity of this correspondence, Aor maintained, quite unexpectedly, that such considerations were beside the point and without importance.

As I manifested my surprise, he said in an irritated tone of voice, "It is as unimportant as is, for example, the matter of Fulcanelli's true identity. Somehow these words have gotten into print in this form, and I want you to know that they are not lacking in content."

With the book open before me now, I remember the last time I perused it thoroughly; it was almost ten years ago, at the time I first attempted to note the events occupying us here. It occurs to me that much of the ground we must now cover has been well prepared in that first attempt of 1975. I have alluded, in the introduction of this present essay, to a pencil sketch made by Aor of Fulcanelli. Here is what I had written earlier on this topic: *The upper stories of the house could be reached in two ways. Toward the side of the house a service entrance led to a steep and narrow spiral staircase rising directly to the second floor which Aor shared with Lucie. This way was used for the daily climb to the library where my meetings with Aor took place. There was also a broad staircase which led from the main foyer to the first floor where Isha had her quarters and Dr. Lamy his clinic. I took this way when consulting with the Doctor who was giving me "phonophoresis" treatments, a method he had devised of applying musical tones to acupuncture points. I suffer from an asthmatic sensitivity to Mediterranean winds, and he was attempting to control the condition by nonchemical means. He did not succeed, I regret to say, nor did his failure surprise or disappoint me. My susceptibilities to environments are complex pathologies which no one understands better than I do. However, he did succeed in* provoking *a particularly severe attack; according to Aor, this was a first step in understanding the condition. I willingly concurred with the logic of this pronouncement, but the second step, namely the ability to break the attack through the knowledge of its cause, never followed. I should mention that the Doctor's technique is well-known and respected in Parisian medical circles. The system was based on Aor's ideas of harmony and sound, and on traditional correspondences between musical tones and the organs of the human body. All these ideas merged with the principles of Chinese acupuncture, a discipline the Doctor had studied with Soulié de Morant, the foremost French authority in this therapy. Aor was insistent that it was the* tone, *and not the vibration, that held the healing power.*

Mounting these stairs to the doctor's office, there was a stately wooden balustrade on the right. On the left, the stairway ran along a wall hung with prints, photographs, and drawings. One drawing in particular, one drawing alone, I should say, of all the graphic work that was closely hung there, had attracted my attention from the very first. It was a pencil sketch of a man in his forties perhaps, or older, a small, intellectual face with delicate features, a high forehead and deep-set eyes, long sparse hair combed backward and falling somewhat untidily toward the sides. It was a Gallic physiognomy which reminded me of photographs I had seen of Paul Valéry. The most characteristic feature was the dense, drooping mustache, so typically French that it is called "à la gauloise."

I hardly ever passed this drawing, hung about midway up the flight of stairs, without stopping for a closer look. I did so again one time when for reasons I cannot recall, I found myself climbing this staircase in Aor's company. It was the only time I found myself alone with him in front of this drawing. The first time I had climbed these stairs in his presence was in the very beginning when we were shown through the house, and then both Goldian and Isha were present.

He preceded me slightly. I had stopped in front of the drawing for another look at that face which held an undeniable fascination for me and stood out so sharply from the other images on the wall. He turned when he felt me lagging, stopped and saw what I was contemplating: "It's Fulcanelli," he said. "I did the sketch when he was here."

I had a spontaneous reaction which resulted in a halftruth.

"I knew it," I couldn't help saying. What I meant was that all along, I had this special feeling about the portrait, and when Aor revealed its subject to me, it was as if he had enounced an evidence, something I had somehow known all along and which now had merely been put into words to become conscious. It was in keeping with the tenor of our relationship and communications that I felt no necessity to

elaborate, nor he to question my pronouncement. We merely
continued climbing the stairs, and the matter of the drawing
never came up again.

I must admit that upon rereading the passage, I am left
dissatisfied with my description of the events. The half-truth
of "I knew it" was in fact more truth than I dared affirm at
that time. Did I fear disbelief from an eventual reader? What
else could have led me to disguise what was never less than a
certainty: that in some recess of my being I *did* know the
identity of the subject of the sketch, and that Aor's revelation
did no more than confirm this intuition. It matters little that
this idea never found conscious expression; it existed nevertheless in an intuitive moment of presence whenever I scrutinized the drawing. Is it so unlikely that I would recognize
the features of the man who occupied a prominent place in
our conversations, when all I was being told must have added
up to a description of some sort? Although I was never offered
an account of the physical particularities of our subject, I had
gleaned many traits of character and behavior, and while they
did not add up to a definite portrait . . . well, it is useless to
approach this occurrence with conjectural arguments. I know
in my own heart how matters stand, and the reader will have
to draw his conclusion to the best of his ability.

It even seems to me now that I might have harbored this
intuition from the very first, from the moment I first heard
about Fulcanelli. There is no doubt that I noticed the portrait
before being aware of its subject. Our first ascent of the broad
staircase, the visit through the house, was a very early episode; it belonged to an introductory time. I am quite certain
that Fulcanelli had not as yet entered my life. But it seems
that the very next time I saw the portrait after hearing about
Fulcanelli and his relationship to Aor, the very next time, I
knew. I am aware that I shall not convince anyone who has
not had a similar experience. However, I tend to believe that
occurrences of this kind are more frequent than is usually
admitted. Fulcanelli seemed to have been a fairly constant

preoccupation with Aor, and in view of these circumstances, with my frequent exposure to a strong projection of his personality, my intuition would be less than extraordinary.

I also question myself at this moment whether over the weeks and months of writing, I have not neglected to mention a number of events and facts which the reader should be fully aware of by now. Have I provided the contextual information needed by the reader to follow me to this point? Enough to know, if not precisely, at least approximately as much as I did *then* about Fulcanelli, about the glass, about the salt experiments, about the various subjects which occupy us? The story of the staircase, somewhat delayed, reminds us that I knew practically from the start of my involvement what Fulcanelli *looked* like, although I only found out recently for certain who he *was*. Believers in his existence had long ago narrowed down his possible identity to the principal figurants on the Fulcanelli stage: Dujols, Canseliet, Champagne, Boucher, Sauvage. As I knew none of them, pinpointing a personality to these names held little interest, especially since Aor insisted that the name "Fulcanelli" was to be applied to the phenomenon of Hermetic renaissance in Paris during the first third of the century, and not to any one individual. Yet he himself used the name Fulcanelli to refer to one particular individual with whom he had had a lengthy association. He seemed absolutely comfortable with this device, never misspoke although it is most likely that in his mind, he must have thought of his associate by his given name and surname.

I return to the book open before me, and the letter Aor had recommended to my attention. Addressed to "My old friend" and with its signature scratched out, according to Canseliet, this document, if it ever existed, is truly a model of anonymity. I shall not take the time to offer an English version of the entire document, as the book exists in translation. It is a letter of congratulations on obtaining the "gift of God." The writer has received news of this great event through his wife, and finds his certitude confirmed by what he thinks he understood. He describes it in three-and-one-half italicized lines as the fact *"that the fire dies only when the Work is done and*

*that the glass is impregnated by the entire tinctorial mass
which, from decantation to decantation, remains absolutely
saturated and becomes luminous like the sun."*

Even if it were to stop short of playing out all allusions and
tracing all references, a detailed analysis of this letter would
carry us too far. Certain aspects, however, bear mentioning
even in our restricted context: the insistence, marked by ital-
ics, upon the successful adept's "goodness," for instance; his
"good works," along with his faith and constancy, and his
"perseverance in sacrifice," make him worthy of this "Treasure of Treasures," it is said. The achievement is called "a
beautiful and victorious answer" to a previous letter from the
writer, a letter now recalled to have been replete with "dialectics and theoretical justice, yet still very distant from the
True, from the Real." The letter, a "strange epistle" even to
Canseliet, himself no stranger to Hermetic imagery, abounds
in equivoque of this kind. How are we to interpret the heral-
dic function of the writer's wife, were we to imagine a social
context for the two men? If we presume that the letter was
addressed to Fulcanelli (which we are led to believe, and no
more), then it established a strong character witness for the
addressee.

Below the scratched signature, there is a sentence that
seems entirely out of context in style and content. It is an
impersonal dictum, a very hackneyed precept of such absolute generality that it conveys no practical meaning. Bad texts
are made of such syntax, and it stands in shocking contrast to
the rest of the letter. It says that the *Oeuvre* can be accomplished with Mercury alone, or only with Mercury (there is
ambiguity in the language, as there is throughout the letter),
and this accomplishment will be the most perfect discovery
for the adept, in that he will have received the light, and
accomplished the Magisterium.

Pronouncements of this sort give the alchemical arts a bad
name. The correctness of the statement cannot be faulted, of
course, no more than could the proposition, for instance, that
unless he be blind, he who has eyes shall see; let us not argue,
however, that profundities have thereby been delivered when

nothing has been said at all. I learned that such sentences are traditionally injected into good texts. In fact, they can only exist in good texts, as they are fragments of "bad" texts, by which I mean texts (and they are numerous!) which consist entirely of such pronouncements. Bad texts are not meaningless texts written as a hoax; they are the earnest efforts of scientific minds. They are coherent, they treat with facts in all honesty, but they are "bad" because they do not evidence the personal involvement of the practicing manipulator. They are rationalizations instead of being descriptions. It is difficult to explain what brings the adept so securely into the manipulating presence of an author like Basil Valentine, while any number of seventeenth- and eighteenth-century texts are but hollow frameworks of mechanical exactitude.

Now all good authors, when they felt they were speaking clearly, have marked that fact by alchemical clichés, injected out of context, so as to stick out like sore thumbs for whomever had been truly following the development, while remaining invisible to those who were merely reading the words. It is to be taken as a signal by the good reader, and it remains nonexistent for the puffer. This traditional inside joke has been mimicked by the writer of this letter which, up to the scratched signature, is an insider's hidden tribute to a mastery of science, agility, and patience, an effort sustained over many years in order to achieve a result at once grandiose and splendidly useless. In its remarkably concise prose, it describes a key experiment attempted since the turn of the century, and eventually achieved: the creation of tinted glass in the absence of pigmentation, a technique that produced the reds and blues of the "stained" glass windows of such Gothic monuments as Chartres, Bourges, the Sainte-Chapelle . . . as well as of the fragments, bound by broad beads of lead, which formed the shade of a modest lamp hung over the de Lubicz's dining room table. There was no doubt in Aor's mind that this glass which he had manufactured at an experimental scientific station he had organized in Switzerland during the 1920s replicated the process used for the cathedral windows by the medieval adepts. In her description of the scientific station of

Suhalia and its various workshops, Isha speaks of the glass-
works where

> ... Aor rediscovered the quality of the glass of the old
> stained glass windows and the secret of the two "royal col-
> ors" which no chemical product can produce: the blues and
> reds of Chartres.[1]

⊖

All I know concerning the historical and physical aspects
of the Chartres glass came to me through Aor. I have not had
the leisure, nor have I felt the urgency since then for further
inquiry into the question. At the moment of committing myself to an orderly syntax, a search through academic scholarship would seem to be warranted to determine the extent of
public participation in the matter. Yet that is not the manner
in which I conceived the present undertaking: if a bundle of
yellowing notebooks may be excepted, research in this case
can look only to the treasure trove of memory for its essential
material. Nothing seems more certain, more secure and closer
to a chronicler's reality than the experienced self after a time
of due reflection. The immediate presence of fact might even
be misleading through its very nature as appearance; yet facts
remain one of the best bonds of consensus to be found outside
of ourselves. They are also among the most useful forms of
information to be conveyed in print and a necessary foundation for all reality. In a naïve epistemology, however, they
become valorized as reality in a surrender to the immediate,
a capitulation to our limited sensorium and a clue to a ridic-
ulously self-centered vision. Nor is such confusion absent
from the scientific laboratory, where greater circumspection
might have been expected. It is a thorny question indeed:
what is fact, what is reality? Is it a fact that the sun rises in
the East, travels across the sky and sets in the Western horizon, or is it a fact that the earth moves in a variety of fashions,
while the sun, relatively speaking, moves not at all? Or is this
latter proposition an approximation of some reality? And in

our desire to know, do we seek facts or reality? Or might they be identical, after all?

Having long ago bartered encyclopedias of fact as well as anthologies of speculation for a sylvan solitude where certainty lies primarily in self-remembered evidence, I need not hold the substance of my theme and the success of its exposition contingent on an exhaustive presentation of facts or on their speculative interpretation. Should the reader perceive this attitude as a shortcoming, he will be prompted to fill in on his own the gap in objective documentation; thus spurred into action, he will prove my memoir's efficiency. He can rest assured, furthermore, that he holds in these pages *all* I know of the matter; and though I merely gathered what came my way, without effort to reach out for what more there may be, the extent of what I can establish is by no means negligible and should provide valuable leads for detailed research. In the pursuit of knowledge and understanding, my own preference remains for the broader lines of discovery, and in the present scientific impasse, I believe, access to physical nature by the unburdened self might bring greater epistemological insight than does the availability of tomes of formulas. In other words, after the exhausting effort of our intellectual past, a greater chance for epistemological discovery lies in the synthesis of relaxed and prolonged contemplation rather than in the refined laboratory tools of analysis. Wherefore I hold that discovery, be it philosophical, artistic, or scientific, is an autobiographical process as much as it is a methodical accretion of knowledge, an edifice of studious patience. It would be unfair, of course, to disparage the possession, expansion, and transmission, through the apparatus of academic scholarship, of received ideas and proved demonstrations (practically a definition of the scientific life for the great majority of its exponents). It cannot be overlooked, however, that there is considerable doubt within the history of science itself about whether discovery blooms with such conduct. Discovery is unexpected, it is irrational; in our terms, discovery is breakthrough. In the mind of at least one contributor to the history of scientific discovery, Professor Gerald Holton,[2] it is as if there were two sciences, one approximating what we have just described and corresponding to the employment of most scientists; the other, the rare, the exceptional science, which according to Holton pursues the "nascent moment" of scientific insight, and was termed a "personal struggle" by Einstein. This latter private science seems to partake of the spirit of discovery with which I came in contact while working with de Lubicz.

Remarkable in retrospect is the measure of information concerning the Chartres glass that *did* come my way despite my avowed lack of method in gathering it. As concerns the historical aspect, I mentioned earlier that Aor found traces of the glass in Egypt. While a link is most unlikely between these Pharaonic artisans and the courts of the caliphs of Bagdad, the glass next becomes known in Mohammedan Araby. Spontaneity of appearance and nontransmission being characteristic of the glass, as the Middle Ages will show, there is little point in speculating on the extent of the contribution by Greek and Jewish doctors from Constantinople who were much in demand in Arab-occupied cities, and were basing their knowledge on the texts of Greek antiquity. The fact remains that the glass did not reach Europe directly through Greco-Roman channels, but, like so many gems of antiquity, through an Islamic adaptation. Nor can the influence be assessed on Arab scientific development of contacts with Hindu science in the wake of extensive commerce between the Indian subcontinent and the Persian Gulf region. But whatever may have been the eagerness for knowledge exhibited in the days of Harun-al-Rashid, it seems out of the question that contact could have been made with the Pharaonic ancestors and the procedures and manipulations of the science of Al-Kemi. Yet the glass is typically an alchemical result encountered only within Hermetic circumstances. The Pharaonic temple institutionalized such circumstances, so that not only language, science, and art, but even history and geography appear as meaningful Hermetic genesis. The substance of this esoteric organization sought transmission along three paths of succession, all of a Western orientation and unavailable to the Islamic world. Knowledge left the temples first through the ideas of Greek visitors such as Thales, Pythagoras, and Plato; however modified by the sharpness of Greek concepts, it came to establish its presence at the roots of Western philosophy; a second path was through Egyptian Gnosticism and heretical Christianity; a third through the images of the Tarot whose cards, just as surely as the Emerald Tablet of Hermes Trismegistos, are said to portray the structure of the sacred science of the Egyptians (as Gypsies were still called in the Middle Ages).

Under cover of the Crusades and organized as Knights Templar, a European elite made contact with the caliphates and their refined approach to life and matter. In the name of the Black Land on the Nile, they brought back a science fit to build cathedrals. Found as a symbol of such science wherever practiced was the colored glass, destined to become known as the reds and blues of Chartres. Its manufacture was by no means continuous throughout the Middle Ages; whosoever produced it gained knighthood by that fact. Nor do the knowledge of the manipulation and the noble title seem to have been hereditary; it was the art of a philosopher and not transmissible as method. Aor maintained that the material processes of the alchemical opus are banal, that they occur at every moment in every laboratory in plain view of everyone. There are no special or hidden chemical events, and the alchemical processes are of the most usual sort, so common that they escape notice, as is repeated again and again with regard to *materia prima* in alchemical texts. The difference in the esoteric manipulation lies entirely in the apprehension of the event: it is a matter of perception, of vision.

There is no way for me to ascertain the extent of the awareness and acceptance abroad of these facts and assertions. Though my casual glimpses at the literature of medieval Europe has yielded no specific information, I am convinced that thorough scholarship will find a number of clues. Alchemical texts abound with recipes for the manufacture of colored glass, precious stones, and rare metals, but there is a dearth of

interest in a possible product, such as the glass of the cathedrals would represent. Yet the facts here proposed are not
obscure and perhaps not even unorthodox, as we shall see.
Orthodoxy in the matter of cathedral glass can certainly be
expected from an authority such as Jean Quievreux, curator
for the stained glass windows of the French nation (*Conser-
vateur des Vitraux de France*). I did not personally know
Monsieur Quievreux, but my good friend Maurice Girodias,
then director of *Éditions du Chêne* in Paris, came to know
him well in 1942–43 when publishing Quievreux's *Les Vitraux de la Cathédrale de Chartres*. It was on this occasion
that my friend first heard of the mystery of the blue and red
glass. The curator spoke of it as a puzzle for modern science,
seeing that there seems to be no analyzable cause for the blue
and red light which the glass transmits. Quievreux did not
present any hypotheses as to the manufacture of the glass, at
least none that my friend recalls. Nor does Maurice Girodias
remember whether mention of this riddle occurs in the book.
I have attempted to locate Quievreux's work, unsuccessfully
thus far, and with very few expectations as to its usefulness
for my concern. For I do not fancy a French government official during the German occupation as a proponent of controversy or a gadfly of esoterism. Yet what he told his publisher
conforms most exactly to what I learned from Aor: the
Chartres glass is different enough to be incomprehensible.

⊖

Although I had worked on Basil Valentine's *Twelve Keys*
almost daily, several brief appendixes which followed the
main body of the work had somehow escaped my attention. I
recall noticing quite accidentally that one of these pieces
bears the title: *I shall also present my opinion on the Salt of
the Philosophers*, and I therefore began reading these pages.
They led to a discovery which confirms the liveliness to that
date (the edition dates from 1956) of Aor's involvement with
Fulcanelli. It confirms both collaboration and experimental
subject.

I read the first three pages of typically arcane prose and could muster only distant resonances of our recent conversations, although the latter concerned this very topic; my interest, consequently, was skimming but lightly over the colorful imagery. But when I turned the next page, I discovered a previous reader who had been much more committed: in the left margin, about three quarters down the page, there was a penciled remark, situated at the beginning of a lengthy editorial footnote by Eugène Canseliet. I recognized Aor's writing immediately. *"Il en ignorait tout"** the inscription reads, and it refers to a passage where the same hand has vigorously underlined two words:

> What remains there to be said concerning the topic of Salt, after <u>our Master</u>, who has discussed the matter elsewhere in all possible detail, though often in a cabalistic manner, so as to be understood only by the 'Sons of Science'? (*Demeures Philosophales, op. cit., passim.*)[3]

"Notre Maître" are the words of Canseliet that have been marked by two emphatic lines. The marginal exclamation is closest perhaps to a cry of indignation. We know who *"he"* is, of course, the dunce, here promoted to Master . . . it can only be Fulcanelli. And how could an ignoramus have engaged in detailed dissertations concerning our subject, Salt, as Canseliet further maintains? Nor is there the slightest hesitancy in the accusation; the hand which here writes and underlines is dead sure of what it means: the so-called Master does not know whereof he speaks! Could this unkind opinion stem from the "cabalistic manner" Canseliet attributes to his author, a manner impermeable to all but the "Sons of Science"?

Most importantly: for whom did Aor write these four words, to whom does he address them? There is no question in my mind that he wrote them solely for himself, and this at the time of a first reading, four years ago at most, which is the

* "He didn't know the first thing about it"

earliest he could have perused the book. During this time and until the moment I inadvertently roused them from their splendid privacy, these words had not been contemplated by a second pair of eyes, for no one, I am sure, had had occasion to read this particular copy or even to leaf through its pages. I knew this specifically with regard to Lucie, the only person who could have had access to the book. Aor had explained to me her absolute nonparticipation in the Hermetic subject, her discretion, and her distant respect for the arcane and ritual framework of alchemical practice.

Would he have given me this book, had he remembered the inscription? Certainly not, to my mind. It contradicts a detachment from the Fulcanelli legend, a detachment Aor attempted to maintain consistently; he certainly would not have wanted a witness to his emotional involvement and concern. The graphic traces of his reaction had been so thoroughly forgotten that he could casually hand them to me now, imprisoned on the page, for me and everyone to see. There had been sudden flashes in the past, akin to this revelatory outburst: when he had spoken of his cathedral research, for instance, which had ended up in Fulcanelli's book. And perhaps one other time, when I had first been struck by his uncharacteristically impassioned sensibility while relating the Fulcanelli saga; so struck, in fact, that I no longer recall the context of the occasion. No matter. The question is rather: why should this footnote on salt by Canseliet (a writer whom he presented to me as a mere *littérateur* of superficial Hermetic lore) warrant more than a curious glance, a raised eyebrow? The damning pronouncement perpetuated in the margin of the text is too strong to have been anything but an overt disagreement, not in opinion merely, but in a matter of *fact*. The extent of Fulcanelli's knowledge is here not approached as idle speculation, but with the assured tone of a certitude that comes from experience. By its tonus, the calligraphic gesture in this case conveys a lived and shared experiment, not a theoretical judgment.

⊖

Some time in early June, Aor mentioned the festivities of midsummer, when on the longest night of the year bonfires are built on the surrounding hills of Grasse as well as all over the countryside. Families and friends gather in large groups, much wine is consumed, and there is a ritual of jumping over the fires at midnight.

"Come over on that evening," he said, "we'll find a moment to slip upstairs. I want you to look at something."

Midsummer's eve of 1960 must be seen as a watershed in my experience at the Mas-de-Coucagno. Some days before the event, Aor spoke to me in an unusually serious and formal vein. The afternoon had started with some further insights into the Fulcanelli biography.

"It must have been during the first year of World War I when Fulcanelli approached me with that manuscript, the one he lifted at Chacornac's; he told me he had been studying it for three or four years without any results at all. I was then working for the French Army in a chemical laboratory, testing supplies; nothing very exciting, but it gave me access to a well-equipped shop. I had plenty of time to myself and the circumstances were ideal for working on something like that. I did have some hesitations about an association with that fellow, but his manuscript was a great find. We entered into a strict agreement. No one was to know we worked together. This suited him fine, as he intended to use for his own aggrandizement whatever information we would come up with, although I didn't suspect it at the time. And this despite my having further stipulated that any contribution *de part et d'autre* was to remain strictly between the two of us. I always kept my part of the bargain. He violated our agreement, as his and his friends' writings clearly show, and it did get him into trouble. The fact is that he never had anything to share, he didn't seem to be getting anywhere, and whatever information I passed on to him during that time seemed to be way over his head. He was too materialistic to appreciate the laboratory events, but that never got in the way of our collaboration. He was able to devise a procedure for any operation one could propose, and that was his importance, as a manipulator. His practice was fabulous, and I had it at my service. He did all the manipulations, a little the way Lucie drew all the figures when I worked on geometry. But the ideas that moved those hands, the ideas always came from me. At least Lucie doesn't propose geometric theorems, the way Fulcanelli started to propose alchemical theory. Remember, when I say 'Fulcanelli,' I mean that whole group of literati and puffers: Canseliet, Dujols, Champagne, Boucher, Sauvage; they all contributed to give shape to Fulcanelli's production, once he had spread my ideas among them. He uses my cathedral work as a vehicle, and a lot of talk about operations he has had contact with, thanks to me, but whose function, whose form, whose nomenclature he doesn't understand. And then the glitter all around it, the fantastic erudition, much of which can be traced to Dujols and some to Canseliet; add the art-work of Champagne, and you have a very salable book. They made a career out of it, but in the process, they missed the moment, they missed the Word . . . " (with empathy), "the Word of the time. They missed *medu-netr*, the hieroglyphic staff words lean upon. But they did collect renown, and in the end, that's what most of them were after. Not a scientist in the lot! I'm not saying they were absolutely devoid of ideas, of course, in their obsession with Greek etymology. But they did not possess the language of their time, *le Verbe de leur temps*.[4] They did me a favor, though; they saved me from identifying my work with cathedral symbolism, which kept me available for Egypt, for Al-Kemi instead of alchemy. It is the same work, of course, only in the language of our time, whereas Fulcanelli speaks in the language of the great medieval alchemical renaissance. But what we must be involved with now is not a renaissance, it is a resurrection. The *Oeuvre* as Al-Kemi is a work of resurrection.[5] That concept went beyond Fulcanelli's reach. Fulcanelli and the cathedral symbolism were necessary, but I was not to be identified with it. It is the closure of a past moment, whereas the opening of Pharaonic Egypt as symbolique gives us the clue to the future. The further back you can see, the farther ahead also. The past is Man crucified in space, represented by cathedral symbolism, but the resurrection is best read in the symbolique of Al-Kemi. Well, but this is not what I wanted to talk about. I was saying that Fulcanelli took it upon himself to publish what he had advised me not to bring out, as well as what he had sworn to keep to himself. You see, one good thing about observing a vow of secrecy is that at least you will not talk about what you do not understand. In Fulcanelli's case, what came out in print is hopelessly garbled, full of unnecessary obscurity, and certainly of no use to any seriously practicing adept, although it gives much ammunition to puffers with its nice-sounding phrases. It does not represent a symbolique, because it is not the voice of its time. But it has the underlying symbols in common with Al-Kemi, and they were what I practiced on. I could not have recognized the cosmology of the Pharaohs had I not known the medieval book of the cathedral. As to Fulcanelli, he represented a case which is not unusual in the arts, Hermetic or otherwise, the case of a marvelous technician without an ounce of philosophic insight. Very cultured, very well read, as they all were, but no docrine, no vision. As he was absolutely destitute at the time, I financed him, gave him the opportunity to install a small workplace and provided a monthly stipend so he could live and work. And I kept this up almost to the end, I kept it up until we got together here, at the Mas-de-Coucagno, for the crucial experiment. After that, I saw him only one more time, not long thereafter, on his deathbed, in a garret in Montmartre."

He had stopped speaking, but remained leaning forward, looking at me with a kindly and polite smile, his head tilted and his hands on the table, fingers intertwined. We were both heavy smokers at the time, and I recall the disarray in the heaping ashtray. I believe Aor spent much time in cafés during his youth in Paris; he often spoke of the atmosphere in the Closerie des Lilas in the early years of the century. There had been a measure of bohemia in his life in those days, and he liked to recall it. At times there entered into our way of spending these afternoons a reminiscence of their urban counterpart around small marble-topped tables, and I felt his loquaciousness as if prompted by this memory.

Now he remained silent, but I did not feel that he had as yet reached what he wanted to discuss, and I left him to his cogitation, loath to interject myself. Perhaps there would be nothing further to be said about Fulcanelli's death, nothing more than what Isha had already told me: that when Fulcanelli lay dying, he had sent word to Aor to come and see him, and both Isha and Aor had been with him shortly before he died. Isha's account had alluded to a painful agony, and the veiled words, more cryptic than usual, seemed to imply a punishment, perhaps the expiation of some sin or crime. In keeping with my resolution, I had omitted all questioning, and this remained my intention now as well. Speculations concerning Fulcanelli's disappearance (which, along with his identity, continues to be presented, as late as 1980, in the guise of a persistent mystery)[6] were here being laid to rest in the most cavalier fashion, but I bridled my curiosity despite the piquant directness and factual tone. The protracted silence was getting to be somewhat uncomfortable, however, and I was beginning to think that he might wish to be alone. Yet before I could devise a gentle way of breaking into the hushed atmosphere and perhaps take my leave, he started to speak again.

"After we left Suhalia, we installed this place here, and as soon as I had my laboratory organized and had solved some remaining problems, I got in touch with Fulcanelli to show him what I had come up with. Remember, I had been helping him financially all this time, notwithstanding his treachery with his cathedral book. It had been nineteen years since he had shown me the color manuscript, and he had not made a step in all this time. *Dix-neuf années sans faire un pas, c'est long!* I had set up the experiment that I hoped would prove the theory of the text once and for all, after which I intended to terminate my relationship with him. There is no use going into the technical details of all this. We have spoken very little as yet about salt, but you have some idea about the shift in its structure that was suggested by the color theory in that manuscript. If you have read *Le Temple* carefully, you will have gathered quite a bit of information on what we mean by salt. By the way, do you ever read in the third volume of *Le Temple*?''

I had to admit that I hadn't gotten to it as yet, but I did so gladly, and rather volubly, relieved by the opportunity to say a few words. Our conversations were not usually so one-sided, but "Fulcanelli" was a subject to which I was unable to contribute, and my usual inquisitiveness was reduced to mere receptivity as soon as this subject surfaced. Salt might be within my domain, or at least I do feel qualified to question it as a scientific concept in its process of definition. It implies a logic I describe with my implicit functions, and I am able to apply myself in the communication of this type of knowledge. The subject of Fulcanelli, however, unlike a topic such as the study of salt and its function in the mineral world, was not a matter into which I felt free to dig at my leisure: for Aor, Fulcanelli was a page of autobiography. Therefore I felt the communication to be a self-revealing gesture rather at odds with the voluntary anonymity of his retreat, with the atmosphere of discretion, and yes, secrecy, which surrounded the Hermetic Aor, if not R.A. Schwaller de Lubicz altogether. If Lucie's word can be trusted, these revelations had been kept from his closest associate, his stepdaughter and collaborator. Now they are freely submitted to an acquaintance of less than six months!

At the time, I was unaware of the exclusive nature of the information; I assumed that Lucie was *at least one* other inclusion besides Isha. It is true, however, that the subject never came up in Lucie's presence, that is to say at lunch, by now practically the sole occasion for our meeting. And unless she was an intrepid mystifier indeed, it could well be that she was living entirely outside the world of the Hermetic Aor, as he had in fact told me she was. It had simply not occurred to me to take him literally and at his word.

In conclusion, this unilateral self-presentation carried our relationship further and faster than I could efficiently handle. It was running through me with too much data to process in too little time. The geometry had been a giant step in consolidating my language, the physical study of Al-Kemi had laid the basis for a philosophical cosmology, form and function had projected a blueprint of universal design, and now an autobiographical factor was offering a page of history, a subtle vignette placed in a landscape that sets it off: the intense search beyond Newtonian physics, the destruction of a world in World War I, the search for new directions everywhere—in society, in the arts, in literature. Was there a Hermetic Aor at that time, at the time when de Lubicz published a book later revendicated by André Breton for the Surrealist cause?[7] It was the same time at which the reds and blues of Chartres were being crafted in Alpine furnaces. It was the year when Aor wanted contact and said so.

$$\ominus$$

But before we harken back to hear him ask himself the question of his name, I would like to point yet once again to this moment where personal history breaks through shielding anonymity in the guise of a teaching, or at least of an instruction. For reasons I was just beginning to fathom, a part of his life had been lived unseen. Did he realize that I represented his adventure's last chance of survival according to the spirit in which it had been lived, and not according to voices who in an earlier day would have favored burning "Schwaller the occultist" for witchcraft?[8] Did he recognize qualifications in me that made it worthwhile, and perhaps imperative for the gist of these events to survive in this transmission, and if so, would it not force me to consider what such qualifications might be?

I recognized the confidentiality of the communication, and was acutely aware that a story barbed with secrecy was here let out free and without strings attached. He knew my opposition to being tied by vows and pledges, but he admitted its validity, though with some sarcasm, and accepted its reasons. Autobiography is a private matter only as long as it escapes observation; once it becomes a public fact, it takes a stand as one more possible life, as one more wager in the game of living. It would be of interest to a theory of values that in our

time, a creatively successful life was lived in terms of Al-
Kemi. For Aor, the wager paid off.

Was *I* to be responsible for the survival of this story? It did
not occur to me at the time, as I thought that others, more
knowledgeable of the facts and more interested in the endeavor, were carrying the burden of responsibility. This erro-
neous conception played its part in my casual attitude. I
admit that at times I felt impatience with the Fulcanelli
theme, or felt my thoughts gently straying from its thread,
not to dream, but to engage in more active cogitation on an
aspect of philosophical cosmology perhaps, or on a theory of
evolution: it was *there* I would have preferred roving with
Aor. A generation later, the human circumstances seem to
me at least as weighty as the knowledge of the spheres, and
insight into the human being as revealing as an understanding
of mankind. The concrete feels more durable now than it had
seemed at the time, the abstract less eternal. It may be that I
underrated the force of *inscription* in those days, and have
now learned to value the salty pearls of experience.

A tacit understanding between us may well have marked
the story for survival; yet I needed no vows of silence to make
me respect its privacy. I willingly extend such courtesy to
friends and acquaintances, expecting equal consideration in
return. Aor was certainly aware of this, and aware therefore
that his indiscretions to himself were committed at minimum risk. By the same token, however, this state of affairs
did not permit me to exhibit even a semblance of prying, and
my unquestioning passivity meant to underline the point. I
knew he did not take it for indifference, although it was cal-
culated to preclude an impression of excessive interest or concern. I would *accept* autobiography, but I could not pursue it
the way I felt free to pursue the impersonal knowledge I assumed to be the mainspring of our relationship.

One time only do I recall forgetting myself. The personal
nature of the question I framed might seem minimal, yet it
sets it apart from the free hunting grounds of ideas. As is
frequently the case, I do not recall the context of the exchange, but I remember that it occurred at table. Perhaps the

conversation had to do with languages, for I asked him quite innocently where he was born. There was an abrupt change of mood and he looked at me rather coldly.

"In Pharaonic Egypt," he replied after a pause.

In return, I was never in any way questioned concerning my past, or my ancestry, and when I attempted to present any such details, my information was received with an apparent lack of curiosity that might well have been the counterpart to my discretion. For all intents and purposes, I was made to feel that my life had begun with my entry into his consciousness, and that no further information was needed to guide our relationship. As for myself, I was fully occupied with absorbing what I could of what was presented here and now, a material fully pertinent to my concerns. Historical considerations were of secondary import.

And yet there had been an Aor who had published his name in a declaration of identity. This is the earliest autobiographical statement by Aor, and it answers all at once the fundamental autobiographical question: "Who am I?", which in the true Hermetic spirit translates into: "What is the meaning of my name?"

"Aor! . . . Que veut dire Aor!"[9]

It was 1925, and the events surrounding the "crucial experiment" were still several years into the future. If the Hermetic Aor is to be kept hidden, who then is the Aor who publicly questions the meaning of his name? He is a teacher and he demands to be transmitted. His very first lesson is on the use of the senses, a theory of perception which establishes the role of ear and eye in functional and formal identification. Once that teaching is acquired, then Aor will show the student the origin of things created. There follows an italicized admonition:

You are not allowed to keep for yourself what you will learn; you will have to transmit it, say it, and write it. This not for your pleasure, but for the Eternal.[10]

We must not forget that *this* Aor is not as yet born to Pharaonic Egypt. His name is old and does not change at the various births. There is a continuity, but there is also a break. The continuity is in the name, the break is a birth to Pharaonic Egypt. Birth is preceded by death, affirmation by negation. To consider his birth to Pharaonic Egypt without his death to alchemy is seeing but one side of the coin. The bright side born in Al-Kemi hides the dark side of the reverse, and this creative death is the end of Fulcanelli. For when Aor breaks with Fulcanelli, Fulcanelli ceases to exist. In 1927, Aor is still in Suhalia. By 1932, Fulcanelli is dead, having published his second and last work, *"Les Demeures Philosophales"* in 1929. For R.A. Schwaller de Lubicz also, it is the beginning of a great silence of twenty-two years, a silence broken in Egypt, in Al-Kemi, with *Le Temple dans l'Homme,* the timid and imperfect feeler which preceded *Le Temple de l'Homme.* By now the public Aor has vanished, and the Hermetic Aor has found his language. He now truly exists, which means that he has covered his traces, shed his atavisms, has entered the Temple and become high priest, builder, Pharaoh.

Aor appears very rarely in *Le Temple de l'Homme,* but never more strikingly than when kneeling on the parvis of the Mystic Temple, fighting the curse of Ashaver, the Wandering Jew.[11]

Had I known the self-representation of *L'Appel du Feu,* I would have been less surprised at his propensity to lock the past into words. The oral autobiography (the contradiction in terms is unavoidable) which was presented to me belonged to the time of the vocal Aor, to an apocalyptic prophet of the cosmic cycle: the end of one world, the beginning of another.[12] This Aor wants to talk, he wants to teach. He even publishes a "Doctrine,"[13] and in its introduction might well give us a clue to his later predilection for anonymity and silence. If it is true that no subject can be understood save through its genesis, then we should not overlook the odyssey from Suhalia to Luxor, via the "crucial experiment" and its consequences.

It must be pointed out that publication of the early work

(even in fragments such as organized by Isha during the year she survived him) is contrary to all his wishes. He wanted everything preceding *Le Temple de l'Homme* to be forgotten, and refused categorically to show me his early writings, although I asked him more than once. He had completely rejected all works that preceded the Pharaonic symbolique. When I questioned him on the content of the strangely titled *Adam, l'Homme Rouge,* his reaction was akin to embarrassment. I do not believe that Isha's tribute to the early work did him much of a favor. Her indelicacy toward his pre-Pharaonic life is not surprising in light of her position vis-à-vis the Hermetic Aor. She operated outside him, facing him, barred by her sex from the ultimate Hermetic intimacy such as Aor understood it: the abstraction of *l'Oeuvre* proved in the concreteness of nature, in an equation where the sense of "nature" is close to the Greek *physis.* It is a scientific procedure through and through, beginning with the logical rigors of esoteric geometry and harmony, to arrive at a thing, a stone, the most common component in a gravitational world.

The dialectics of abstract-concrete escaped Isha; she felt equally as uncomfortable with things in their laboratory concreteness, with physics and chemistry, as she did with mythical abstraction. It was, Aor would say, a gender characteristic, a matter of mental circuitry and physical constitution. It came from the lunar function, the reflected existence. It brought with it an irresistible coercion to fill up with matter, imagery, and usefulness what was meant to be purely abstract form, function, and substance. No amount of application could close this gap. It was a hopeless, an inescapably basic congenital deficiency. Right or wrong, such was Aor's oft-expressed persuasion.

Discrepancies would spring chasms between Aor and Isha on quasi-theological grounds, differences to be debated with an empathy that showed the seriousness of the involvement. On those occasions, Aor would soon sense that a breach had opened which could not be straddled and which neither side was disposed to jump, and he would gently back away. I first became aware of these tactics after I brought up the identity of myth and hieroglyphic language in a conversation with Isha. This point of view, admittedly extreme, had been a topic I had broached with Aor from time to time, and always discussed in perfect agreement. To my surprise, Isha refused this notion, which seemed to me perfectly in tune with the primitive originality of the Pharaonic spirit. She would agree to an identity of myth and nature, but I knew the extent to which our definitions of "nature" differed. We later had occasion to bring up our disagreement with Aor, and to my surprise, he tried to evade the entire discussion, refusing to take a stand, hiding behind his pipe.

At the first opportunity he took me aside.

"Don't you know yet that Isha cannot cope with such abstraction? She needs the personages of the myth, she needs the imagery."

These sudden walls of noncommunication were the limits for her of the Hermetic Aor, and they must have contributed to her valorization of other areas where she had been an equal partner. Most of these lay in his past; they did not survive the meditation of Palma de Majorca, where the couple spent "two fruitful years of solitude in the silence of an ancient hospice of Raymond Lully,"[14] after the social and political phases had run their course. After that, Aor set up a laboratory in Grasse, eventually inviting Fulcanelli for the final manipulations on the crucial experiment. Once the consequences of these events had been absorbed, he was ready to inhabit the temple of the Pharaohs. Although there were women in that temple, they were priestesses and not philosophers. If anything, the ancients knew the difference between sun and moon.

Yet there had been a public Aor at whose side Isha had flourished, and she refused to have this overlooked, to have those vibrant years wiped out as *he* would have it, perversely, to her mind. She managed to place them in the limelight as soon as his constraint disappeared. The story should be a warning to all who leave behind memories and memorabilia. In the painful and exhausted aftermath of his illness and death, she thinks not of silence, rest, and retirement, but resurrects a past he had wanted to forget. Her effort is misplaced to the extent of making us consider it a case of willful disclosure, or else of an abysmal ignorance and lack of consciousness concerning both their lives and the events surrounding them. She chose to violate the parameters set by Aor for his autobiography. Was this a grave misjudgment, or a gesture of honesty and frankness, or again, was it merely misguided adulation? Any conclusion we might draw would be pure speculation. The impulse to reveal may have been benign, but the many years of constraint and anonymity could not have been voluntary, judging by her reflex as soon as she was free. Aor died in December 1961, and by 1963, her book had exposed his political identity. It may be difficult to believe she was entirely unaware of the implications of this identity, but it is certain that she never imagined the actual effects of the disclosure. Her impulse may have been naïve and innocuous; its effects certainly are not. They alone would compel me to compose this memoir and to confront the questions raised, even if such questions were the memoir's only theme. Although she must have known that his desire for occultation was here not related to the esoteric, she may have thought that it signaled the yearning for privacy which tends to accompany spiritual maturation. Such a propensity would be considerably weakened, and perhaps eliminated altogether at the end of that private person's physical existence. A "now it can be told" breathlessness pervades the prose of her hasty biographical pages. Be this as it may, it was certainly never clear to her that with her revelations she had entered a purely *political* domain.

7

*Les Veilleurs and their language.—An ugly word
translated.—A signal from the lunatic fringe.—A 1919
publication reviewed.—Salt, bones, and symbolique.—The
arms of Eze.—Indestructible remnants.—Evolution,
cellular and metallic.—Perception and endless cycles.
—Inscribing the mineral salt.—On metal.*

The group of "Les Veilleurs" has recently been presented to
this country[1] as a benign "sociospiritual" group, and there is
no one to say that it was not intended as such. Yet the few
other references I have encountered, all of European origin,
unfortunately point to a shadow zone where the activities
seem to reach beyond these qualifications. We will point to
both the blatant misinformation contained in these allega-
tions and to the undeniable evidence of the group's problematic nature. If some material realizations of the sociospiritual
program have been left to posterity, they have eluded me so
far. As testimony of their activity, Les Veilleurs have left us
words, and it is to the political implications of their language
that Isha's biography drew my attention.

Words and terms in their syntactical arrangements; these
are elements that have preoccupied us from the very beginning. Now we are here examining a practical manifestation of

language as living entity, and the management this vehicle of
creative thinking deserves and demands. Living, because with
every new terminological context, the word is expanded by
live thinking in a truly organic and functional process, in a
ripening of words. But not every fruit attains its harvest after
perfect gestation; there are mishaps, injuries, deaths even. An
entire language can be sickened by perverted perception and
ineptitude of consciousness, and there corresponds, to this
systematized deficiency of the higher faculties, a monstrous
political machine of tyranny; this much we know from history and from recent experience. Such a criminal system
starts by starving thinking life and silencing the nation's
poets. The ripening of words is meant to be a civilizing enterprise, available to the human being only, but I am afraid that
in general, and certainly since 1919 when Les Veilleurs were
coining their propositions, we have nurtured our inherited
languages with more brutality than care. The responsible
writer must guard against the degradation of his text through
such a crisis in his language, and there have been extreme
cases where, facing the loss of a mother tongue, this responsibility toward language has lead the exile to despair, even to
suicide. An educated and trained perception will find its safeguard in theory of language, in a technique of thinking. If the
writer fails in his communication, if the latter is distorted in
time because the language has been twisted by falsehood, the
highest ideals and most spiritual expressions will be prey to
interpretation in the light of historical change, and even of
spurious fashion. In our case, it is political events that twist
these unguarded words into shapes their authors certainly
never intended, were unable to foresee, and would most likely
regret, could they witness them today. We can blame Les
Veilleurs for a lack of foresight, but we cannot convict them
on the strength of an anachronism. The charges, if there were
any, would not be of guilt, but of irresponsibility.

Therefore I shall refrain, as much as possible, from using
political labels the terms of which had as yet neither past nor
future at the time Les Veilleurs formulated their policies,
while now they have shown themselves and proved them-

selves for what they are in a great variety of contexts. These
concepts and their symbols, the words, the terms, the images
today are loaded with experience, some of it brutal to the
point of inhumanity, the point at which language fails and
words deteriorate, emptying themselves of meanings: inhumanity possessed of language, an unbearable, maddening contradiction which is the locus of semantic degradation.

I have no doubt, then, that this unguarded syntax of 1919
which Isha brought to my attention, this language as yet not
tested by experience and encounter, had in its day advanced
under a banner of shining light and for the good of all mankind. Today however, smothered with past, the terms remain
imprisoned on the page, their comprehension unconditioned
by a tone of voice, a gesture, an action offering irrefutable
truth. The intention has vanished, the text remains, a prey to
interpretation. How is this received by the public for which
Les Veilleurs have become a topic, a public too young and too
remote to have a feeling for those days, too ill-informed to
picture not only the seeds that were sown then, but even to
remember the bitter fruit at maturity, rotting on bloodied
soil? And how is it seen by the ones who cannot forget?

An important link to those early days is through O.V. de
Lubicz Milosz, the source of the de Lubicz name. At the time
of Les Veilleurs, Aor was de Lubicz Milosz's closest friend. It
was the period in which Milosz wrote his most esoteric pages,
the time of the *Cantique de la Connaissance*.[2] But it was also
the time when the ground was laid for the great left-right
struggle that engulfed all of Europe and from which France,
or at least the French spirit, has yet to recover.

What I know of Les Veilleurs from Aor is direct, singular,
and potentially compromising, even while concerning a matter as harmless, apparently, as the garb he devised for himself
and his disciples. It had been a lighter moment when he
talked about the fashion industry, which he considered, quite
rightly to my mind, a shameless exploitation of people and a
contributor to the moral decline.

"In Paris after the First World War, I had a group of people
I worked with, and in protest against this fashion nonsense,

all the men wore the same attire: boots, riding pants, and a dark shirt. *Ce qui plus tard est devenu l'uniforme des SA."*

I have a painter's memory for moments and a musician's memory for tone (rather than a storyteller's for duration), and although twenty-five years have passed and it is difficult to define the complexity of my first reaction, I do know exactly what was said and in what spirit. And I remember quite precisely how it was received by me. I never flinched, primarily because his language (which I present verbatim) offers a neutralizing ambiguity to the nexus of cause and effect. Watching him lay this out for me so simply, with his charming smile and a youthful surge which moved his body toward me as if the memory had quickened his blood, it never occurred to me that his syntax might indicate a causal relation between the clothes he had designed and those that would costume barbarity. Surely he was merely bringing out a strange coincidence in this vestiary transmission *outre Rhin!*

I knew nothing about Les Veilleurs at the time, and although a group of booted men in the 1920s would raise my hackles on either side of the Rhine, I did not attempt to gain more information on the group. I would have been quite content to let the matter rest forever on its uneasy bed of doubt and coincidence, had not Isha, later, presented me with her artless revelations.

My desire to sidetrack this issue in favor of the good work I was doing with him easily made me overlook the convictions he shared with his social class and tradition. The French bourgeois is right wing and anti-Semitic, and although Aor as a rule restrained himself in my presence, he did express himself forcefully on the subject when he felt he had good cause. A most remarkable transgression comes to my mind: he was venting his anger at an entertainer who was playing at the Cannes Casino, a popular pianist and singer whose name I never saw in print, but who, according to Aor, called himself "Beethove" (or so it sounded when Aor pronounced his name). Here was a cheap entertainer, he thundered, taking in vain the name of a genius.

"Alors ici, il faut le dire: Ça c'est vraiment le youpin!"

As I have already indicated, I laid this type of outburst to a relatively inoffensive xenophobia coupled with religious intolerance. One is prepared to pay the price of encountering these reflexes when one frequents the French middle class (where anti-Semitism is inbred and strengthened by Catholic schooling), yet prejudice is always disappointing when it stems from an intelligent and respected source. Still, one is disposed to forgive, also because such revelations can be interpreted as a sign of trust, of intimacy. I was indoctrinated neither by my Catholic mother nor by my Jewish father, and I never concerned myself with either religion, nor with any other for that matter. Nor do I in any way fit the Hebrew caricature which lives in all anti-Semitic minds, and it was quite clear to him that I could suffer no personal offense by his remark: he did not think of me as a kike (which is the fairest translation of "youpin") any more than I thought of myself as Jewish. Furthermore, and more subtly, he doubted that I, who had agreed so closely and easily with his most difficult ideas, could foster a serious disagreement on a question as plain as *race*. His anti-Semitism (which I still presumed to be merely social and religious) struck me as predictable, although I found it deplorable nevertheless. A good part of the French population will thus express themselves on this matter in private, while maintaining a polite silence in public. And I took this to be his case. His anti-Semitism was part of his right-wing position, and politics was irrelevant to our concerns.

⊖

Even Isha's biographical sketch of Aor and the material it contained about the time of Les Veilleurs did not prod me, after I saw her book in 1963, to investigate this matter further. Aor had been dead for two years, and I had by this time presented my paper, *Knowledge and Implicit Functions*, to a Swiss journal of epistemology, *Dialectica*, where it had been read by Professor Ferdinand Gonseth, who was then in charge of higher mathematics at the École Polytechnique fédérale of Zurich. The correspondence and encounter which ensued are beyond our title, and I bring them up only to justify my frame of mind at that point. I had found it preferable to distance myself for a time from the teaching I had chosen to leave, and the Gonseth exchange had offered a creative opportunity to that effect. However, it had led me far, not only from Al-Kemi and alchemy, but also from all biographical aspects of Aor. My reading of Isha's book was therefore cursory, but some aspects of the material couldn't help but strike my attention. Isha had selected a number of texts from *Le Veilleur*, each one addressed to a specific sociopolitical topic or segment of the population. These must have appeared in the first issue; together they formed a general statement of policy. There was first of all the sweeping *Adresse aux Français* anonymously signed by the council of watchmen, *Le Conseil des Veilleurs*. In a footnote to the signature, Isha reveals the constitution of the council:

> *de Lubicz-Schwaller, chef des Veilleurs; Jeanne le Veilleur (Isha Schwaller de Lubicz); Jacques le Veilleur (Carlos Larronde) secrétaire général.*[3]

Next came a variety of signed articles: A *Lettre aux Artistes*, a *Lettre aux Socialistes*, a *Lettre aux Philosophes Occultes* and a piece on femininity signed "Jeanne le Veilleur." It was the topic of the "letter" signed "Aor," however, that fairly stunned me. It was entitled *Lettre aux Juifs*.[4]

I remind my reader of the accommodation I had reached over the years with the ingrown social and religious prejudices of the French bourgeoisie, accommodations that had conditioned my relationship with Aor. But the publication of a "Letter to the Jews," whatever its eventual content, had to be a highly visible gesture in the Paris of 1919, and it certainly reached beyond the limits of my exemption. What . . . ? In a new publication representing his ideas, he lets others address philosophers and artists, and he chooses to address . . . the Jews? Such involvement lacks all common measure with the passive narrowmindedness that is the national malady! Actually, the letter turns out to be a bit of advice and a call for action by one who is

> not one of you, but to whom you will listen nevertheless, for I speak with knowledge and I know who you are.[5]

Whatever the content of this article, I would be able to judge its intent, for I knew who *he* was, and I knew the provenance of the ideas. True, my acquaintance with his feelings on the subject was of later date, forty years later, at the end of his life. Yet it was easy to extrapolate from here what he might have felt *then*, at the height of his temporal powers, with disciples, all turned out in boots, riding pants, and dark shirts. The effect of age, known to erode extremes, had to be considered, as well as the sobering horror show recently presided over by Nazi Germany, which could not have been witnessed, one assumes, without some modification of consciousness. In 1919, these occurrences were barely in preparation, and it would rather have been the echoes of the Dreyfus case he would have heard, and a furtive typescript of the "Protocols of the Elders of Zion" he might have seen. The revision of the Dreyfus trial which ended in 1906 had by no means defeated anti-Semitism in France, as was widely held by an idealistic left, and definitely disproved a generation later by the population at large. Yet it had helped to keep anti-Semitism under cover, so that a Gentile *Lettre aux Juifs* as late (or as early!) as 1919 must have seemed to a secure French Jewry a signal from the lunatic fringe. Whatever its content, this article must have raised Aor, its author, to a position above the general public's routine prejudice. In 1919, in preference to any other subject with which he could have launched his new publication, Aor chose to address French Jews; and they, the most assimilated in Europe, could only interpret his proposition to

> Go build your country and construct a square tower in Zion[6]

in the way I knew perfectly well it was ultimately intended: as an invitation to leave a France which was not really their country.

⊖

Allow me to wonder once again: what made her do it? Could it be that she thought this piece would prove him in the avant-garde of Zionism, and thus perhaps silence

> ... certain rumors spread by ill-informed, or perhaps even ill-willed persons concerning Les Veilleurs as well as the very name of Schwaller de Lubicz[?][7]

Unaware of any slander, I find more danger in the remedy than in the alleged ill. Yes, the footnote by Jean Rousselot[8] is obviously misinformed (in 1955, this Paris intellectual believes the name to be "Schwaller-Milosz," itself a commentary on Aor's obscurity at the time), and it is speculative as to the aims and practices of Les Veilleurs and of their chief ("black magicians and practitioners of conjuring books"), but the speculation was fed by the subjects themselves: the "secret-society" aspect of René Schwaller, the esoteric and occult aspect of Aor, and most of all the testament of silence left by the later Milosz. According to Rousselot,

> Milosz, at the end of his life, implored his friends not to question him concerning "Les Veilleurs" ...[9]

The offending contents of the *Lettre* is adequately couched in heroic terms, so it is possible that in her haste, Isha overlooked what it implied in the light of events. Or, more likely perhaps, it might never have been present for her in the first place. Her prejudice had yet another character, stemming from a mystic disposition nurtured by a strict Catholic upbringing no paganism would ever displace. This data is the only clue for coming to grips with the insanity of the publication. In a last effort of her iron will, she must have pushed this project past blinded editor and publisher and into print.

Yet I paid scant attention to the contents at the time. What alone mattered was that at a very early date, Aor had chosen this visible identification with the "Jewish question" as his banner in a public enterprise. Even before being aware that his text in fact proposed a *solution* to the question (thus assuming a *problem* many thought had been laid to rest for good in civilized society), I knew the pages boded no good for the respect and admiration owed this man, and I both regretted and resented this. But I am straying from my subject . . .

Rather, the point is that here, once again, I had encountered the pernicious weed that grows wild at the extreme political right, and once again I had encountered it in the name of spirituality. Theocracy, a spiritual monarchy, is the structure of tyranny when debased to political materialism. The difference between abstract and concrete is not a different reality, but a different consciousness, and is therefore easily blurred. Theosophy would certainly be a misnomer if the wisdom it enounced in the name of God were not applicable to the political sphere as well, toward a Godlike organization of the *polis*, the city-state. I have found the true believer in God-made-in-our image vulnerable to political excess the moment he falls from the abstraction of this language into an imagery requiring concrete support. A "liberal" image of oneness exists, of course, but it is less vocal and not at all aggressive. I have not been aware of spiritual pretensions on the Soviet left, but I know that a spiritual pursuit wove through the sick fabric of the Nazi mind in a paradigm of esoterism abused, of myth degraded and, in the end, of humanity renounced. The glorious abstraction is made to fit the concretion of the everyday hurly-burly. Hierarchies reduce to class concepts, while superiority and inferiority become the terms through which value judgments are reached.

I knew firsthand Aor's everyday prejudices concerning Jews. I cannot presume to dissect his feelings on the subject; it suffices that I know his overall sentiment for certain. He conceded an important role to the Jews, and invites them to play it in Zion, where, left behind, they will inherit the earth, while initiates inherit the Spirit. The letter expresses this truthfully enough. The addressee may also hear the implication that the play does not run in Paris board-rooms nor in the casinos of the Côte d'Azur, and perhaps not even in the departments of the great French universities.

It gives me small solace that his views, actualized in great part through the excesses of persecution, after the fact of Nazi Germany, were indeed widely acclaimed as at least a partial solution to the "problem." While alone the apologetics of a necessary bloodbath to prepare the reality of the State of Israel fulfill the meaning of the term "holocaust" in its recent application, such cold paganism feels contrived in view of the magnitude of the events. In conclusion, there is to me no acceptable interpretation of Aor's *Lettre aux Juifs,* and hardly an excuse for the condescending and paternalistic tone.

Beyond these particularities, the texts from *Le Veilleur* espouse the standard "new society" whose image had been variously molded by esoteric tradition since Rosicrucian times: a society based on excellence of work and a sense of duty, on qualitative values, on valorization of regional characteristics, in all a program it would be difficult to quarrel with. A reaction against inertia is called for, and the tendencies are antimaterialistic and antimechanistic. They were predictable and taught me nothing new.[10]

$$\ominus$$

Aor had commended to my attention volume III of *Le Temple,* which I had initially neglected, and he pointed out a short appendix of two pages in the section dealing with the knees of the temple-man.[11] This particularly interesting example involving the evolutionary salt illustrates the difficulty of deciphering glyphs in the absence of a thorough insight into myth. The topic of fixed salt was by now central to our discussions, and the importance of this Hermetic principle for a theory of evolution had impressed me. The brief note in volume III (example #2) has a companion piece in volume I[12] (example #1), where a tradition of psychic transmission is presented in a most arresting manner. While both examples are based on a figuration, #2 is concerned with hieroglyphs and their decipherment. The hieroglyph concerned is the "iwa"-group of three figures to which is added the determining sign of a *femur*, largest bone in the body. Now the femur had been defined in example #1 as to its function:

> The absolute fixed salt in man is formed in the femur, the rock bottom fundament and support of the physical body (the Egyptian *men.t*).[13]

Together, these two examples present a remarkable case for an esoteric theory of evolution first signified in Pharaonic Egypt, where it was incorporated into a Pythagorean science that resurged in Europe in the early Middle Ages. The "iwa"-group and its determinative are infrequently encountered, and a general meaning is difficult to induce from the particular instances that have been studied. The general orientation of the signs is clear, however: it points to a part of the lower body which has to do with posterity and descent. The range of meanings therefore spans from "organ of generation" to the concept of "inheritor." To view the femur as a euphemism for the sexual organs is in contravention of Pharaonic practice, which deals unabashedly with all parts of the body through a realistic picture language. Unaware of

> ... traditional knowledge concerning the fixation of the indestructible nucleus in the *thighbone* ...[14]

the classical Egyptologist misses what de Lubicz sees as evident:

> ... the idea expressed by the femur bone necessarily comprises that of inheritor and of regeneration.[15]

De Lubicz explains that the sense here is one of

> ... "personal reincarnation," transporting the acquirements of a lifetime.[16]

Such, briefly put, is the context of example #2. The question must be raised: what is the nature and the mechanism of this inheritance which contains a physical and material component, yet involves no genetic transmission?

Example #1 was considered by Aor as the most direct Western reference to an esoteric theory of evolution which he studied through the philosophical salt. It also showed the involvement of the Knights Templar who had carved the coat of arms of their fortress-town as surely as the ancients carved their hieroglyphs. The arms of Eze-s/mer (Alpes-Maritimes) show the phoenix reborn of a *femur*, with the legend *"Moriendo Renascor"* (see Appendix B).

"It is not surprising, after all, that clean senses and an unspoiled mind would recognize the mystery of ashes. One of the natural phenomena that primitive man registered early, one of the first scientific observations of a process of nature, if you will, must have concerned the death of his own kind and the physical decomposition, rapidly down to the skeleton first, then the much slower disintegration down to the ashes, and the relationship of the end result to *earth*, to the soil with which it assimilates so readily. Such an observation would valorize the residue for its permanence, for its being all that remains. What remains is mineral salt, the vehicle for the fixed mineral nucleus, but don't be misled by atomic theory such as it might exist in your head from your studies. Still, we can say that fixed salt as principle of inscription is the neutron of the fixed nucleus. See it as the inner kernel of materiality, the ultimate physical presence. Nucleus of inscription, that is the fixed salt! Even in the popular expression, the biblical salt of the earth is ultimate reality. But ultimate reality has to do with change, so you might call the Hermetic salt a locus of formal change, an instrument of time, *enfin*. What can I say, I can't put it more clearly, just remember that it is the key to all evolution!"

It was one of the times he would grope for words to structure the abstraction. I had gathered much on the subject from *Le Temple de l'Homme*, but I had not had time to establish a coherence among the many elements involved. Salt as the

juncture of being and becoming, as an agent both of permanence and change, was a new step in my understanding.

"Don't forget, in the primitive mind, the mind of nature,
these intuitions do not take the shape they take in our learned
heads. The greatest benefit of reading a symbolique like the
Pharaohs' is the practice of participating in the natural mind
of the primitive. We can never duplicate the unspoiled clarity
of it; that's the price we pay for the breadth of our knowledge.
Yes, the temple has been enormously enlarged, and whoever
enters it now has other vistas than our early *Sapiens* with his
heap of ashes. *His* temple probably didn't extend beyond a
few things like ashes, bones, and rocks, but he saw the heav-
ens above him more clearly, and it must have helped him to
an early emotional perception of his sacred affairs. And that's
what counts, after all!"

I had lost the thread somewhat, as the "salt of the earth"
had brought to mind the notion of *Sal Amon* and its six-
pointed seal of materiality, balancing Fire and Water. Aor had
talked about this some time ago (I was involved to the extent
of having borrowed a chemistry book from him and informed
myself as to the nature of ammonium chloride), and I felt the
notions were connected. Yet, as so often in this pursuit, the
elements of information were free-floating in my mind, occa-
sionally joining in more or less complex molecules of understanding, then separating again and regrouping into diverse
meanings. When I mentioned my frustration at this haphazardness, he laughed and maintained it was better that way,
preferable to setting up structures that would have to be torn
down later anyway.

"I'm sorry," I said now, "I didn't quite . . ."

"It doesn't matter, it never is the way it sounds anyway;
language is always a long way from the reality of it. This just
happens to be the best way I can put it now, in this context.
Don't let the sound of words fool you."

"I won't, but please continue."

"Yes, I would like you to understand the palingenetic factor
in all this. And also the relation of salt to form. Don't forget,
salt rigorously determines form. That is how we are able to

think about it today, but imagine mythical perception of the ash as mineral, as earth, as rocks, as the most permanent matter the primitive mind can sense! Are they aware that the mineral content of the earth's surface circulates as constructive element throughout the vegetal and animal realms? You may be sure they are, for this is precisely the kind of intuitive knowledge that is very visible to the primitive. It ranges on instinct, on animal knowledge. Intelligence lets it waste away, probably because it is no longer needed for survival. They see the *eating* of the realms, one realm suffering the other. So they know that the substance of the earth is captured by vegetal forms which in turn are subject to ingestion by higher forms of life. Does the stone-age man appreciate the difference of vegetation, of the living life? I'm sure there were philosophers as soon as the cerebral cortex was complete.

"The breakthrough to thought," I murmured, mainly to myself.

"Well," he went on, "the chlorophyll function is a second manifestation of the fundamental creativity that makes something be rather than nothing. First is the manifestation of existence generally, and it is mineral, salt. That is a *percée*, as you say . . ."

"A breakthrough, an opening . . ."

"Yes, always from the unknown to the known. Out of what to the mind is nothingness, something becomes, an element, a volume. Something out of nothing. But for life and growth and generation, the mineral is nothingness. The vegetal has suffered the mineral, but it has broken through."

"Don't you count the distinction between plant and animal as a similar jump, a breakthrough?"

"It is different, it is a question of movement, of mobility, outer and inner, motion and emotion. An important difference in color form, red out of green. But no, we have seen only three stages: existence, life or animation, and mind. Three great openings. And whatever came into existence had form as well as structural, material, and substantial elements. Form always has an aspect of impermanence, and upon destruction of form, those elements return to the surface of the globe, so that the topsoil is in large part constituted by the remains of biological entities. No form disappears entirely; when destroyed, there remains the physical residue of a mineral salt. Again, a very primitive intuition knows that this life-giving nucleus which has participated in the life experience of the formal entity does not suffer such adventure unaffected. The experience of the living form is inscribed in this element of permanence. *Ça vous parle?*"

"Then there would be two survivors of the living form: the seed, or offspring, and the mineral remnant?"

"You are quite right, and considering the effort expended in speculations about survival beyond physical disaggregation, it is surprising how little attention is paid to the indestructible remnants of every physical entity that has appeared on the globe."

We sat a while in silence before I started to jot down some notes. I would have liked to cover this terrain once again, systematically, from the beginning, and I told him so.

"Good," he said, "where is the beginning?"

"We'll just have to make one, I suppose. Where would you suggest. . . ?"

"No, this is *your* idea."

"Well, let me try. It has to do with a creative way of experiencing through an emotional state. The nature of the organism is somehow affected by such an experience . . ."

". . . as salty tears best prove . . ."

". . . affected by what you call an inscription into fixed salt . . ."

"*Attention, cher ami*, if you really want a beginning, you have to find a totality, a oneness, and where experience is concerned, that oneness must be achieved in the *perception* of the experience. You can fragment it through an analytic view, which is what we have trained our cerebral cortex to do, or you can identify with the formal and functional essence of the experience and intuitively place it in its cosmic context. That takes a reeducation of the senses for modern man; we have talked enough about this. Without adequate perception, you will encounter a world of objects to register into your brain matter, but you will only rarely be inscribing experience into salt. Perception, in the average person today, manages this inscription into the very nature of his organism only accidentally, when emotional sensitivity happens to be aroused by circumstances. The rest of the time, it is at best merely filing impressions into the brain's memory, and they will disappear with the disintegration of the tissues, if not earlier. Anyway, most of the time it doesn't even do that much, most of the time, all there is, is just time, precisely, just time, time going by, with nothing done. Well, that isn't entirely true, time in itself furthers evolution, but left to its own devices, it is the slowest vehicle there is. Those are the watery paths of the Western horizon, but there is also the direct way of Fire, the flame straight up to the zenith. Consciousness, the consciousness of identification, is the instrument through which we can move ourselves along. The genetic concept of evolution through the generations, with mutations thrown in to justify the incomprehensible jumps, this Darwinian thinking is unbelievably childish. The old Egyptians knew more about it than our universities today!"

"Strange indeed! Evolution as an expansion of consciousness seems so much more natural than natural selection and survival of the fittest or whatever it is. It's always been difficult for me to remember how it is supposed to work."

"Still, you should know about it. There are important ideas in Darwin, and in Lamarck and Haeckel, even if their theories don't hold up. These ideas had to be thought, worked out, yes, inscribed like every other experience. There are also some basic errors in that theory, and they have blocked all possibility of a correct understanding. Perhaps the most damaging hypothesis concerns the causal relation of function to organ. The idea that an interior drive of the organism can create an organ for a particular function is a monumental misconception. You'll agree from all we have said that 'function' is the most abstract concept of all, and the least likely to have a direct influence on a physical entity. Yet for Darwinism, the complex and subtle interplay between the living entity, its environment, and this general natural disposition we experience as a complex of functions has been reduced to the simplistic slogan of 'function creates organ.' There is no doubt that our organs *bear* those functions, they adapt themselves to them, and there is usually a certain development of the organ through its functional activity, but *creation* of the organ is an effect of the energetic environment, of ambient forces that affect the living entity much in the way a flowing river affects the surrounding landscape, little by little forming its path into banks that are molded to the very shape of the waterflow's formative energy. Sound does not exist for the entity which lacks the organ to capture it, so there can be no drive by the entity toward the faculty of hearing. The vibratory phenomenon, however, will make its imprint onto matter through the organism's reaction: it will mold substance in the image of its energetic impulse. The function will take possession of an existing organ, and use it at the level of consciousness presented by the individual, be it as an awareness of danger, of mating calls, or of the laws of harmony through a fugue by Bach."

Insufficiently conversant with received ideas in biology and theory of evolution, I was unable then to judge relative innovations in Aor's point of view. Yet, as so often with his concepts, it struck me as the simplest, most obvious way to envision the problem. Today, twenty-five years later, I still find myself but spottily acquainted with the academic state of the art such as it might be taught in our institutions of higher learning, having pursued only those avenues offered to me by his indoctrination. Even were I capable of doing so, I would in no way intend to offer here a coherent plan of his views on the subject. The topic, nevertheless, is fully within the limits of my enterprise, being a body of knowledge centered on the Hermetic salt and its avatars. All I can do within the limits of my format and my competence, is to gather notes and memories, which, together with some pertinent references in his printed works, should present, to a more specialized mind, ample material for investigation.[17]

"These are but details and finer points of an eventual theory of transformism," he continued, while I was jotting down some cue words into an outline of his talk. "What you must realize is that the knowledge of evolution and of species, the knowledge of the ages of the earth, which is also an evolution, the knowledge of time, in the end, and the secret of genesis in the beginning, these things have an esoteric content that escapes the analytical mind. It just doesn't fit into the logic we have established for ourselves. The facts, the end results of the analysis, the quantitative event, all this is important and must be observed, but it is only a shadow, a reaction, whereas *causal* action is the thing that interests the Hermetic philosopher. The secret of genesis, a spontaneous existence out of a state of equilibrium, out of a homogeneous causal state that separates into the heterogeneity of above and below . . . , well, you know what I mean, the becoming of number-form through the function *phi*, that is a path totally missed by analysis. *Je vous le dis*, it's a different mentality!"

And he shook his head in wonderment at this blindness where there was so much light. I, however, was intent on keeping him on the subject of salt, which had come to intrigue me enormously.

"Is it correct to say, then, that salt accumulated in the bones is the seat of a hereditary transmission through somatic cells, and that it complements the hereditary transmission through the germ cells?"

"Well, yes, except for the idea of complementation. The transmissions are really quite different one from another. One concerns the individual, the other the species. The germ cells are passed down directly from generation to generation, along with adaptations to climatic conditions, available diets, and other local circumstances, all of which produces varieties, subgroups, and races, but always within the species. Fixed salt, after it has spent a lifetime in the bones of the individual, starts circulating in nature, unless it be prevented from doing so by special burial procedures. It will remain a tremendous focus of attraction for a formal expression commensurate with the inscribed experience, which means that it will need more and more evolved forms in order to express its accumulated experience. If we were limited to the activity of germ cells only, we'd have to come down on the side of poor old Cuvier and his fixist ideas, or else bring in a *deus ex machina*, mutation, random mutations supposed to bring about a process of evolution that doesn't look random at all. I'm simplifying, of course, and that may be unfair, but let's stop talking about theories that have already been discredited by academic biologists themselves. The only reason, in my opinion, that they have not as yet been dumped into the overflowing dustbin of nineteenth-century conceits is that those biologists have nothing to replace them with."

"So the importance of perception is to insure the quality of experience and guarantee inscription into salt, which in turn will call for a more evolved form in a later incarnation?"

"Yes, and don't forget that perception depends on a state of consciousness, or better, it is a measure of consciousness. The faculty to perceive, to experience, is usually wasted on some kind of esthetico-hedonistic pursuit, or else applied to purely practical purposes; if correctly channeled, however, that is, if placed at the service of intuitive knowledge by a technique of identification, it will contribute to the expansion of consciousness that is the driving force of evolution. The power behind the entire cosmic drama is this evolution of consciousness, and not a propensity of matter to metamorphose. Matter can do no more than express consciousness. Why do you think I insist on this effort of perception? Why the effort to perceive even what is clearly beyond our present norm, such as a spherical spiral? Because as long as your perception remains routine, remains an ascertainment of objects, a psychological interpretation of events, you will not make a step toward a broader consciousness, you will inscribe nothing, you will make no evolutionary gains save those that time accomplishes through its endless cycles, through what the Egyptians called "Osiris." The gains are not personal gains, of course, but they are ontogenetic, they are an evolution of salt due to the inscription of experience. What is thus inscribed, this modification of the mineral base, is permanent; com pared to it, the genetic material is downright fragile."

"But . . . but . . . there is evolution from the mineral to the plant to the animal and human, and if the role of perception and experience are so crucial, how does the rock experience and perceive?"

This question seemed to amuse him considerably.

"Ah," he chuckled, "I believe Monsieur thinks of the mineral as a lot of dumb, dead rocks! But you forget that the affinities of atoms and molecules, their associations and combinations, are the very essence of perception; they are the pure and unadorned revelation of inscribed salt, proving the bias of the mineral entity, its identification with certain atomic groups, its rejection of others, truly an exercise in comparing and choosing. These are true experiences, don't you think? More than that, I would say that they are consciousness in a search for an expanded experience. The *will* to experience does not exist, of course, nor the emotive catalyst toward inscription; these elements which speed up the evolutionary process exist only in the upper levels of organized entity. The mineral by and large depends on aeons of time for its progress. It evolves mainly because of the evolving environment. For we can't be shortsighted and look at the evolution of our biosphere only in itself. The entire solar system evolves as an entity, and each one of the planets in turn evolves through cycles. These are complex matters, certainly too vast for our poor brains. They are not meant to be thought about, but experienced as anthropocosmic reality."

After a moment of reflection, he continued in an unusually gentle voice.

"I don't want to discourage you; I know you are trying to understand these things. But with the notion of salt, we are reaching a point that represents the limit of rational and irrational, where metaphysics and physics meet; it is a moment that can only be described as transcendent, yet it must remain inseparable from the concrete. It is not something that can be explained. But it can be shown, yet there is no guarantee that even when shown, you will see. For actually, the entire universe and every detail of it is such a juncture of transcendency with concreteness. So why don't you see it right here and now?"

He was looking at me with utter seriousness, and only very slowly did his severity resolve into a smile.

"Are you tired?" he asked. "Have you had enough of this for today?"

"I'll never get tired of this subject, if you don't mind going on for a while. We do have a half hour before teatime."

"Très bien, cher ami, à votre service. We were speaking of this ligature of concreteness and abstraction in the salt, a juncture of root and germ, and you shouldn't forget for a moment that the mineral salt we are talking about is the same salt we subject to laboratory manipulations such as the color experiment from Fulcanelli's purloined manuscript. That might give you a measure of the responsibility involved in such an enterprise. The idea is to effect an inscription into the mineral salt that will change its specific characteristic, speeding up its evolution, making it experience what would take millions of years for nature to inscribe, then to destroy the present form and to allow the salt to become the center of attraction for a new and more evolved form. When I talk about destroying, I mean a creative disintegration, a putrefaction without trace of violence. It is possible in this way to have a mineral form become vegetative. Every molecule of mineral salt has its specific inscribed characteristic, and at this level of consciousness, the form which expresses that specificity reflects the inscription perfectly. This is less true with more highly evolved entities . . . "

"So the alchemical transmutation of lead into gold, if such a thing exists, must be the result of a succession of inscriptions into salt and subsequent destruction of the resulting form."

"Well, well, we're going a little fast here, are we not? It's interesting to hear your conditioned hypothesis, though: 'If such a thing exists . . . ?' It doesn't really matter if such a thing exists, does it? For no true adept has ever set out with that purpose in mind! He has a conviction concerning the nature of the universe, and he attempts to prove his conviction by laboratory procedures, like any other scientist. In fact, considering your hypothesis, you are quite right to wonder if such a thing exists, because the mineral does in fact *not* play the role of fixed nucleus for the metal. The mineral is the *mine* of the metal, it is the site of gestation for a metallic world which has an evolutionary destiny of its own. What is remarkable is that the mineral here plays the maternal and environmental role as matrix for the gestation of the metals, whereas in biological evolution, it plays the paternal role of the fixed salt, the function of specifying the form of the incarnation. This double role of the mineral is rarely taken into consideration, and yet it is an important facet of successful practice. There is a strange prefiguration of terrestrial evolution in the evolution of the metal. I am now speaking of the metal within the mineral gangue, the metal being gestated in the belly of the earth. Exposure to air and light, and particularly the extraction from the mineral matrix by melting at high temperatures, interrupts this process, and the lower metals, such as we know them once the mine is opened, are arrested phases of an evolution the finality of which is silver and gold. Quite similar, you see, to the living plant and animal forms on earth which are arrested phases of an evolution that has its finality in the male and female human being. Metallic evolution is a paradigm, within the very restricted environment of the mineral matrix, of evolution in the cellular world. Note that the environment of light and air, essential to the organs of assimilation and reproduction taking form in the plant world, is in fact deadly for the metals which can live and evolve only in the mine, and these conditions will eventually corrode them. This means that no experiences of light vibrations are inscribed in the metallic nucleus, and that the passage to the plant realm cannot be achieved through a metallic entity. I insist on this, because you cannot imagine the time and effort that has been wasted on misguided experiments in this direction. In fact, true metals have a fixed nucleus of inscription of their own. They are an evolutionary process more closely tied to the larger planetary evolution of the solar system than to the particular biological evolution on planet Earth. And remember, *le milieu crée l'organe!* Before the organization of photosynthesis can occur, therefore, there must have been a prefiguration through an exposure to light during millions of years. This cannot occur through metals, obviously, but it does occur through the mineral realm. So when metallic evolution reaches gold and silver, it has attained its finality, limited by the particular milieu of the mineral matrix, just as the human being is the finality within the milieu of this planet. Is all this a bit clearer to you now?"

"What I gather is that the transmutation of metals is a different line of work than the passage of the realms?"

"You could say that, but both are closely connected. Without the work on fixed salt, I couldn't have achieved the results on the red and blue glass, which is a problem involving metallic entities only. With metals, the exercise is to separate the fixed from the volatile, an aspect that needn't concern us in the biological evolutionary sequence, because in the cellular world, this separation occurs quite naturally at death in the process of putrefaction, and can in no way be influenced by manipulation. With metals, we have a different situation. First of all, the metals we work on are dead; they die the moment they leave the mine. Metallic death is different from cellular death, there is a contraction involved, but no putrefaction, and the metallic body retains its specific characteristics for a long time. Furthermore, even in the metallic death that occurs when the metals are melted from their milieu of gestation, they retain that sulphurous, fiery nucleus that plays for the metals the role the alkaline salt plays in later realms. The dead, extracted metal can be revived in the laboratory, furthermore, provided an environment is created that reproduces the mineral matrix. Once this is achieved and the metal is live, it is possible to separate the volatile part, the soul of the metal, from its body. The fixed nucleus, which is one and the same for all metals, is often referred to as the seed of the metal, and this shouldn't confuse you when reading texts that describe this process. The best way to consider true metals, what I call 'metallic metals,' the planetary metals from lead to gold, is to assume a single metallic body in various states of purity, with one fixed metallic nucleus or seed. We might consider the metals as one species, within which the variability is a matter of somatic impurities. So you see, the evolution of the metallic body from lead to gold is really a purification process. It is the adept's intent to cleanse the metallic body. To that effect, there are four steps: revive the metal, separate the fixed from the volatile, cleanse the body, and rejoin the fixed to the volatile. This is quite different from biological evolution, where the fixed salt remains the attractive focus until it is reunited with the volatile through the processes of nature."

"If I understand correctly, there are in the metallic world only two elements to be concerned with, the fixed and the volatile, whereas in the cellular world, we have the fixed, the volatile, and the seed?"

"That is surely an oversimplification, but I guess our cerebral cortex has to live with such rational schemata. For our present purposes, it will have to do. One thing is certain: biological evolution rests on the trinitary foundation of Sulphur, Mercury and Salt, or function, substance and form, where function is the creative element, the spiritual, life-carrying cause; seed the regenerator of substance; and salt the guardian of form. Metallic evolution on the other hand, is not a palingenesis, and the volatile component remains indissolubly joined to the fixed after the metal leaves the mine. In fact, it is only after the conditions of the mineral matrix are recreated that we can obtain a dissolution to liberate the volatile that will appear to us as the characteristic color of the metal. I will show this to you some day: the metallic lustre separated from the metal!"

"Can I assume that this is the first step toward the colored glass?"

"It is indeed. The Chartres glass is tinted in the mass with the volatile spirit of metals."

8

*Introspective interruption.—Pythagoras in Pisces.
—A voyage on the sound of words.—An azure-blue
recrudescence.—Emotive states and inscription.—Cycles
and lost time.—Experimentum crucis.—Revelations
between one and two.—Lubiczian majuscules.—Politics
and the elite.—Enlightened anarchy.*

If I choose this moment to interrupt my narration, it is not to signal the end of our conversation (which in fact prolonged itself to the point of making us late for tea), but to acknowledge a discomfort felt upon rereading my last few pages through the eyes of another who might stumble unprepared across my recollections. This situation can unfortunately not be allayed, for I hold no clue toward the possibilities of such propaedeutics, unless it be a faithful repetition of the very ones which destiny reserved for me. A sequence of events managed my receiving the audacities I am relating, having not only steered me physically into their presence, but mentally within reach of meanings more readily grasped by a sort of visual sense of touch than by astute intellectuality. For while the lessons on perception which I was subjected to (and upon which I have duly insisted) would seem to be useless in a conversational context, they nevertheless showed an unex-

pected efficiency in keeping the mind on a narrowly formal
track, restricting the imagination to an imitative empathy
meant to situate the feelings of an interlocutor, instead of
adapting his words to one's own definitions. Of great assistance also were the hours spent poring over specific passages
in alchemical treatises which Aor left with me in the library
while he took his afternoon siesta. Upon rejoining me he
would launch into exegeses that cleared obscurities in an almost magical manner, relating seemingly chimeric reveries
to solid physical principles and transforming fantasy and su-
perstition into handbooks of laboratory procedure.

Evidently our conversations found me in a unique frame of
mind, the receptivity of which my reader cannot be expected
to duplicate. Without it, however, in the cold percipience of
common sense, and within the sobering congruence of his
everyday surroundings, how will he let worn words guide him
to these configurations in which his intuition is to recognize
a palpable reality? Even should he observe the rigors of a theory of language promoted earlier in these pages, and thereby
distinguish "terms" that must remain two-dimensional along
with the page that holds them, from "words" that must be
left to fit themselves unfettered into the very form of what
really *is*, even then, where will he find the guiding sound of a
teacher's voice? I recall several times spending hours on a
short passage, unable to liberate a meaning from its syntactical ties, yet being immediately released from this mental
cramp by the mere intonation of the words as Aor read the
passage aloud, accenting certain vocables, repeating others,
stopping in mid-sentence to give a fragment its chance. Such
sagacity will be difficult to find once more in our time, and
infinitely more unlikely its coincidence with this text. It was
Aor's opinion that the conditions essential to the accomplishment of his work were deteriorating rapidly, and that atmospheric disturbance would soon make entire aspects of it
impossible in most locations on the globe; an indication, according to him, that certain powers had withdrawn from the
present state of the planet, thereby dooming mankind to inevitable cataclysms. There would be survivors, and it was

understood that a new start would be made on the basis of Al-Kemi. I asked him whether he was aware of other individuals or groups engaged on work along the lines of an esoteric science, and he told me that he was not. There seemed to be no question in his mind but that he was the ultimate repository of the Pythagorean line in the precessional month of Pisces.

So it is once again to encourage my reader that I have stopped *in medias res,* interrupting what I hold to be a lecture on an alternative and unified approach to those various disciplines encompassing the Earth and its inhabitants, but which a less accommodating point of view could easily consider to be no more than the wildest of inventions. I sympathize with a position that must needs confront improbable concepts of impossible realization, and must do so alone, without peers or masters, on the mere bidding of a written page whose language avowedly is lax in covering irrational reality through its rational organization . . .

Nevertheless, I am not writing fiction, and I want to take the time to reassure the reader to that effect. I have encountered nothing in the last twenty-five years that would have me reconsider my initial conviction: whatever the terms in which the notion may be couched, a revolutionary insight resides in the mysterious thesis of the ashes. Revolutionary to our scientific establishment, I hasten to add, for the idea of "inheritor," determined by the femur, such as it appears in Pharaonic hieroglyphs, is perhaps the oldest biological notion of which we have found traces. Paralleling a specific descent through the seed with a personal lineage through the fixed salt of the ashes, as the result of either long and patient observation or sudden divine afflatus (probably of both, as deities of all times have been said to be kind to him who helps himself), is a remarkable intuition in any case. Nor is it, after all, as speculative an idea as it seems at first sight. De Lubicz himself points to experiments that can lead to proof in the plant realm.[1] It is a pity, therefore, that the surfacing of these ideas in our time does not draw the attention it manifestly deserves. It seems, furthermore, as if the visibility of this material might have been diminished, consciously or uncon-

sciously, by those left in charge of our author's work. Thus
the most valuable pages on the subject have not been found
worthy of appearing in an English translation of selected
texts. Is it because they are judged to be too difficult of access,
and perhaps too conjectural? Or could it be that their hypothetical nature is felt to compromise equally advanced theories in the field of Egyptology, branding the author as a
"fantaisiste," dreaded epithet that has indeed been thrown
his way by some archaeological gravediggers? Nothing ventured, nothing gained.

⊖

*"Le verre de Chartres est teint dans sa masse par l'esprit
volatile des métaux."*
There are privileged moments when a sequence of words
adapts itself to our state of being with a precision such that it
espouses comprehension perfectly, and thus is able to possess
it, seize it, and lead it far beyond the proposition's intended
design. I am saying that this sentence, the terms of which
were chosen and arranged in their declarative order for the
sole purpose of expressing that which is the case, of enounc-
ing with reasonable exactitude and sufficient economy a factual state of affairs requiring transmission; uttering no more
and no less than what is to be communicated, and uttering it
without philosophic or poetic intent; this sentence whisked
me free from the circuitry of mind to an intuitive moment
present here in a beginning impossible to will, a moment
attained only by abrupt negation of all the means which usually yield an answer to a quest. For some unknown and im-
material reasons having to do perhaps with the extraordinary
weightiness of the individual vocables and the delicate balance of their combinations, or maybe with their rhythmic
cadence that calipered time in an arcane computation; or
again, because of acceptations certainly beyond all help from
etymology or glossaries; for all those reasons and more, this
sentence swept away in a majestic gesture the scattered
shards of information that had littered my mind, and by a

metonymical effect elusive to analysis, positioned me to witness the subtlest vision of the infinitesimal shift from sameness to difference, from identity to opposition, from self to
other, from one to two. Poised on the edge of multiplicity
(and all the while aware of his expounding on coppery lustres
and blue vitriol), I held firm to this inchoate initiative, a differentiation which in the absence of all else becomes the absolute measure, a yes or no without gradations.

Undoubtedly related to the fatigue he had noticed earlier,
and facilitated by the accumulated weariness which bespoke
my exertion on the geometric work over the previous weeks,
my divagation nevertheless was clearly triggered by a magic
akin to incantation, where the meaning of the chant yields to
the power of the sound. It was a *sonant* quality in the sentence that caught me and conducted my journey, and while I
continued to hear his description of the ore particularly
adapted to extraction of the tincture, and of the advantages of
native semi-metals in solid solution (and undoubtedly looked
at him with an air of consummate interest betrayed only by a
puncticular vacuity in the depth of the pupils, where the optic
nerve had disconnected all concatenations and no longer
transmitted a stereoscopic image to the inner screen), the picture is replaced by a volume of cyclical nature whose motion
turns upon itself yet all the while progresses (somewhat akin
to a cosmic Archimedean screw), a figuration in which I ef-
fortlessly recognize a perfect spherical spiral. The spatial exercise now applies itself to a formal reality which contradicts
all relativity by the uniqueness of its configuration, progress-
ing while somehow remaining the same, playing out a paradigm of simultaneous being and becoming. And as his words
echo mightily in the orchestra, this cosmic stage is peopled
by an exhaustive referential personnel pertaining to the event
proclaimed: THE CHARTRES GLASS IS DYED IN ITS MASS
BY THE VOLATILE SPIRIT OF METALS.

Now he describes a paste of quartz and calcium carbonate
from which the vase is to be blown, but due to the peculiar
spatiotemporality which has overtaken me, the mixture is
hypostatized into a kernel of materiality representative of all

possible substantial forms the aggregate might assume; I mean the *mass*, recipient of spiritual fragrance, a breath too subtle to be scrutinized, but manifest in its magnificent gown of reds and blues. With the normal static dimensions superseded by these kinematic sinuosities, the convoluted helix is able to place all temporal events into immediate reach, be it even that distant first conversion of indifference into partiality which I mentioned earlier and which started it all, that primeval event being as close to me now as is my vis-à-vis across the table with whom, in fact, I entertain a similar relationship of identity and contrast, of sameness and distinction, of equality and hierarchy. And he, still apparently unaware of my remoteness from his drift, yet with every word fueling an imagery that flares in blatant contravention to the abstract and geometric mind, now somewhat heatedly defends a procedure (which to my knowledge no one has attacked), a course of action toward the recrudescence of a subject wherefrom the tinctorial spirit is to be obtained. I am softly drawn toward his exposition, although his voice is distant and my body inert, a heaviness possessing it up to my neck. Above, the head is clear and light, and I realize that I am able to follow him with great attention and yet to continue my contemplation of an abstract function, the function of scissiparity, the creative function *phi*. Furthermore (and absolutely fixed upon his exposition, where every additional word comes to people the spiralo-spherical scene with yet another figurant), I am able to remove this function from an impossible beginning beyond the bounds of spirit itself, and I resolve the absolution, and arrest the devilish infinite regression, his Ashaver, his Wandering Jew, see the separation here, between him and me, because there is a separation between me and everything, between me and cosmos. Now I am drawn to the facts expounded, the news that one single subject yields both reds and blues, which seems remarkable, and that there is controversy on this very point; although the parties to the argument are not made known, I understand it having been Fulcanelli; yet I fade with the details of a copper chloride mine to be created within a tightly sealed vase where the oxidation forms a mineral matrix that could breathe life into our metallic corpse. I gather that this is all one needs to know in order to assist an azure-blue recrudescence, and suddenly I am aware of my infinite sympathy with the subject's inertia, measuring my temporary lassitude against its transient torpor (death plainly being a misnomer for this hedged demise which allows the undecayed cadaver possession of its spirit, albeit contracted and condensed by the ordeal of metallurgical crematoria, yet live in its innermost substance). We are to awaken the metamorphic agent of this subterranean evolution, but before any procedural instructions can reach me, I register yet another level of removal from my factual environment as the sensory quintet forsakes its usual subservience to automatized unification, abandoning sensation, conation, conception, and the entire psychological construction in order to engage in a kinetic activity of its own. A momentary confusion reigns among the senses, between color and sound, and his voice paints shades of brown while a cluster of light is reflected from his steel-rimmed glasses in a crisp D major. Most surprising is the interaction between smell and touch as the latter's restrictive need for contiguity is compensated by an increased awareness of the subtle emanations which issue from the element earth, agent of all tactile experience whatever its medium of physical resistance, solid, liquid, or aerian, as in this case. Just as all things have their sound, so do they have inherent effluvia available to heightened olfaction, it seems, an odoriferous presence independent of any incidental smell the thing may have acquired through contact or manipulation, but the redolence inherent to the state of physical existence, the fragrance of bodily being, the scent of objectivity. I have been told that divine creation manifests only through the odor which congeals substance into form, and I experience the emanation it lends forever to the earth-body, seat of resistance to touch. Vastly expanded as well is the sense of taste, fully justifying its root of "tasten," which in modern German has affirmed the sense of "feel," "touch," a meaning also carried in Old French, as well as in Middle English.

Just before this etymological reflection brings my mind back into play and makes me realize I am on the verge of dropping off to sleep, an equilibrium is reached in the inner ear, anterior to the cerebral cortex, and as gloriously as any swelling chorus of baroque polyphony, the phenomenon strikes its chord, earthy bass setting the tactile foundation in close cooperation with the fluent tenor's sapid line, while above, pneumatic alto relates to fiery soprano through the ethereal flame they carry in common, and with unanimous consent, the tetrad relates to the pentad: dry—Fire—hot—Air —humid—Water—cold—Earth—dry, the nine stages of phenomenal creativity. They affirm and inform, through volume, number, color, sound, unified into an imitative gesture I could imagine arrested on a plane surface: the symbol, the art.

So much more fits into that moment, abundant beyond what can be told. In this context, language distorts the temporal component of the event; temporality and occurrence in themselves are misguiding, furthermore, when only silence and immobility adequately represent the creative experience. The esthetic aspect of the occasion reconciles me with artistic creativity, as all is present in the timeless moment, l'instantané, the cosmic snapshot. The event is too insignificant to register on the book of temporality; we do it violence when expanding it, when stretching it into time and space. We must choose: truth or communication? By and large, the two are incompatible, and woe to the biographer, doubly so to the autobiographer who carries the full onus of telling the truth, having been the only total witness. The moment, always creative, falls into an in-between without dimension, without perspective. In that "no time," which is the time of inspiration, art is created, cosmos first, a masterful gesture of imitative imagery even then, being "in the image of." This does not happen within time, and any language concerning it not only diminishes it, it demolishes its truth from top to bottom, so that the reality of it, its permanence beyond irrational presence, exists only through experiential inscription into the major bones of our body.

With the peculiar little start of fright that pulls us out of this momentary ambiguity into which I had fallen, a delicate flotation equally in touch with wake and sleep (our personal day and night, the most fundamentally contrasting states of our earthly consciousness), I have drawn myself up in my chair, clearly aware now of Aor's voice, and of the fact that it is lowered, and that it drones in a monotone. He is quietly singing the praises of salt, principle of individual immortality situated in the thigh and divinely empowered for personal resurrection, cause of all mutation, of all contingency, irrepressible and indestructible even in corrosive solutions or extremes of heat . . .

It is this incantation that has directed my waking sleep, and I realize with some embarrassment that he has been conscious of my state for some time and has adopted this delivery in order to direct my fantasy. As I begin a few words of apology for my lack of concentration, he waves me down with his hand.

"No, no," he laughs, "to the contrary, I wish you could spend more time in that state, you might pick up knowledge that will never surface in your cogitations. The second before falling asleep is the most valuable moment of the day, when the cerebral cortex cuts out while you are still in a waking consciousness. It is really the perfect meditative state, and word associations made in that state don't obey logical rules; they can bring true revelations by breaking out of the routine of rational meanings. As the mind has abandoned control, but not consciousness, it leaves the field open to the emotional complex which usually is quite suppressed and tied down by the mind. Note that the ultimate presence of the higher intellective functions, though in a completely passive state, is essential, for without that presence, you are simply asleep and dreaming, and no one has ever achieved anything in a state of deep sleep. Dreams, while having their importance for psychological consciousness, are in no way instruments of knowledge. Certain states of consciousness may be compared to dream-states, but if they are to serve consciousness, they must be a heightening and not a dulling. But listen here, *jeune homme*, are we not going to be late for tea?"

And indeed, a good half hour had gone by since that topic had last come up.

⊖

By the time we met again, a day or so later, I had realized that all I could summon from those strange few minutes in the twilight of consciousness was the sound that had started it all: "*Le verre de Chartres est teint dans la masse par l'esprit volatile des métaux.*" The sense of this phrase had become multidimensional, however; every word expanded until the ordinary terms of language no longer were able to form the boundaries of the new meanings. I told him as much.

"*Très bien,*" he said with an air of satisfaction, "let it go at that. The material is securely inscribed, it will never leave you again. Thanks to the blessedly abstracted state you found yourself in at the time, the experience had a minimum of struggle with mental interference, and that is the best condition for achieving inscription. The less the head is present, the more will be inscribed by emotive vibration. The emotional component is usually an effort to overcome mental resistance, or rather, it is the effect of a resistance within the total emotive state. What I am stressing is the role of emotive states in the process of inscription. This has nothing to do with the sudden emotional shocks of joy, sorrow, fear, or rage, with all the passions that have been suffered in the animal world. In man, they are supposedly unified and synthesized, and even when we regress and let particular emotions flare up wildly, there usually remains a background of emotive stability that establishes a measure, a norm, at least among sane, average human beings. That state can be cultivated in the solar plexus, the center of emotional action. Emotional functions have adapted this locus of intertwining nerve endings for their purposes, but behind their chaotic impulses, there is a general emotive tone that must be listened to, in other words, a general disposition corresponding to a sensorial instrument that bypasses the higher centers of the brain. It is a meditative practice of the ear, but in certain states of consciousness, such as the wake-sleep moment you experienced, the emotive state reigns supreme."

"In fact, I connect no feeling of emotional involvement to that experience."

"Of course not, it is the absence of specific emotional shocks that permits the audition of the emotive state. We may talk about it, but words are useless, it is a process that precedes thought. I'm merely pointing out an emotive awareness that we can work on to help things along. There is so much that needs attention! You know, when I was younger and we lived on a yacht, people would go on land to amuse themselves; well, I stayed on the boat and worked, and still, *j'ai perdu beaucoup de temps.*"

I had heard this before, and considering the breadth of his knowledge and culture, the idea of his wasting time was truly preposterous.

"But you always tell me that nothing much can be done before the age of forty-two!"

"Ah, that is different. You will see for yourself, once you are in your seventh cycle, your understanding of these matters will change. Mark my words, the effects of the seven-year cycle, whether consciously realized or not, are inescapable. For most people, I admit, life is just one straight line, day after day, and they will have to come back and try again, in roughly the same formal parameters. Before the age of forty-two, I myself thought there were other activities that would further the work of consciousness, activities involving people, concrete applications of the abstract ideas in the form of group organizations, esoteric schools, if you want, but once I entered the seventh cycle, I realized my error. It was during that cycle that I finished the practical work on salt, here in this

house, and that I proved the work experimentally, with Fulcanelli handling some crucial manipulations. But the aftermath of all this once again showed me what I should have
already learned in Paris: it is dangerous to use the *Oeuvre* and
the knowledge it affords in any other way than for inscribed
experience. The voluntary obscurity of adepts all through history must in part come from that realization. The desire to
pull those abstractions into the concrete is legitimate; it is
the essential wager of the scientist, and that is what I consider
myself to be, but this process has to be carefully controlled,
and the only real control is practical laboratory science. Furthermore, whenever the work-context becomes social, the
tendency of making the concrete facts fit the abstraction is
unavoidable, and that is more than an error, it is a calamity.
Well, these are typically the experiences of the first six cycles,
the drive of youth and a certain exuberance that characterizes
the early adult cycles."

We had often talked about cycles, and he had told me that
each cycle is brought to consciousness by a major experience,
une expérience décisive, a *crucial* experiment (*experimentum
crucis*). Isha had mentioned this, and Aor himself had talked
about these essential episodes which inscribe entire blocks of
reality, entire sections of consciousness that sometimes have
been worked on for long periods of time. An experience which
might be quite minor, quite innocuous, can then suddenly
play the role of this determining incident of realization, and
inscribe the material in question. I understood the fact (and I
was later to understand it more and more thoroughly) that the
experience itself was without importance, that it might be
just any experience somehow espousing and activating the
inscribable abstraction. Isha had told me that Aor had experienced a revelatory insight at the age of seven, when the handling of a coin had prompted a metaphysical realization
concerning the nature of God. He talked about it now, saying
that it had been the realization of the two sides of the coin
that had made the experience unforgettable; it had been his

first grasp of duality with respect to unity. This experience was clearly the breakthrough of number as form, and the extent of the inscription, which reached to the end of his life, shows the enormous preparation brought by the fixed salt. He told me that number never ceased to obsess him from that moment on, whereas earlier the notion had been practically nonexistent for him. He also spoke of the event which opened his third cycle, an experience with broad inscriptive consequences: the breakthrough of the color-form at the age of fourteen, which was not an artistic experience, as one could have expected from a budding painter, but a chemical experiment. Here at this early age he would make a breach meant to occupy his thinking for many cycles to come. He mused over the fact that each cycle begins with a birth, with a new life that sometimes eclipses the others.

"These cycles must each have a definite character that manifests itself in all people," I ventured. The topic was of special interest to me, as I have strongly experienced these periodic "life-changes"; they can be radical, and they raise havoc with the bourgeois idea of a settled life. I had never examined them as regular cyclical occurrences, however.

"How could it be otherwise! Each cycle concerns a specific stage of development which every individual conforms to in his particular manner; some put more emphasis on one cycle, some on the other, but the basic character of the cycle is invariant for all individuals of the species. The first birth is the experience held in common by all living things, the physical appearance on the planet. After that, each species falls into a time-measure of its own, which for the human being is a seven-year cycle. The second human cycle is characterized by great intuitive input, usually with spiritual overtones. This is when lasting attachments are often made to particular religions, or to particular religious personalities. The third cycle as a rule is marked by intellectual development, and the fourth usually concentrates on the emotional complex. It is here that emotive tone, so important to inscription, starts becoming firmly established. It must be said that some individuals travel through these periods of particular sensitivity for one faculty or other without profiting hardly at all from the general bias of their organism toward certain aspects of the functional milieu. The earlier the cycle, the more clearly defined its formative specialty. Starting with the fifth, cyclical character becomes more diffuse, as personal orientation affirms itself and begins to displace the influence of the natural cycle. The cycles of later life are less and less distinct. If the first three or four cycles are not fairly clearly marked, therefore, it is unlikely that the later ones will have any influence whatsoever. And for some incarnations, the only birth is the very first one, the physical entry into the world, and they by and large live out the implications of that birth and are aware of very little beyond the physical context."

"If I understand correctly, the species undergoes a necessary development through the infinite repetitions of the cyclical process in each individual."

"Yes, and through the consequent exhaustive variety of inscriptions into the fixed salt of the species. The infinite repetition of the same process will exhaust the variability within the invariant law, and thereby accomplish the law, actualizing its finality. You find the endless repetition of the same process in the Hermetic work as well, based on this natural logic. It can only be justified by the urge to inscribe the total spectrum of variability of a particular aspect, exhausting it and thereby accomplishing its finality. For man, individuality is the analysis of the functional process that spans twelve cycles from birth to death, an ideal lifespan of eighty-four years measured by seven-year cycles."

He then told me in considerable detail about the experience that had opened his third seven-year cycle. Here, in a few minutes, his entire scientific orientation was determined. The experiment took place in his father's laboratory, and it was the father, a pharmacist, who manipulated a mixture of chlorine and hydrogen gas in the production of hydrochloric acid. As is well known, these components maintain their individual character as long as they are kept in darkness. Light, however, even when diffused, will prompt a reaction. Under direct sunlight, an explosion occurs.

This experiment made an enormous impression on the young man, and his interest in color phenomena dated from that day. It had become evident to him that for the objects of perception, light ceases to exist as such, as it diffuses into the color phenomenon. A part of knowledge concerning light would have to be gathered through color: color had become a form of perception. He instantly felt that the state of consciousness which accompanied this intellectual opening was connected to another decisive moment in his life, the moment of his "metaphysical" discovery of number through the two-sided coin. Number was present again, the unity of light fracturing into the ordered multiplicity of the spectrum. The revelation of one becoming two had been fleshed out by the analysis of the *space* between one and two. And that space was a scale of color.

While color joined number as instrument of knowledge through form, light became abstraction, metaphysical entity. Color occupied the scientific domain where the phenomenon would be examined, and theories concerning the nature of light would have to prove their findings in a world of color. Light was the oneness of color, somewhat like the coin had been the oneness of its two sides. But this new unity of color no longer contained merely its own duplication by mirror image: its division yielded multiplicity and a new number, the sevenfold spectrum. Light became an agent of another kind. It provided him with the first entry into a world where intuition felt closest to knowledge: the world of causal states, to be known as "functional principles."[2]

Yet it was in the nature of *fire* that he found the essence of this moment of intellectual discovery which opened his third cycle. Fire had been the principal agent in the little experiments he had undertaken since childhood with a toy chemistry set; hitherto, he had known heat from the flame of a Bunsen burner to activate most reactions. Now he realized what a shallow conception of fire he had been entertaining. It appeared to him that a universal element, best named "fire," existed in the physical world, and was contained in a degraded state not only in flame and heat, but penetrated physical existence through and through, its most refined occurrence being *light*. The eye therefore conducts a privileged relationship with this fire, this constituent element of physical appearance. The experiment turned his entire attention toward this illuminating and unifying presence his intuition had shown him as pervading all bodies to a greater or lesser degree, an animating factor common to all levels of matter, from mineral affinity to human intellect. It was a ready step from here to the conception of light as the spiritual origin of matter, a step that launched him on his lifelong search.

About later cycles he spoke only in general terms.

"There is a great force of exteriorization in the first six cycles, in the first half of human life. That ended for me precisely with the end of the sixth cycle, at the age of forty-two, with the dissolution of Suhalia. You must understand what I mean when I say: "losing time." The social contact can really lead you astray. It is normal, of course, to accept a restraint of one's freedom of action and of thought whenever placing oneself in a social context.[3] The only way to avoid it is to dominate the context, to lead it.[4] That brings access to power, which is very attractive in early manhood, but is dangerous also. There is a great temptation for the intellect to abstract social notions from a group of individuals and centralize this abstraction into a political entity; to take concrete structures, as it were, and make them fit the abstraction. This can easily lead to a state of tyranny. *Caveant consules!"*

At the time of this dialogue, I was unable to appreciate all that was being said with these words. I was as yet unaware of my mentor's political past, although I knew quite well where his sympathies lay. Politics, usually any Frenchman's favorite topic of discussion, were proscribed from our relationship by a tacit and instinctive convention. So was the German language. Although we were both fluent in German, we violated this interdict only when a philosophical concept found in that language its most adequate terminology. As the sound of the tongue had been abhorrent to me since the 1930s, I did not miss using it. I was well aware, however, of a strained complicity whenever these harsh sounds imposed themselves on us by their conceptual power. My political involvement having found its finality in the defeat of the Nazi State, I no longer had patience for political exchanges. For him, the topic was fraught with frustration, although I did not know this at the time. I had supposed that he considered politics unworthy of study, as did many artists and intellectuals. Beginning with the information he had proffered about Les Veilleurs and the odd destiny of their uniform across the Rhine, it became plain that this was somewhat of a misjudgment on my part.

Then there was the circumstance that at the period of my knowing him, colonial questions were in the foreground of French politics, with the nation deeply divided between left and right, and we both knew where the other stood. It had been forty years since de Lubicz declared in *Le Veilleur* that there existed "an unsurmountable partition between one race and another,"[5] and if the passing years had mellowed his tone, it had certainly not converted deep-seated convictions. Again, we must be aware of the calamities that have struck language during those forty years, and realize that the word "race" has irrevocably forfeited a title of nobility it might arguably have claimed before the 1930s. Broadening the context somewhat to include related concepts such as "hierarchy" and "elite," we gain more insight into the career of these terms within his thinking, from the first cry of *HIÉRARCHIE!* in *l'Affranchi,*[6] to the reign of Pharaonic theocracy in *"Le Temple de l'Homme."* On the term "elite" he has in his later years expressed himself in typically Lubiczian fashion: majuscular anointment, consecration to reality.[7] This singular elite is formed of individuals who have a reach beyond nature as their common attribute. The accent here is on an individualism that will afford us a rare glimpse of de Lubicz's late social philosophy. The excerpt is from the *Reflections* that follow

Nature Word,[8] and it could well be a reflection on the quotation that occupies us. It is preceded by a prayer, a constant repetition: "The whole Work of the Universe is in me."[9] In the rather loosely knit sequential logic of the *Reflections,* this relentless reminder quite naturally introduces a philosophy where the other disappears into the same, and egoless individuality encompasses them both, as it encompasses the rest of creation, being absolute. Because the subject as individual represents the whole, its responsibility is toward the whole: true solidarity (certainly an optimum condition for a perfect social order) does not grow from exchanges between you and me, but from the responsibility toward the whole, which for the human being is a responsibility "toward all humanity, [his] own kind, [his] species . . ."[10] We know that such individuals can aspire to reach beyond nature, and for them we need not fear.

Pausing for a moment to consider the man who expresses these ideas, we readily perceive, in his life, a social withdrawal for the sake of universality. The reach beyond nature cannot help but be a removal from the natural, the social in man, and a retirement, therefore, from any political stance. At the time I knew him, the *polis* led a marginal existence in de Lubicz's consciousness, this much is certain. Yet these statements in the climate of our day contain the seeds of controversy so that the difference must be drawn between this language and the language of 1919. There is a great change, but it is still the same man speaking: in deeply essential ways and despite the convenience of differentiating between René Schwaller, Schwaller de Lubicz, and Aor, the man is of one piece, and among the number of motifs occurring from beginning to the end, there is a sense of "hierarchy" and there is a sense of "elite."

Will anyone really take umbrage at this elite so strategically placed at the source of spiritual manna, providers of food that stills hunger and thirst, guardians of a wealth to which the elite by its work has gained access, with no other intent but distribution, in a suprahuman altruism?

Probably, for if the elite, the best the species has to offer, "eliminates the 'you and me' " and dedicates itself to the universe which constant prayer has realized within it, where will it find the *alter* its vocation demands, the multitude for which the you and I are the stuff of everyday existence? The critic will be quick to point to the guidelines that cover this distribution to the needy: the sustenance will come "in the form which is suited to them."[11] Temple structures weave through this expression, political structures derived from Horian and Osirian myths; those inside and those outside, and what laws of nature may be divulged and which must remain hidden. A secret of the elite, evidently, a judgment of suitability . . . Galileo . . . And therewith we have come full circle.

But a further step must be taken before we can be satisfied, for whatever *I* can think, another can think just as readily. If this philosophy of individualism is to trickle down, as it must, from "the Elite" to "the elites," I shall certainly be asked what manner of oneness will be the oneness these less accomplished consciousnesses feel responsible to. By definition, the universe they comprehend is in some way deficient, wherefore they are *not* the elite. What will be the measure of *their* cosmos? the size of their God? From metaphysical oneness to spiritual humanity, down to the physical universe, to their "own kind," their "species" . . . perhaps their race, too? or even their State? And maybe just their local bureaucracy!

Again the wounded language chokes with memory, loses its live creative force slipping from abstract to concrete, from universal to particular, from spirituality to politics, all by the agency of one and the same syntax, a terminology devised to fit exalted concepts and nevertheless unable to make us forget how in the middle of this century, a group of criminals and insane racial elitists was empowered with decisions as to who would genetically further the species, and who would not. The excesses of this satanic mandate possess the primordial grandeur of irrational imperatives, and as such, they exert a hideous fascination. Their trauma must be overcome and its causes remembered. No less a voice than George Steiner[12] in a stunning mise-en-scène reminds us that self-proclaimed elites have been around since the Chosen People at the dawn of our social history. The most cursory observation, furthermore, will confirm a pecking order in nature, an order that becomes unnatural and problematic only with self-consciousness in man. There are experiences, readily situated within an hierarchical and elitist structure, which yet are of immense value on the simplest human level. I have already spoken of the circle of my masters. Would I be open to such experiences (which I value highly) had I not, in some part of my consciousness, *known* elite? Didn't Rilke *know* his *Engel*? In his late philosophy, de Lubicz's concepts of "hierarchy" and "elite" are of a similar order of knowledge.

And yet, as I may have already indicated, I was never comfortable with the elitist undertone mainly cultivated by Isha, and we shall see that this topic was one of the conjunctures where I resisted his ideas and therefore must have been one of the subtle forces that converged in my departure.

As to the early days . . . What did he really mean by "having lost much time?" Perhaps this was the closest he could come to a confession of error, not to me so much as to himself. What do I recall of his demeanor during this admission? Was it regret? With certainty I can attest to no more than a shade of melancholy.

Only with the publication of *Le Roi* does a full acknowledgement of the problem obtain. Hidden in an appendix dedicated to the life of Pythagoras, we find the following judgment:

> . . . the revolt in Croton was the consequence of Pythagoras' failing in his duty to heed the precept which forbids every disciple of sacred science to establish a school and to engage in politics.[13]

The elite de Lubicz proposes in *Nature Word* is unimpeachable save for its name. Understanding the function of terminology in a theory of language, we are able to disarm the

concept and perhaps even to call it a misnomer. By its individualism, the elite refuses the power of organization, and therefore abjures its single most objectionable aspect. De Lubicz's
later elite is a set of solitaires, absorbed in their individual
totality. They spurn utilitarian collectivism, and presumably
also the State. In fact they evoke nothing as much as they do
the free denizens of an enlightened anarchy. De Lubicz's individual elite, egoless because recipient of the entire cosmic
work, is logically incapable of political concerns, the organization of which would pull it down into the plurality of "the
elites." As far as these individuals are the real elite, they are
already beyond nature, in the realm of upper-case abstraction.
I no longer perceive them as a threat, actually or potentially,
intellectually or socially, and time has enabled me to condone
the elite of 1952 while continuing to condemn the hierarchy
of 1919. But most importantly, the interval has also persuaded
me to look squarely at the early syntax, still smoldering remains of wasted times, to bring them to the fore and show
them for what they are: a remarkable individual's astonishing
mistakes. This should come as no surprise, as I have shown
how error was prominent among the impressions that first
struck me about his work. Conscious rectification of error,
the faculty of saying *no* to what is negative is a creative tool
of consciousness. Error plays an important and necessary part
in evolution, through the path of suffering that guarantees
emotional inscription.

9

*Isha's "Aor."—Hierarchies.—A triad of abstractions.
—"Qui est Aor?"—Some academic philosophy.—The
question of responsibility.—"Il faut toucher à tout."
—More about fixed salt.—A cluster of happenings.
—Starched white napkins.—The island of the elite.
—Facing the issue of secrecy.—Fulcanelli's downfall.*

Bereft of his guidance for her unauthorized biography, Isha's discernment flagged miserably when deciding what should be brought to light in 1963 and what should be discreetly forgotten. In the Messianic chorus that broadcasts the program of *Le Veilleur*, we isolate some proud voices of esoteric racism. Here is an elite, *"un petit nombre,"* ready to show us "the path of our Race [*sic*] . . . a sleeping human Race [again *sic*] awaiting the day of its Resurrection. . . ."[1] Though not from Aor's hand, these words are nonetheless quite in the spirit of his ideas. We know him well enough, furthermore, to feel confident that Veilleur and Chef would not disagree on basics. Nor does the *Lettre aux Juifs* contradict our assumptions in any way. Forty years had changed nothing in his thinking on this point, as a hierarchy of races is fundamental to his concepts both of universal evolution, and of color-form as knowledge-medium in the perception of the natural phenomenon. I didn't need to ask him who he thought was fit and entitled to rule French Algeria.

The intuition of a hierarchical world is certainly borne out by nature, but the analysis of race into a number of impermeable enclosures is pure ideology. Therefore it contributes to the *malheur* against which Aor warns us later: abstraction in unprepared hands. In the Pharaonic Temple, he would remember that such hands are tied to concrete minds and would abide by the principle inscribed above the Pythagorean portals: Only geometers enter! Therefore *Le Temple de l'Homme* is a geometric study first, a training in abstraction. It is a safeguard against questions he hoped never to face again: who, under theocratic law, receives the divine Word? Who speaks for deity, who puts it into language? The king by divine appointment? The sage by his manifest superiority? And who, in the end, represents the public interest, and by what right?

Whoever attempts to organize society along the lines of a natural hierarchy will eventually confront such questions, and by that fact reach the ultimate political dividing line. The scission, true to all primordial divisions, separates oneness from the many. The many are on the left and below, the one is on the right and above: pyramid of political hierarchy. Thus the right is monarchic, monotheistic, and traditional; the left democratic, agnostic, and revolutionary. The left will praise equality and human individuality, the right will point to hierarchy and profess divine, inescapable order. From this basic cleavage flow all political nuances, at least in French society. The twentieth century appears as paroxysm of this confrontation, the time of definitive inscription through a multiplicity of experiences exploring this relentless political enmity in its ultimate excesses. It has made our time the most barbaric in history.

Not surprisingly, Aor's personality expressed strongly the exteriorizing character of the fifth cycle. It put him on a path that proved to be a misdirection. He withdrew from his public political role precisely with the end of the cycle. Had he then already understood the error, and was his withdrawal a renouncement of this particular work? According to Isha, it was not. To the contrary, there seemed to have been a cadre of Veilleurs in place, and the various branches of the organization continued their work, presumably with the blessings of the departing Chef. According to Isha, he left, and she with him, because their mission was of a more spiritual order, and because Aor's function on the sociopolitical level was merely a *seeding* function: now the fruit had to mature.[2] Aor did not disband the Association, as he undoubtedly would have done had he already at the time had misgivings concerning it. For he of all people must have been aware of the responsibility of the seed for its fruit. Had his ideas been mismanaged by disciples, as would happen again in Suhalia? Isha would surely not have brought this involvement of his to light at the first possible opportunity, had that been the case. For her, the Association of Les Veilleurs was part of Aor's work, and the world the better for it.

Possibly Isha never became aware of a problem. Aor, as we know, came to condemn the infringement of philosophical abstraction upon political institutions. As presented in the pages of *Le Veilleur* chosen by Isha, sociopolitical concepts seem hardly weaned from metaphysics, which gives them a vibrancy that accounts in great part for their power. The philosophically impeccable hygiene of living proposed here and intended as lifestyle for the "new Times," echoes, hideously distorted, just a short way down the road of history, in the most pernicious institutions men of brute force have yet devised to turn the abstractions of Hierarchy, Race, and Work— of special interest to the Association—into a State of tyranny, genocide, and slavery.

This triad of abstractions made its way in Europe between 1923 and 1945. In the murky depths of a concept intended to express the highest ideals of human government, the predominantly Jewish intelligentsia of central Europe was worked to death in camps whose portal carried the inscription: *Arbeit macht frei!* The abstraction, once broadcast, can no longer be managed and directed as it sinks into concrete applications where it will be degraded and will eventually succumb to the inertia that tears down all things physical and man-made.

Again, who speaks for these concepts, once they become public domain? Who strives for their application?

In a hierarchy, he who hears the voice and understands the language.

How shall he be found?

Not to worry. He will find himself, and loudly claim the apex of the pyramid, usually while waving a big stick.

Could Aor's abandonment of this line of work be totally without bearing, furthermore, on his friend Milocz's later refusal to speak about this time?[3] Isha specifies that "almost all" the disciples placed in charge when Aor left to settle in Switzerland remained faithful to their apostolate until their dying day. Was Milosz one of those who didn't? Isha doesn't acknowledge a problem, and yet we know Aor's warning in *Nature Word* against applying philosophical abstractions.[4] The discussion I related, which was very close in spirit and substance to the quotation from his work, confirmed this for me personally. I do believe this conviction was formed later, and that the lesson to be learned from the experience of Les Veilleurs only ripened after the events, after the fall of Nazi Germany and Vichy France.

In hindsight, it is all too easy to identify the mixture of politics and esoteric ideology as a dangerous explosive. Aor issues his warning in 1952. At the time of World War I, however, who in their wildest dreams could have imagined the extent and significance of esoteric ideas in the politics of the coming generation? It was in early 1918 that the Theosophical Society, fecundated by contact with the precocious René Schwaller, was delivered of a brash offspring, a paper called *L'Affranchi* that acknowledged its filiation with the defunct *Théosophe* only through the date on its masthead: it took up where the latter left off. Yet theosophy was never mentioned

in the sheet.[5] Behind the publication stood the group of Les
Veilleurs which René Schwaller had started. Soon thereafter,
L'Affranchi gave way to the publication *Le Veilleur*, which is
fully representative of Schwaller's ideas and entirely under
his direction. A close associate, along with Isha, is O.V.de
Lubicz Milosz, who bestows upon him a title of nobility. Yet
this public exercise lasts but a few years. He retires to the
mountains above St. Moritz and away from politics. The fifth
cycle has ended, the sixth begins. The latter also has a public
aspect, but it no longer addresses the Nation, nor does it aim
for the State: it is a philosophical teaching for an elite, and it
harbors an aspect of confidentiality.[6]

It would be possible to draw the bottom line and chalk the
experience up to not-so-youthful folly, had his departure from
Les Veilleurs spelled the end of the movement. But ideas of
such fundamental reach, broadcast onto such fertile ground
with such vigorous authority, are bound to achieve a life of
their own. They shoulder themselves into history, at the cost
of an interpretation. We know much about the later Aor, but
very little about René Schwaller and the early de Lubicz
Schwaller. If various signatures were used for his articles in
Le Veilleur, it would not be indifferent, considering the author's concern with the symbolism of names, to know which
ones were signed "de Lubicz Schwaller" and which were
signed "Aor."

What is signed "Aor" comes from a mystic source revealed
in *l'Appel du Feu*, a private source of knowledge with which
Aor alone had contact, and he took its name. But he certainly
never presumed to usurp its place. Aor is "He [who spoke] one
evening at sunset, from a frozen fire-red mountaintop."[7] René
Schwaller, or de Lubicz Schwaller or R.A. Schwaller de Lubicz
(we cannot be certain which one) heard the voice and understood the language and became Aor. We know some essential
things about the speaker: he lives in frozen heights, his elements are fire and ice. His topic is cosmological, cosmogonic:
the history and origin of things created. He is acquainted with
St. John, and places the Word in the beginning. His first ges-

ture is to say: "Listen," which implies the functions of the ear, the hearing-intuition which the French capture with *"entendement."*[8] It implies also the function of equilibrium and orientation, as well as the synthesis of harmony and therefore the knowledge of number and proportion, of volume and situation. To make sure of our awareness of that faculty of hearing, we are bid to "become ear" altogether. Henceforth we can be reached only by what is accessible to the ear. The rest disappears. Listening under those conditions, we hear only the living rhythm of the heart, which is its basic intelligence. On this concrete foundation, the abstract intelligence-of-the-heart shall be built, once it has been found in full hieroglyphic context. The lesson of the fifth cycle has been applied: the abstraction is securely anchored to the concrete fact.

We are experiencing the auditory system within the milieu that has created it: the general natural disposition carrying the auditory possibility is perfectly complemented by the form expressing it. We have form carved into resistance by a constant activity of the environment, until action and reaction have reached a compromise that is able to carry the function. The function cannot create its organ, as we have seen, because the drive to audition does not exist without the instrument. But the vibratory possibility of audition exists in the environment, and in time will carve a tool the function can adapt. The substantial form will carry the auditory function in its widest acceptation, the world as sound, the Word as tone, before thought. And what do we hear in this pure audition? The *history* of things created, says Aor.

Thought belongs to a second gesture, it comes next, *ensuite.* "Look!" is its command, "become eye and thought." And what shall we see? The *origin* of things created, says Aor.

Immediately thereafter, he emphasizes: *"All I tell you must be passed along."*

Aor, as we see, teaches primarily perception and communication.

"It is debatable," he now pursued, "whether in the end the

cost in personal freedom is worth the meager comfort of the
company of others. One feels a duty to communicate knowledge that can be helpful to others, but more often than not,
one is misunderstood, and one's words are distorted by students who speak before they know.[9] All this I had to learn in
the first part of my life. In the second half, I began to feel that
most of that kind of effort is a waste. After the age of forty-
two, I understood that the most direct path is the solitary
dedication to inscribed experience, facing the physical
Oeuvre. Make no mistake, practical concrete application is
essential, the theory by itself is not enough. It takes the art,
the sign on the flat surface, the study of harmony in sound,
color, and volume, and that is best put together where art,
philosophy, and science meet as *Ars Magna,* or *Scientia sacra.*
As soon as I took the solitary path, I found the great treasure
trove of inscribable material in Egypt. Here was the symbolique in the language of our time; I felt sure of this from the
beginning. The intuitive effort needed to decipher it made it
a perfect field of action, and it came to supplant almost entirely my scientific laboratory work."

A disenchantment with group interaction and discipleship,
as brought out in the introduction to his "Doctrine," must
have played a part in the eventual withdrawal that would
soon find him on the path to Egypt. Isha's testimony, that a
secret instinct drew Aor to Luxor, must be tempered by Aor's
own version of discovering the Pharaonic symbolique. While
Isha herself had been attracted to Egypt for years and had been
studying the hieroglyphs for some time, Aor spoke of his initial indifference to the monuments that surrounded them
once they had dropped anchor in Alexandria. He was working
on a medieval text at the time and did not participate in the
frequent sightseeing excursions organized by Isha. I believe
that for him, the conscious motive of the sea voyage had been
less an approach to Egypt than a move away from Europe.
Concerns for his own time had diminished, if not ceased; he
had withdrawn from it, and was about to move into another
and very different era, where he would truly find himself. It

probably did not matter much to him on which Mediterranean shore the yacht was docked. Persuaded one Sunday to visit the Valley of the Kings, he was taken to the tomb of Ramses IX, where a figuration impressed him by its geometric implication: the Pharaoh as hypotenuse of the triangle 3-4-5, with a gesture of the arm determining a measure of five to six.[10] He instantly recognized a mentality familiar from his studies in cathedral hermeneutics. I gathered that the quality of surprise, the haphazardness, the unconscious and unprepared inevitability carried a special significance for him.

It is most unlikely that he would have left his disciples and dropped the teaching of his "Doctrine" for the sole reason of financial setbacks, as has been maintained.[11] Even with Suhalia on hard times, had he had an enduring contact with his students, and had he really believed in the teaching he had evolved, he could easily have arranged for a more modest setup in order to pursue that path. Instead, he took to his yacht, and spent two years on Majorca, in an ancient hospice once inhabited by Raymond Lully. If he withdrew from Suhalia as abruptly as he withdrew from Les Veilleurs, it was because he had found this particular pursuit as unsatisfactory as the previous one. At the end of the Suhalia experiment, he is forty-two. The seventh cycle begins with a definite withdrawal from the exteriorization which had marked his life until then.

The very existence of the "Doctrine," an uncharacteristic piece of intellectualism, shows the extent of his compromise for the sake of the master-disciple relationship. It hints at the price he paid for contact with an academic mentality in matters philosophical by adopting a terminology and logic that were probably common coin among Suhalia residents, but that could in no way convey his own philosophical worth. It is painful to see him draw on Descartes, Schopenhauer and Nietzsche, battle with psychologisms of "Moi" and "Ego," parody the *Cogito,* and espouse a rationality that he would eventually come to recognize as his worst enemy.[12] What is manifestly missing here is not *knowledge* (a knowledge unexpressed, though constantly referred to), but a *language* that belongs as yet to the future. It is also painfully evident why Aor refused in his last years to acknowledge the texts of this period. Even then, he must have considered the doctrinary, along with the hypothetical and theoretical, as the devil's invention, so that the very title of this treatise gives a measure of the aberration. A doctrine would arrest those notions that live in a state of flux, the way the concept "tree" kills all hope of contact with the living entity. This attempt at logical formulation is shocking for whomever knew the later Aor, and we are relieved to find out that it was produced under duress and distributed only to Suhalia disciples, making the indiscretion of Isha's presentation all the more incomprehensible. It is, parenthetically, exceedingly difficult to give credence to Isha's claim on the back cover of *Aor* (the biography she edited, where this material appears) that the book was produced in obedience to a clearly formulated wish (presumably her husband's, although this is not specified, so that we cannot exclude one of the disembodied voices that always stood her in good stead as a source of unverifiable information). It is even more incongruous to imagine Aor *in extremis* adopting Isha's psycho-spiritual "Witness" terminology[13] which he had derided all along, referring to her notion of "spiritual Witness" and "permanent Witness" as *"les deux petits bonshommes d'Isha."* * They proved, according to him, the incapacity for abstraction of a female constitution, a theory of which she herself approved.[14]

As to the "Doctrine" itself ("a nasty word," he admits in the introduction, "a prison of ideas"), we are told that it was developed in order for his students to make contact with the teaching in its entirety and see it as a connected whole. The master is forced to do this, because the disciples have "squandered" the teaching in disconnected bits and pieces, giving the impression of "gratuitous affirmations and speculative fantasies."[15] His disappointment is palpable as he chides

---

* "Isha's two little fellows"

them like so many irresponsible children:

> You are known to be my students. What kind of teacher do I then appear to be when you translate me through ideas that have been insufficiently studied?"[16]

Yet it is treason not only to his image as a teacher. It is more than just a case of *traduttore, traditore;* it is treason also to a broader cause.

> Do you not betray me by dropping words that any intuitive person can snatch up and from which he can draw conclusions leading to a science not only false for certain, but probably seductive as well?[17]

What have we come to here? There is anxiety in this accusation of betrayal directed at disciples who have furnished in his name and behind his back confidential elements for a false (and yet seductive) science. The sense of responsibility in the dissemination of scientific ideas is manifest, a sense never encountered when the broadcast was political. Had this new-found prudence risen in the wake of the Veilleurs experience? Much had happened in European politics in the years between the shrill rhetoric of *L'Affranchi* and the logic of the "Doctrine." Was he aware of the events across the borders, where movements were coming to the fore with programs that closely echoed the ideas espoused by his Veilleurs?

It has taken me a long time to open inquiries of this kind, and it is a relief to be able to set them down now [1985], at a time when questions of responsibility are reexamined by the general citizenry in the light of the magnitude of past events. Crimes so excessive, so successful, so openly committed, had to have a broad base of support. Perhaps they needed overt or covert complicity from every single member of the human species, if only through a token concurrence, or even just through inattention, through sloth. No human being on the globe could then avoid his share of guilt, greater or lesser according to the circumstances, and particularly according to a quality of *consciousness* he or she otherwise expressed. We could not distribute equal responsibility to the uneducated and uninformed citizens of a backward country, for instance, and to the erudite and informed philosopher of the Western tradition. All would be responsible to some degree, as all are responsible for the extinction of animal species hounded off the face of the earth by the spread of civilization; the more civilized, however, the more responsible. Cases of political mass murder and genocide (affording ample occasion, unfortunately, for study in recent times) prove that the victims, when by chance they had escaped destruction, yet could not evade the guilt of their salvation: having inscribed in their bones and known in their hearts the isolation of the condemned, they tend to construe their own escape from the common destiny as an additional betrayal of those left to die. This could be seen as an expression either of animistic primitivism within the clan, or else as ultimate consciousness of the unity of life. And the conjunction of spiritual intellect with radical paganism has not been lost on historians of our time.[18]

Generalized infringement of human law makes particular punishment impractical, and the law will eventually be changed or revoked. When humans make laws, even fads can change society. Yet an infinity of wrongs do not make a right, and diffusion in no way diminishes iniquity. It does facilitate the individual assessment, however, and it certainly eases my inquiry. Whatever its extension or restriction, responsibility in matters such as these can no longer be evaded.

For many years after Isha had brought Aor's early activities to light, I did not allow myself to reflect upon the facts and upon my feelings. I had been forewarned and had made concessions. I had dismissed my diagnosis of a postwar anti-Semitism on grounds of generality: French bourgeoisie is monarchic perhaps, right wing most likely, but anti-Semitic for sure. The events of Nazi Germany and of the Occupation seemed to have had no more impact on this inborn hatred than had the vindication of Captain Dreyfus. The diffusion of iniquity had spread the offense thin enough so that I could permit this transparent film between him and me, unwilling as I was to let these facts of "life" interfere with a fascinating relationship based on abstractions such as number, geometry, function, and form. The spiritual value of the teaching lay in its abstraction, and if there was a sociopolitical indoctrination here, it was not made apparent to me. Nor was I involved with Isha's psycho-spiritual side, an aspect he himself criticized mercilessly and which I had successfully bypassed as soon as it became feasible.

These largely unconscious adjustments were made at a time when I tried to keep our discussions centered around two related pairs of topics: salt and inscription; form and perception. But although these topics were clearly also foremost in his mind, it still was difficult to tie him to an agenda, as he preferred to let the conversation drift freely with whatever subjects came up incidentally, from the olfactory organ of serpents to the extraordinary intuition of a cook he once had, who could sense from a distance the peaking of a soufflé. One time when I had hoped to discuss certain aspects of fixed salt that I had ruminated on for days, he brushed aside my carefully prepared questions and managed to involve me in considerations of Karl May's novels, the only books written after 1850 he now deigned to read. He read them in German, as I had when I was a child. He usually brought to spirited heights any subject he approached, and this method of flitting from topic to topic was an accurate expression of his intuitive use of words as well as of his horror of specialization (*"Il faut toucher à tout"*). Almost invariably though, his considerations returned to the topics of salt, inscription, and form, and this preoccupation of his during the months I spent with him has led me to believe, in retrospect, that had he had time to produce one more "cosmogonic" work, it would have strongly leaned toward the definition of form, as *Nature Word* leans toward the definition of function, and *Esoterism and Symbol* toward the definition of substance. Such a treatise would have gone a long way to clear up certain aspects of the fixed salt that remain obscure to me to this day, despite the many questions I asked at the time.

"*D'abord,*" he responded to one of my queries, "let us be clear about one aspect of this: the inscription into the individual's fixed salt can in no way affect the destiny of the present bearer, who is living the fortunes of the inscribed salt which his form expresses. This is the importance of the old Hermetic teaching: the passage of one form to the next is accomplished by an essential decomposition, a putrefaction.[19] What does that mean? Well, simply that the salt must be liberated. The entire reality of the form is in the fixed salt, you understand, and once it has been expressed, no further attraction exists to keep the form together. The disintegration is slow, it precedes physical birth and lasts beyond physical death. It starts with the fixed salt, the first cell of the individual, so to speak. It is around that cell, around the purely energetic site of the nucleus, that the form becomes visible, similar to the formation of crystals along lines of force in the saturated solution. For the fixed salt, those lines of force are *inscriptions.*"

"Ahhh," I let out, as this twist somehow had connected some terms hitherto isolated.

"Yes?"

"No, nothing, do go on, please. I hadn't seen it quite . . ."

"I do hope you didn't see inscription as done with some kind of stylus on some specially permanent material, *non?* Force fields, of course, patterns of energy, like everything else; only in fixed salt, they are very highly distilled, *pour ainsi dire.* Anyway, *passons!* We were talking about putrefaction, the essential destruction of form. Here again, be careful not to narrow the concept down to one particular aspect of form —such as volume, or color—but remember that number and plane-image are also form, and you will see that many forms are very longlived. But there is a creative dissolution of all aspects of form, and it is only after form has been wholly decomposed that the fixed salt will become the point of attraction for the next form. It can take a long time for this to happen, or it can happen almost immediately. It just depends

on the state of inscription, the qualitative state of this particular energetic complex."

"Is there advantage and disadvantage in its taking a longer
or shorter time?"

"Advantage? It depends on what is needed for the entity
involved; it depends on necessity, and also on the state of the
environment. By the time the ancients had evolved their fu-
neral rites, for instance, with embalming and canopic urns,
they seem to have had a pretty clear picture of organic functions, and also of the function of the mineral salt that gathers
in the skeleton."

"Do you mean that the embalming process has a bearing on
the fixed salt?"

"No doubt about it! The awareness of absolutely indestructible remains once a body has appeared, a residue that remains
even after fire: this must have made some impression on the
primitive mind. It must have appeared as a kind of antidote
to death, to absolute disappearance. They must have imbued
these remains with tremendous power, and they were right:
they had put their finger on the vehicle of evolution! Did they
realize that the ashes of their ancestors, kept over generations, were still not the absolute permanent part, that there
were still volatile elements that were merely somewhat
slower in disintegrating? Did they know about the indestructible nucleus of inscription at the center of the mass, about
an energetic entity where experience is abstracted into a
metaphysical force that will circulate through nature, once
the ash gets into the soil? Primitive intuition is a powerful
tool, and it may well be that what I express here in intellectualized images was present to their minds in a different manner, but no less correctly, and possibly more so. We can't
know exactly what their intuition had revealed to them, but
we do know that they attempted to prevent the circulation of
the fixed salt of their Pharaohs and other notables, and that
they went to great pains to keep the ashes from being reinte-
grated into the crust of the earth. Do you give much thought
to the crust of the earth?"

"Do you mean geology? Unfortunately one of my more neglected subjects."

"Well, there are a lot of ways to look at the mineral realm,
and the most interesting ones won't be found in books. Geology is a good book of past history, of course, but it hardly tells
us anything about the everpresent moment of the mineral,
where fixed salt is inscribed. Remember now, once a natural
entity has appeared on the globe, it will leave behind a mineral presence. Let's go back to the ashes. Burn them, grind
them, do whatever you want to them, some part of them
remains. The heap will diminish with the years, or better,
with the centuries, with the millennia, but something will
remain for tens of thousands of years, while the last and least
volatile elements disperse. But what remains forever, that is,
until the end of form, until the end of even the most subtle
form, Number, what remains forever is the fixed salt. Now
with each appearance of form, that salt is *nourished* by inscription."

"Nourished?" My concept "fixed salt" was undergoing active modifications today, back and forth between abstract and
concrete.

"Every natural entity needs nourishment, and the nourishment can only come from its source. Fixed salt has existence
as a mineral entity, as the crust of the earth. It is substance
and needs a nourishing substance. It receives it through the
agency of the sun, origin of substance in the solar system. The
sun is the seed of the earth, and like all seed, it contains an
active fire that will control the assimilation of nourishment
in the growth of the mineral, the earth part that is closest to
God, as the saying goes. We call the nourishing substance
'dew,' and Lavoisier wouldn't believe in it, he had no use for
a spiritual *apport*, which is what 'dew' is. But then, *we* in turn
no longer believe in Lavoisier nowadays. The 'dew' image is
quite accurate, a condensation through a fire in the air. Now
this nourishing substance is attracted by a central nucleus;
there is an affinity of the volatile nourishment, the watery
dew, for the fixed earth; the volatile is captured and remains

in the crust of the earth. The earth is involved in a process of growth along with the entire solar system, and it manifests that process by an actual increase in volume, as mineral remains accumulate in humus and geological strata.[20] If you want to study geology, be sure to start with these premises. They might sound irrational to you, but as always, begin with the irrational to come to the rational. When Einstein eliminated the ether from his calculations, he was being irrational too, according to the rationality of his time."

"And inscription is a 'nourishment' of the fixed salt?"

"It is a modification of the fixed salt; it conditions its needs and affects the quality of nourishment needed. It has even been said that the Hermetic dew is in fact not a water, but that it *is* a salt.[21] But that is another story, that's alchemical language. Let's stay with the inscription as nourishment for the salt: it conditions the form expressed by the salt, therefore it determines the quality and quantity of substance the nucleus attracts by affinity. As long as there is active fire in the genetic seed, the fixed salt must find another form. *Enfin,* 'find,' *trouver,* that is a *façon de parler, n'est-ce pas*? Perhaps you prefer 'choose,' that would be more accurate. Such necessary choice is the freedom of nature . . . and . . ." he leaned toward me, his head fairly close to mine, placing his hand rather heavily on my arm in an unusual gesture that must have contributed to the acuteness of my present recollection . . . "the freedom of nature is the only freedom known to the human condition, notwithstanding the *Liberté, Egalité, Fraternité* of our Revolution."

⊖

A cluster of happenings here fit into my story. Each has a bearing on subsequent events, and they all fall within the two or three weeks preceding the summer solstice, the night we were invited to spend at the Plan-de-Grasse. With the exception of Christmas Eve, we never spent evenings with the de Lubiczs, and therein lies the first of my vignettes.

I had been working for some time on a perplexing problem pertaining to Pythagorean geometry such as it was presented in *Le Temple de l'Homme*. It seemed inadmissible to me that a discipline which did not recognize point and line as true geometric entities (in plane geometry, only planes express geometric truth) should demonstrate an essential function, the function *phi*, by means of a routine section of a line into two parts. The solution to a "*phi* by surfaces"[22] came to me suddenly one evening after supper, as I was doing some reading on an unrelated matter. It took me but a moment to sketch out my argument on some quadrilated paper, and I was rather excited by the result. *Original* geometric ideas, be they Pythagorean or Euclidean, are by no means easily come by, and it seemed to me that I had one by the tail!

Now it should be understood that Aor and I had been mulling over this point for some time, and that he agreed on the desirability of an alternative demonstration. He could not readily propose one or even an approach to one, and this is not surprising. Geometric inspiration, more perhaps than any other, is partial to a constancy of application, and he had done no geometric work in years; he was at the time putting the finishing touches to a new book.[23] I was understandably eager to share this idea with him, even at the unconventional hour of 8:30 P.M. As we did not have a telephone, I folded the sheets of paper I had been working on into my pocket, took the car, and drove to Lou-Mas-de-Coucagno; Goldian accompanied me.

I shall make a short story even shorter: Aor was visibly upset at this breach of routine. He was just finishing supper with Lucie. I spread out my papers and quickly indicated what it was about, but he didn't seem able to warm up to it, nor to our presence at this odd time of day. We quickly withdrew. I saw him the next day, at our regular time, when I presented the idea again. This time he expressed his appreciation of the work I had done, and spoke of a possible inclusion in an eventual second edition of *Le Temple de l'Homme*. I shall not pretend to analyze why this occurrence, insignificant as it may seem, was yet of significance to me. In hindsight, I admit to an error of spontaneity, although spontaneity, even irrationality, was what he preached. It showed me a distance between him and me that I thought no longer existed, but that I now realize (in hindsight once again) would persist to the end. It also showed me an unexpected distance between him and his ideas. I know I probably made too much of the incident, but such feelings do not bow to reason, which is why they matter, as he would have been the first to agree. My explosive exhilaration of creative discovery fell, as it were, like a dud into his ordered world of lace doilies and starched white dinner napkins.

While I move on to another incident, perhaps I should qualify this particular moment more closely than with mere temporal indications. Yes, it was shortly before the midsummer night that marks a watershed, not so much in our relationship, as in my positioning myself within the situation. I had fine-tuned the balance of feeling and intellect that seemed to reach Aor most directly, and our discussions were effortless and relaxed. Yet I had begun to isolate a small number of areas around which I felt uneasy. The nature of my hesitancy had to do with the difficulty of remaining true to myself in those regions. It will be remembered that I arrived in Plan-de-Grasse on the premise of a *logical* problem, and that I had willingly let myself be persuaded to consider its answer in Al-Kemi. On the whole, I was not being disappointed. But my original concern had been much narrower than what I found here, and it was in the surplus that I discovered those islands of reversed polarity which repulsed where all else attracted. We would enter these domains together, but I would usually leave alone, while he remained, absorbed in a twilight of unknowns. One such domain was the island of the elite, which lived by rules different from those that bound "the multitude." The laws of the island of the elite were well founded philosophically; they were based on the One and the many, on an irreproachable theory of number. Yet the elite that represented the One (pre-

sumably because closest to It) felt more foreign to me than
the multitude from which I had merely tried to distance myself somewhat. Isha was godmother to this elite, and she had
introduced me to its island; now she didn't forgive my deser-
tion, for I stopped following him into that cold and mountain-
ous region of duty and blood.

At the time I held the conviction (and perhaps I still do)
that an elite organized by a leader, albeit under the auspices
of benevolent guidance, sooner or later admits of a sense of
rule, an aspect of control, an ascendancy which de Lubicz
sustains with his definition of theocracy, the elite's favored
form of government: ". . . true theocracy is the domination of
the entire life of a people by spiritual truths."[24] There are
many obvious dangers lurking in such regimentation under a
set of ideas. Who will determine and define these truths?
Who, in a theocracy, has access to the mind and to the will of
the divine? And how do we prevent identification of diviner
and divine by an organized elite positioned to structure a government by domination?

It is implicitly assumed, furthermore, that universal agreement exists as to what is "spiritual" and what is "truth." We
need not belabor this point further, as memory is still fresh of
a tyranny that certainly "dominated the entire life of a people." What is less well known, yet well worth knowing, is
that the Nazi regime was built up on the idea of "spiritual
truths." The spirituality was perverted, making the truth a
falsehood, but nevertheless . . . The origin of Nazism is a
weaving of ideas taken from some of the world's most spiritual texts; its sword was honed by acknowledged spiritual
exercise; and its aim identifies with the aim of all spiritual
teachings: a Man beyond man, a cosmic Superman.[25]

Whatever the module of its constitution, the organized elite
is an unacceptable solution to the problem of diversity. Convenient in the short run, perhaps, but necessarily destructive
in the end. Aor to the contrary felt that elites alone could save
mankind. I understood his drift, but I simply couldn't follow
him in a traditional belief well characterized by Jean Saunier

as "the image of initiates having reached spiritual realization of a level such as to have become capable of knowing what suits individuals and societies."[26] Aor himself had unwittingly given me reason to be wary of a social life and political structure governed by exalted beings variously called "Superior unknowns" (eighteenth-century Freemasonry), "Great White Lodge" (theosophism), or "Spiritual Masters," a key word of occultism which Isha posthumously applies to him.[27] My experiences in later years did not prevail on me to drop my guard in this respect.

So I had begun careful entrenchment around positions I was not ready to concede, at least not without further discussion. Aor was unaccustomed to adverse opinions and he was no model of patience when confronted with even the slightest critique. One had to tread with care. But just days earlier, he had afforded me an occasion to bolster my defense against the notion of secrecy by letting me read some parts of his upcoming book. Here I found notions I had last encountered in conversations peppered with *"gardez cela pour vous!"* and *"de ceci, pas un mot!,"* admonitions that had led me to consider the entire domain of practical Hermetism off limits, and this for a spectrum of reasons: governments, Jesuits, puffers, swine with pearls, to name a few.

I was somewhat confused, but made no mention of my feelings, realizing that he had a perfect right to reveal whatever he wanted of whatever he had asked me to conceal. But it further degraded the notion of secrecy for me, and it reinforced my skepticism. In the conversation that took place one or two days before the night of St. John, the topic came up in a context of genesis, as *"le secret de la genèse,"* that irrational necessity of the beginning. I wholeheartedly concurred with this use of the term, because the ever-present moment of beginning manifested by nature is indeed the secret she keeps from reason. But he wasn't in the mood for philosophy, and he brusquely came down to rock-bottom concreteness:

"Vous savez, pour la Saint-Jean, si nous grimpons, vous garderez cela pour vous, n'est-ce pas?"

("*Si nous grimpons*" meaning: in the event we climb, and "climbing" meant the ascent on the winding staircase to the study or the laboratory on the first floor.)

This time I took the bull by the horns.

"But Aor," I said, "we have already spoken a great deal about what you want to show me."

He looked at me askance.

I reminded him that in recent conversations, he had described to me this separation of salt and sulphur accomplished on a copper entity; that we had talked about a colored luminosity hovering above the ashes of the form; that he had referred me to various "good texts" where the matter was discussed in a variety of images; that the "tinctural mass" alluded to in the letter he advised me to read at the time (the letter presumably addressed to Fulcanelli after his master heard the news of the experimental success) certainly represented the spiritual dye at the basis of the colored glass. What he meant to show me, I presumed, would bear much reference to all this information and would present a visual confirmation of the theory he had evolved. What precisely, then, was I being asked to keep in secrecy? It certainly wasn't his involvement with Hermetism in general, and his practice of philosophy (as a cautionary measure against the ruthless interests of certain governments and of the Jesuits, as I had been told from the beginning), because that involvement, if not entirely clear in his earlier writings, would certainly be evident after the publication of his latest book. Nor was it the "theory" itself, which was public domain, having been examined in a variety of "good texts," and which he himself was proposing in his writings. Was it the fact that a proof existed of this theory and that he possessed it? Certainly not, because he had at least implied, if not proclaimed as much himself. Nor could this communicative interdict be directed at a formula, or a process of some kind or other, for I was no chemist or physicist and would be incapable of discerning any technical data. Furthermore, neither formulas, mechanisms, or processes had any bearing upon the science that concerned us. The presentation would be a gesture of knowing intuition, so that the only dependable representation would be an intuitive perception of form—as number, color, sound, volume, or plane-image. It would be an inscription into the fixed salt, not a notation onto memory.

I have sketched an outline of the arguments I led, but in fact, we developed the ideas in easy dialogue. I did most of the talking, which was unusual. He broke in several times to further one argument or to contradict another. When I was questioning what a layman (with whom I graciously identified) could bring away from the observation of a Hermetic manipulation, he alleged that the essential component of *any* gesture could be acquired by imitative imagination. The motionless "imitation" which he held to be the only creative use of the imagination would establish an emotional and even mental contact with the inner causes of the gesture, and thereby there would be a contact with the experience itself.

Perhaps he had followed the trend of the discussion with some added satisfaction, knowing it would provide him a most relevant occasion to tell me what was left to be told concerning Fulcanelli. In the end, he questioned me outright as to what I *thought* he might be preparing to show me. I had to say that I rather thought he would be showing me some *thing*, or more precisely, a *gesture* pertaining to some thing, but this thing or gesture would be a spiritual thing and a ritual gesture. Having previously emptied my mind of all the considerations I felt obliged to vocalize at this moment, I would present as best I could a purely intuitive perception according to the precepts I had practiced. Of two things one: either I would undergo a nameless formal experience of number, color, volume, sound or plane-image that would provide an inscribable, but not transmittable knowledge experience; or I would undertake a factual observation that could be of little interest to myself or to anyone else. What, then, was the use of a vow of secrecy?

"I have heard it all before," he said after I had proffered my question. "It is a very reasonable argument, and I'm gratified to see that you take the subject seriously. But the true protective function of secrecy escapes you, because the secret itself escapes you. Conscious participation in a natural function, which is the essence of the Hermetic act, is a magical gesture, and secrecy is magical protection. We are not talking about a secretiveness of some kind or other, of course, or of some personal decision concerning the privacy of a certain domain; we are speaking of a prohibition empowered by a vow. Fulcanelli had worked under such a vow of secrecy, and he died in the effort of revocation."

Isha had previously dropped ominous hints concerning Fulcanelli's demise. The way Aor told it now, the agony lasted nearly two years. It began the very day of the successful experiment and shone brightly in Fulcanelli's eyes as soon as he perceived the event beneath his savant hands. By prearrangement, this was intended to be their last meeting, and all traces of their association were to be eliminated, never to be mentioned again. The monthly stipend would cease. Fulcanelli was to leave directly, there was to be no discussion, no further conversation after the experiment, and regardless of success or failure, no subsequent meeting was envisioned. A driver was waiting, the luggage loaded. Aor noticed the new spark in Fulcanelli's eyes, the new power in his bearing. They parted, strangers to each other in all ways, including their interpretation of what they had made come to pass.

What Aor had seen in Fulcanelli's eyes was the loss of equanimity for dearth of spiritual preparation; it was the sorcerer's apprentice syndrome, the genie out of the bottle, Icarus flying toward the sun. Fulcanelli had a good share of mid-Eastern materialism in his philosophical makeup, and this turned out to be insufficient background for the knowledge at hand. Aor's diagnosis to that effect proved correct less than a year later when he received, in breach of their contract, a brief communication from Fulcanelli, asking for a meeting in terms of such urgency that Aor acquiesced. They were to meet in a suburb of Paris, in a quiet restaurant. Over a copious meal and more than one bottle of wine, Fulcanelli announced his conviction that he could no longer in good conscience withhold the information they had gleaned in their experiment the previous year. He, Fulcanelli, had continued working, and although he had not yet been able to repeat the experiment, he felt that having done it once, he would be able to do it again. It was just a matter of conditions, ambient conditions, just some detail, but with more trial and error . . .

"The fool! He was talking like a doctor from the *Facultés!* But I interrupted, refusing to discuss such matters in a public place; I reminded him of our agreement, got up and left. Of course he couldn't repeat the experiment! There were a great number of concurring conditions when we ran it, and I had chosen the moment very carefully. He knew nothing about all these preparations. He could only repeat the manipulations he had performed at that time, and these had so far proved insufficient for success at a different time. But no matter, he was dead set on talking about it anyway. Although I left him sitting there over his heaped plate, I did get in touch with him later, because I realized I couldn't leave the matter at that. We had another meeting here, in this house."

Aor reasoned with him, tried to remind him that he was involved with powers that would never forgive a broken vow. The malediction went back all the way to the Pythagorean disciple who revealed the existence of the irrational in geometry and subsequently drowned in the Aegean. Aor tried to convince him that anything he would reveal would be degraded by eyes attuned to usefulness only, all the while suspecting that profitability might have a share in Fulcanelli's astonishing behavior. He therefore offered continued financial assistance if only the man would come to his senses.

In fact, he told him that he could make himself responsible for a cataclysm such as might destroy the planet. While the experiment in itself was perfectly useless, it did point to a non-Newtonian constitution of matter that might well be exploited with unpredictable results. This was "temple knowledge" for Aor, and definitely not meant for the multitude.

"He was already sick when he came here that last time, limping somewhat and complaining of circulatory problems. And he persisted in this insane desire to come forth with whatever he thought he had understood. I reminded him again of his vow of secrecy and warned him that no good could come from breaking it. It was useless. Six weeks later he wrote me a line announcing a meeting he had scheduled for a limited group of adept friends: he was going to talk about our experiment."

Aor's voice had lowered to a whisper.

"Il a voulu parler." * After all those years, there still was a tone of disbelief.

He had gone to Paris a few days before the scheduled event, had gone straight up to Fulcanelli's mansarde and been aghast at what he found. Fulcanelli was deathly ill. Gangrene had set in on his leg, and his complexion was dark gray.

"He was turning black," Aor said almost inaudibly, all harmonics gone from the timbre of his voice, "and he could barely speak. Imagine, he could no longer speak! We looked at each other for a long while, and then he shook his head. I think he understood. He pointed toward a pile of papers on a bookshelf and had me look through them. I found the six pages of manuscript he had stolen and that we had been working with, the manuscript, I am convinced, that had brought us both to this moment. He made me understand that he wanted me to have it, and that no copy existed. I put it in my pocket and left. He was dead the next morning."

---

* *"He wanted to tell everything."*

10

*Crops and seeds.—Bare crudeness.—Conscious
immorality.—Affinity among my friends.
—A sorry roster.—Some unfortunate
parallels.—Responsibility rears again.—Aor's
trajectory.—Schwaller de Lubicz in America.
—Examination of the seed.—Departure.—Adieux.*

If we can trust a historian of the time,[1] the crop sown by René
Schwaller during World War I was brought in with utmost
discretion by those left in charge, so that very little is known
about Les Veilleurs. Yet the Association did spawn at least a
progeny of two who made their mark on history and who have
a bearing on our story. Before bringing them to the fore (and
making them, by default, the only members of the rank and
file to represent the issue of the Association), let us speculate
for a moment: seed from the first harvest may have been
collected, according to principles of frugal husbandry, collected and sown in some other spring to bring a second-gen-
eration harvest, when and where we do not know. Were this
the case, perhaps it is the flower and fruit of this second generation that should preoccupy us most. Whatever the fate of
the first harvest, enough seed was produced and gathered to

be sown for another generation. Twice removed, the fruit no longer fully comprehends its seed of origin, the conditions of the matrix that received it, the environment that greeted its germination, the phases of gestation, and the conditions of the birth. I judge by a personal timetable: born five years after the end of the First World War, I never perceived that conflict as an immediate living presence; it is history learned and remembered as dates and events in an abstract time and space. Applying the same scale of memory, World War II, in terms of its complex causes and effects, is a hazy event today for anyone thirty-five or under, particularly in the United States. Because of this shortage of individual and collective memory, denials have even been attempted of well-documented occurrences scarcely more than a generation in our past, and the more extreme the occurrence, the better the chances of success for such revisionism.

A second generation "memory of the seed" is one of the reasons why the original germ must be held up to scrutiny. We have learned that generations inherit through seed and salt; they are heirs to empty figurations if they lack a sense of their history. They ape atavisms in blessed ignorance, suffer inscriptions far beyond their ken (meaning that they have to repeat experiences over and over, esoteric reality of the well-known and evident dictum on history: know it, or repeat it!), and unconsciously espouse formations devoid of content in the present environment. But nature abhors a vacuum, it is also said, and proceeds to fill it with conviction, leaving no choice to the container but to accept the evidence of what so naturally fills it. Being human expresses itself most immediately in a politicized society, and sociopolitical content is an early filler for empty configurations: the artist, the philosopher, the scientist come later, and metaphysical man comes last, if at all. The path of this evolution is no straight line; there are crests, there are troughs. All must be inscribed, or else repeated. As it is essential for mankind not to suffer once again certain events of recent history, no aspect of those events must be left to fester uninscribed.

Still, even such grave concerns might not have moved me to where I stand today had it not been for Aor's own teaching of the "bare crudeness" of facts and of self.[2] *"Il faut voir cela dans sa nue crudité"* was all the moral guidance he would ever proffer. It implies a free vista of the existing state of affairs, unhindered and unembellished by an artificial code of morals. Its function in the psychological domain is analogous to the function of scientific proof in the domain of intellectual conceits: it differentiates truth from falsehood. It is an effective solvent for the heavily encrusted deposit of hypocrisy which he terms *"fausse pudeur."*[3]

An odd pragmatic realism transpires from this moral sense that would refuse to step outside the realm of brute, natural fact for fear of falling into a false modesty of man-made morality. In fact, the text condemns only *false "pudeur,"* and not *"pudeur"* itself, which is indeed the very instrument to eliminate the grossness from bare crudity without disarming the experience. The hypocrisy of false modesty suppresses emotivity, and the falsification inhibits inscription of the experience. An inertia results, an inertia which is amoral not only because it destroys conscience, but because it no longer furthers functional consciousness, thereby impeding the fulfillment of the human raison d'être:

> Functional consciousness is action, action "in itself," not what acts nor the effect of action.[4]

Such action is certain of inscription, and as *all* must be inscribed, *any* inscription is better than none, any movement better than stagnation. Action "per se" is valorized, abstracted from actor and effect. Functional consciousness becomes action without responsibility. There follows the dangerous logic of *"anything* being better than nothing."

> Always consider that conscious immorality is infinitely better than amorality, this inertia of the moral sense that destroys conscience.[5]

Our botanical metaphor carries us one step further: we can scrutinize the seed not only to refresh the memory of its nature, but also to examine its *responsibility* for the form by which it is actualized. The seed is virtually fruit, time being the only distance between them.[6] With the memory of the seed revived, the fruit is known and it can recognize itself. We need ask for nothing more, but this much we must obtain.

The broadest responsibility of seed for fruit is that the fruit is of the same nature as the seed.[7] This allows seed and fruit, upon perfect inscription of the fixed salt, to become one. In fact, or rather, according to Aor who speaks for her, Nature preaches the doctrine of

> ... the hour of the dissolution and unification of "seed and fruit."[8]

The seed is the virtuality of the fruit as well as being its finality: there is a direct and explicit determinism of seed to fruit.[9]

We can concur: by their fruits ye shall know them.

$$\ominus$$

It took three assaults for Les Veilleurs to establish itself in my consciousness. First, the few words of Aor,[10] their revelatory directness comprehensible only as a judgment of nude crudeness, or naked rawness, if you wish, or even bare crudity: his pronouncement responded to a moral sense of truth, a directness which must be respected and which can only come from a deep conviction of righteousness. Confronted with the brutal frontal attack demanded by *nue crudité*, I admit that I took refuge in *fausse pudeur*, although for this particular case, I would no longer translate the attitude as "false modesty," but rather as "false shame."

The similarity of the uniforms of Les Veilleurs with those of the SA, the first paramilitary organization around Adolf Hitler . . . was this an odd coincidence, a tidbit that gave color to the tale, or was there an organic analogy of which the garb was symbol? I did not want to face the question, and my excuses to myself were framed in terms of discretion, mainspring of true *pudeur*. Alas, I can no longer remain sheltered. The experience must be filtered through emotivity, it needs to become inscribed. All along it has been false shame, as the inner eye that needs no proof had seen the raw truth instantly.

Next there was Isha's autobiographical sketch with the texts from *Le Veilleur*. For fifteen years, like a true prude, I did not dare to look, fearing to see obscenities.

But it was the third attack that breached my defenses. It must be told in some detail, as it is an astounding example of the workings of *affinity*, and therefore pertains to one of the more esoteric functions in de Lubicz's cosmogony.

I have mentioned Maurice Girodias several times. He was introduced to me by Aor, and he reciprocated, fifteen years later, by introducing me to René Schwaller, Chef des Veilleurs. For if by their fruits ye shall know them, then René Schwaller must be known by Les Veilleurs, the crowning achievement of his Paris years, from arrival in 1905 to apotheosis into de Lubicz in 1919.

The circumstances of the first introduction are as follows: shortly after we moved from the Côte d'Azur to Paris, less than a year before his death, Aor communicated with us concerning the translation of *Karnak*, a collection of photographs of Pharaonic monuments for which he had written a text. This was slated to be an international publication, and Italian and English editions were in preparation. Both had run into trouble. The Italian because of censorship ("*Les Jésuites, naturellement*"), the English because at Thames and Hudson, the editor simply hadn't believed the text. Aor asked us to check the translation. Although it had to be redone, the ideas were nevertheless quite recognizably represented; what was construed as heresy in Rome had simply been received with incredulity in pre-1960s London: the commercialization of things esoteric still lay in the future, and the public was not as yet familiarized with the possibility of alternative ways of thinking, or for that matter, with a justified absence of logic altogether. The British publisher experienced some difficulty in reconciling a book of art photographs of Egyptian antiquities with the propositions of the accompanying text. It was, admittedly, unusual for the time.

The calamitous destiny of this publication venture is beyond the scope of our subject. Maurice Girodias, an assiduous autobiographer as we shall see, undoubtedly intends some day to tell its story. Beyond the uncontested fact that my good friend is entirely accountable for the failure, all I could relate concerning it would be secondhand and hearsay. Our involvement, Goldian's and mine, stopped with the translation.

What matters is that Girodias had met de Lubicz before I did, had made a trip to Cannes in the company of Georges de Miré, the photographer, for a business meeting with de Lubicz, and had evidently passed scrutiny, so that the project was launched. They knew nothing of a link that bound them. But if affinity is truly the law of nature, as Aor teaches, and if we should strive to live the spirit of affinity rather than an easy rationality,[11] then we are in the presence of a splendid example of the lived logic of choice without decision. And as consciousness, essentially, is selection by affinity,[12] this meeting offers an insight into the workings of such faculties and functions.

I view the event from a coign of vantage, it having been a meeting between two people I know well. Even so, it has not been easy to understand the workings of affinity in this get-together. I do not know if Maurice Girodias's reputation preceded him; it would have mattered little, in any case, to the success or failure of the encounter. Affinity—such as it is presented by Aor, mouthpiece of Nature, by whose laws, we must assume, he lived—is no facile calculation to determine compatibility and dissidence: it is not reasonable conduct. It necessarily projects this irrationality upon the moral sense, upon

> . . . the supreme high judge within . . . [whose] judgment is not reasoned . . .[13]

For if instead of reason, the strict determinism of inscribed experience rules our form and actions (remember that the specificity of the fixed salt determines affinity), then a rational moral sense becomes an extraneous burden. Affinity absolves us of all responsibility of association.

As to my friend Maurice, he was even in those days notorious for his defense of naked rawness in literature[14] as well as on the stage, having produced in his own theater-restaurant a play by the Marquis de Sade that was set upon by the Paris vice squad. Whatever Aor's intuition of the man might reveal, never would it be even a trace of paralyzing *fausse pudeur!* In fact, as they sat down for dinner at the Cannes railroad station where their meeting took place, he was facing a man whose entire life was dedicated to the eradication of *fausse pudeur*, of false modesty, false shame, not to speak of prudishness, true or false. Undoubtedly they shared a certain understanding on an aspect of morality, but while the one enounced this precept as an abstractly impartial moral perception of the bare crudity of things and of self, as a moral sense unhampered by man-made morality, the other shouted from the rooftops the naked rawness of human sexuality. The common enemy, nevertheless, was *fausse pudeur*, the flim-flam of the mind that warps the moral sense. Pornography is perhaps the prime (and certainly the most innocent) example of conscious immorality in our day and age, and in Girodias's opinion infinitely preferable to the inertia of bourgeois French society's amorality. He meant to fight destroyers of consciousness as surely as did de Lubicz, to the same ultimate end, if by different means. The fit between them would have surprised one and the other. In contemplating this puzzle, it helps to remember what we have just brought out, that for de Lubicz, both affinity and moral judgment are of the realm of the irrational; would such a point of view not be a focus of attraction for Maurice Girodias, an expert on irrational living?

Unlikely though it was for this limited coincidence in moral specification to stimulate a meeting through affinity, I had been tempted to assume that the laws of attraction and repulsion could be swayed by subtle magnetism such as this.

In fact, there was a much more powerful polarity at play, as it turned out when Girodias published the first segment of his autobiography. Not only had there been an early involvement with the Theosophical Society, where René Schwaller first exercised his mystical ideas a quarter of a century earlier, but at a Krishnamurti lecture, Maurice had met a certain Vivian Postel du Mas,[15] who was the center of a group of schismatic Theosophists with political ambitions. Girodias, still in his teens, became a member of this group.[16]

In 1976, at the time when he was researching the events of that period, he came to spend a weekend at our home, located in the midst of a New York State forest. He had brought along several books he was engaged in reading, one of which spoke extensively about Vivian du Mas. As I recall, it seemed to have taught him little that was new, and he left the book · behind, out of forgetfulness, or perhaps to lighten his luggage. I only knew the name of Vivian du Mas from him and had no particular interest in the man. The title of the book, however, *La Synarchie*, drew my attention. I had heard about the secret society that is said to have been a gray eminence behind the French governments of the 1930s and early 1940s, and that is believed in some quarters to wield power in France even to this day.[17]

As I leafed through the book, I was struck by the words: Les Veilleurs. Here, in one brief page, was a history of the group. It was an outgrowth of a "curious sociopolitical messianism" that had manifested itself in circles close to the Theosophical Society. The book quotes René Guénon.[18] It mentions *L'Affranchi* and its motto of "Hiérarchie, Fraternité, Liberté." It speaks of Milosz and an associated publication, *Revue Baltique*. It also mentions two more restricted organizations inside *L'Affranchi:* the mystic group *Tala*, and the apostolic Center. These groups later took the name of Veilleurs.

The interest of Les Veilleurs in the context of the book was that Vivian du Mas received his early formation in this group.

Standing at his side, a companion from across the Rhine,

a somber young man destined for renown.

His name: Rudolf Hess.

$\ominus$

This name mentioned, the tale is told, because my chronicle is not a temporal one: the continuity is in a logic of inscription into fixed salt, and not in dates and times. Events have their moment of occurrence when they are perceived, yet it may happen that their experience is creatively assimilated only much later. I have attempted to trace my assimilation of R.A. Schwaller de Lubicz, a process that started in a Brussels bookstore in 1959 and ended eighteen years later with the entrance of Rudolf Hess through the backdoor of Les Veilleurs. The medium for that process I have called *Al-Kemi.*

Al-Kemi is a symbolic mode of life that has best been applied in Pharaonic Egypt. It is a science that guards its proofs in secrecy, for reasons on which we have touched. This stance places it at an intersection of the esoteric and the occult, whence the power of its ideas tends to materialize in a political arm. We have traced this net of motivations in the various aspects of one René Aor Schwaller de Lubicz: René with the coin, and in his father's laboratory, Schwaller with Les Veilleurs, de Lubicz with the Pharaohs; and Aor, the twofold Aor, first the teacher of nature on the mountain of fire and ice, then the private Aor, entirely private to me, Aor as a mentor and friend. I have therefore dealt in biography, in autobiography, and in a relationship between them: the force-field created by my experience of another, an exceptional other.

Could there be a similarity in conduct between the inscription of fixed salt and the labor of the artist with its multitude of gestures that carry the first general sketch, so rich in possibilities by its indefinition, to the final result, so absolutely stable in its inevitability? Or rather, how could there help but be? The artist knows with certainty when the final image stands revealed. Thereafter, an added touch may be needed here and there, a highlight; or a detail may want to be simplified. In the main, however, the statement is complete.

That is the point we have reached.

The tale is told, but if this be the end of the story, it is also the beginning of the completed tableau. I am able to take the step backward that permits a gaze upon the whole, as writing it down guarantees the ultimate inscription. According to a theory of language we have entertained, words can indeed be instruments of knowledge. Irrationalism, an approach to knowledge that denies this fact, begs the question by its very argument which is a syntax of terms, a language. The word, after all, is as close to the divine as is the mineral: the latter is close below; the former above, in the beginning, and therefore in the end.

Above, there can be found a diamond of ideas, each facet sparkling with creative light.

Below, it is business as usual: the same trite prejudices, the same failures of the intellect.

There is ample evidence that the world's most obscene sociopolitical system, the Germanic National Socialist State, drew its logic from the founts of spirituality.[19] At the root of Nazism lies conscious irrationality as well as conscious immorality. Both these concepts also are bastions of the scientific and moral code that held sway within a particular lineage of European spirituality: occultism. We have seen them both represented in the work of Schwaller de Lubicz.

René Guénon has brought out the recency of the phenomenon of occultism, the origins of which he traces to the middle of the nineteenth century.[20] Whatever the nature of this movement, it is remarkable to us because it featured Schwaller de Lubicz.

One salient characteristic of modern occultism is that it presents "a single doctrinal corpus" where hitherto there had been a number of "occult 'sciences' entirely autonomous one with respect to the other."[21] Another is that the "doctrine" generates political opinions, ideas on the government of society as well as a covert propensity to impose them. Older traditions had been involved with ideally structured societies (Guénon mentions Jean-Valentin Andreae's Rosicrucian project of a "Christianopolitan Republic," the "New Atlantis" of Francis Bacon, and even Thomas More's celebrated "Utopia"). Contemporary occultism is further characterized by an evolved and learned spirituality, the spirituality of science. Nowhere has this been more amply expressed than in the work of Schwaller de Lubicz.

The contemporary flowering of modern occultism represented by de Lubicz uses Pharaonic Egypt as symbolique for a spiritual, scientific, and political organization of society: *AL-KEMI*. For her investigation into "cults making claims to paranormal knowledge" (a fair attribution to the "Knowledge" that at times translates de Lubicz's "Connaissance"), Dusty Sklar enumerates certain features they share:

> an authoritarian obedience to a charismatic and Messianic leader; secrecy; loyalty to the group above all other ties; a belief in supernatural possibilities open to the members [initiates] only; a belief in reincarnation; initiation into superhuman sources of power; literal acceptance of the myth of ancient "giants" or supermen who handed down an oral tradition to a chosen people and who were guiding us now . . . [22]

All these features are common to modern occultism; all can be encountered, to a greater or lesser extent, in the words and acts of René Schwaller, R.A. Schwaller de Lubicz, or Aor. He embraced these ideas in a dedicated search for expansion of consciousness and spiritual evolution of mankind. The mystery, then, the tragedy perhaps, is to consider in what other and far less idealistic quarters these features appeared. We return to Dusty Sklar:

> Glaring parallels to Nazi history. Turning back to that history and its antecedents, I saw unmistakable evidence of a direct relationship between the Nazis and occultism. In fact, it was hard *not* to see it. Here was the missing link in our understanding of the beasts who proclaimed themselves gods.[23]

⊖

I have at times been asked the reason for my leaving the presence of such inspired teaching as could be found in Plan-de-Grasse in 1959–60. The ultimate inscription of my departure is an anachronism in terms of sidereal time, for my physical exit from the intimacy of Lou-Mas-de-Coucagno by no means ended my relationship with Aor, which underwent a considerable development as he revealed himself further and further. The two samples from the membership list of Les Veilleurs completed a picture of René Schwaller, thus adding the final touch to de Lubicz, and thereby to my friend Aor. It must be remembered that I knew nothing concerning René Schwaller at the time of my departure.

I knew nothing save his presence. The young man rarely disappears entirely, whatever the later developments of the maturing adult, and that was very much the case with Aor. But more revealing was the presence of the one whom René Schwaller had chosen as companion, and while René Schwaller evolved into Schwaller de Lubicz and into Aor, Isha at heart remained closest to Jeanne le Veilleur. This had been the period of her greatest activity, when she had been most dynamic, most in view, closest to the source of power, most conscious of the materialization of ideas, the bringing down into the concrete of abstract ideas that could be construed into occult and secret conceits. She had been truly moon to his sun, a paradigm of the sexuality of a new mankind. She wrote on femininity, on its principle and on its manifestation, espousing the idea of a necessary inequality between the sexes proved by their obvious complementarity. And she conceded the blind spot of her gender:

> Woman does not know abstraction. Her imagination is entirely figurative.[24]

She specialized in intense psychic exchanges, and became spiritual adviser to the streetwalkers of Paris.

Isha-Jeanne le Veilleur was undoubtedly a strong component in the atmospheric womb that gestated my departure.

⊖

Fifteen years after my withdrawal from his physical presence, it was a chilling contingency that clogged the emotive filter for this ultimate inscription: could it be that I had been spending those months listening to a voice that once inspired Rudolf Hess? R.A. Schwaller de Lubicz, O.V. de Lubicz Milosz, Rudolf Hess . . . they may have a number of things in common, but only one of them has proved itself to me by actions, speech, and publication: a preoccupation with Jews as a race apart, as a problem that needs solution. What did the nonmechanism of affinity achieve by drawing me so close to what is most abhorrent? Considerations that had not surfaced throughout our relationship now broke through in this final engagement. They were accompanied by a closing cadenza on the theme of *responsibility.*

Not that he hadn't expressed his views on the matter. He frequently mentioned Albert Einstein's irresponsibility, not so much for developing calculations that could annihilate the globe, but rather for publicizing them.[25] He also sided with the Roman Catholic Church in the Galileo matter.[26] The heliocentric solar system was known since ancient times, though the knowledge had remained the private property of an elite in the inner chambers of the temple. Control of information was even then recognized as a tool for oligarchy. Again, a principle borne out by nature (and by human nature specifically!) becomes by political application an instrument of oppression: ignorance is bliss. And bliss is an easier political handle than the brooding dissatisfaction of the inquisitive mind.

Einstein also serves our author as model for a description of the perfect type of black magician. We learn that he has the necessary qualities: intelligence, disinterest, compassion, sensitivity, musicality . . . If *his* science is black, it can only mean that the road to hell was once again paved with the best of intentions. What, then, *makes* his science a black art? It is the syndrome of Pandora's box, quintessential femininity (in Hesiod, Pandora is the first woman) goaded by the one vice that will liberate all the others: *curiosity*, as it pries the lid from the jar, *her* version of the male inquisitiveness that drives the prying scientist as well. Better not to accept this present of the gods unless the proclivity—which more learned minds might yet show to be a widespread function in the movements of nature—can be controlled and the lid kept on the jar. Black magic is a Pandora's box not because the practitioner is evil and means harm, but because he lacks the "sense of the temple," safeguard of ideas.[27] It is a science of demotic texts that can be read by anyone who applies himself to the task. Not so for the hieratic writings of the inner chambers, where a teaching is said to exist that penetrates the mystery of the jar without violating its seals. The esoterism of nature as such is not called in question here; to the contrary, Hermetic perception is our interest, the form of nature in its esoteric reality. Nature is the locus for inscriptive experience, however, and that is an individual, not to say a private concern. The group, the association, the clan, the nation, the church; community of any kind, save for the Hermetic complementary, tends to frustrate individual creative perception, and Aor's trajectory from the group-oriented René Schwaller to the solitary de Lubicz speaks for itself.

Through the very definition it received from de Lubicz himself, nature remains open for whoever is born to the abstraction of its Hermetic constitution. This birth is individual; it cannot be the labor of an association: it is the adept's vigil by the athanor.

Problems start as soon as this esoterism materializes into concreteness, is organized, centralized, and protected by vows and laws in occulted vaults where churches and sometimes governments are hammered into existence. The result can be fully as destructive as the applications of Einstein's theories, and the accountability de Lubicz expects from Einstein must by the same logic be demanded of René Schwaller, Chef des Veilleurs.

Evidence is always circumstantial; in the final analysis, it will depend on the extent to which the circumstance has been refined. Like beauty, objectivity ultimately lies in the eye of the beholder, and with secret societies, the eyes are heavily veiled. Could it be, for instance, that the innermost core of Les Veilleurs, the mystic group *Tala*, had more than just a phonetical resemblance to the earliest Nazi organization, Sebottendorff's Thule Society, the first group to distinguish itself by sporting the swastika?[28] They are exactly contemporaneous, and Rudolf Hess was a member of both. They also shared a vocabulary. Here, for instance, is advice addressed to socialists on Christmas 1919 in *Le Veilleur:*

> It is the falsehood of EQUALITY that lies in wait for you like a thief . . . Kill it mercilessly . . .[29]

The same antidemocratic line had already been taken in July 1918 by *Runen*, the organ of the Thule Society:

> We want the freedom not of herds, but of duty. We hate the propaganda of equality . . . Equality is death.[30]

The "herd" metaphor is full of resonances for whoever has known de Lubicz: *"le sens du troupeau"* was his ready sarcasm for mass mentality. The image is too widespread to be of use to the coalition argument. It is no more than what we said, full of resonances, and they are amplified by their immediate context. For it was in the beginning of the year 1918, as the reader will remember, that *L'Affranchi* declared its substitution of *HIÉRARCHIE* for the *EGALITÉ* of the French Revolution, that dream of equality, freedom, and brotherhood among men. Is this all coincidence, or is it evidence?

The very name of the Thule Society's organ, *Runen*, harks back to the familiar ground of decipherment. In fact, the Society's counterrevolutionary activities were hidden behind a study group concerned with the occult meaning and symbolism of the ancient Germanic alphabet.[31] Young Isha, like many occultists, was an assiduous student of the Hebrew alphabet. Grist to the mill of affinity . . . or coincidence?

To bring my reader to this point, I clearly have to play the devil's advocate, to invent, as is said, a worst scenario. But the invention has a rational counterpoint neither texts nor factual events will falsify. We must accept that language extracts dues for its use, for the loan of substantive communication, for the gift of conceptual permanence. Responsibility is assigned by language to the writer for the lasting configurations his syntactical arrangements determine. Once in language, they remain potentially active forever, contributing their infinitesimal part to the everchanging conformation of the world.

It is interesting, therefore, to observe Schwaller de Lubicz making his way through our upwardly mobile popular New Age culture. William Irwin Thompson understands the dangers of a polity hinged to spiritual conceits,[32] but when, without further consultation, he situates the theocratic de Lubicz at this juncture, he is misled into accepting a context that spells guilt by association, a context, furthermore, that would hardly have been recognizable to de Lubicz himself. So sparing of contacts with his contemporaries, so critical of the level of their work and so acutely aware of the uniqueness of his own, de Lubicz, while perhaps not out of place at that intersection, is certainly unbelievable in this company. Whence comes this conclusion that de Lubicz's interest in theocracy evinced a concern with a mystically enlightened future State?

To begin with, it is a misrepresentation of Lubiczian anthropology, which doesn't believe in any future whatsoever, let alone a future social form that would emerge from our particularly specialized expression of mankind. A cosmology of apocalyptic moments on the cyclical treadmill in this precessional time offers a daring opportunity for the Elite, while sounding a warning of destruction to the idle many: the actual and present urgency supersedes all refinements of the social contract. Aor was quite serious when prophesying a new Stone Age where we would all start again by chipping flint, in a primordial instance, it seems to me now, of anarchic individualism.

I have already indicated my feelings concerning such theories; they came up as mere asides to the main concern, and I hardly noticed them. One can admire and respect a man and not like his verse,[33] and maybe not even like his politics, and yet consider his scientific ideas of interest. If we must "become more aware of the set of contradictions that constitutes civilization,"[34] perhaps we are first to note the ambiguities within ourselves and then develop the largess of admitting them in others. Contradiction and ambiguity abound in de Lubicz, but in such a many-faceted individual, it must be possible to appreciate an insight into natural phenomenon while discounting his taste in music, for instance, or his ideas concerning social structure. His cataclysmic vision made him serenely indifferent to the future of government, his concern being escape from any organizational context whatsoever, be it logical, physical, or social. We are speaking of the mature de Lubicz now, who had learned his lesson through a long-adolescent René Schwaller. He entertained to the last the idea that "the cycle of THE END OF THE WORLD [had] begun."[35] Escape from annihilation lay in an *individualism* about which he wrote no more than a paragraph or two, and that he never named by this term in our conversations, but that is amply connoted by his later lifestyle and work. Politically, it translates into a mystically enlightened anarchy and certainly not into a State. Nor does it seem too far removed from that "American mysticism" of Walt Whitman, the "noiseless operation of one's isolated Self, [that] enter[s] the pure ether of veneration, reach[es] the divine levels, and commune[s] with the unutterable . . ."[36] As to his preference for ancient Egypt,[37] we know it never was a "longing for the hierarchically ordered world of imaginary ancient theocracies" that drew de Lubicz to the Pharaonic, but considerations such as measure, number, and symbolique in general. De Lubicz's interest in theocracy is explained even before we have opened his book on the topic: to make sure that *Le Roi de la Théocracie Pharaonique* was understood as the symbol he means it to be, the royal principle, he explains that

. . . this book does not advocate a form of government any
more than would a description of the functional organization of the bee kingdom . . . The aim of the author is not to
'go back in time.'[38]

Nevertheless he now finds himself accused of lunacy for
"seek[ing] to drag us back into . . . theocracy."[39]

The living present is always new, and beyond that here and
now, consciousness encounters only the old, preserved in
concepts. Reality is a present moment lived in language, and
beyond that presence, consciousness sees a receding horizon
of past. The future has a minimal input into reality, it concerns technical predictions and outright speculation, and is
mainly concerned with security, preservation, profit, desire,
and the like. Under these conditions, we always learn in the
past, and there is much to be learned from Pharaonic logic
and hieroglyphic mentality. De Lubicz did not "prefer ancient
Egypt,"[40] he preferred *Al-Kemi*, an experimental scientific
concept with intuitional components that were well expressed in ancient Egypt and that are relevant to certain logical and methodological problems in contemporary physical
science.

We are speaking now about the R.A. Schwaller de Lubicz
who is in possession of Pharaonic evidence, *not* of the young
Schwaller *who had not yet encountered theocracy*. It is the
latter who was social and political, while the Pharaonic Aor
who felt he was born into theocracy had no interest at all in
advocating it for the present or the future. A hermit, he lived
his empire in a room, out of touch with the polis. This de
Lubicz must be read through his symbolique, and with the
understanding that his entire *literary* formation took place
over medieval alchemical texts. The king of Pharaonic theocracy is a symbolique, not a model for a future nation-state.

In Thompson's words, de Lubicz holds in common with
Alain Daniélou and Guénon "a reactionary abhorrence of secular democracy." The terms are far too strong to characterize
the later de Lubicz, yet there is an underlying truth no one

will deny. The sentiment is much more benign, however, closer to a mild, but thoroughgoing contempt. Yet it should be pointed out that all three writers are French, and might quite naturally share a political feeling that has been widespread in their country since the 1930s, if not since 1789. Favoring freedom, even holding its real secret,[41] Mr. Thompson's aim is certainly not to censor privately held political beliefs. He tells us that the secret of freedom is "the ability to deal with ambiguity, the capacity to tolerate noise and yet hear within its wild, randomizing abandon the possibilities of innovations and transformations." Through the noise of Schwaller 1919, the innovation and transformation of the Hermetic Aor?

Much of de Lubicz's early prose has ripened badly; a language created by flawed concepts lacks resistance to time. The themes have remained, have been both anchored concretely and spiritualized, and after the long silence that separates *Adam* from *Le Temple de l'Homme*, have returned not only with a "new" language he called "*la symbolique*," but with an old civilizing principle: Al-Kemi. With that title, I hope to focus the attention where it belongs, on the Hermetic Aor. The failed politician, who shocked me when I first discovered him in Aor, now bothers me as little in him as he does in Plato, for instance. It is the syntax left behind by these fifth cycle surges that alone is of concern. As we have seen, it can easily fall into uncomprehending hands. Is it not the distant echo of Les Veilleurs and the handsome, dashingly booted and uniformed "dynamic and charismatic leader"[42] that distorts the valuable message to be so patiently deciphered? All biographers of de Lubicz will have to cope with the ambiguities, but after Mr. Thompson, we hold that the ability to deal with them will be liberating.

⊖

Having metamorphosed an epistemological inquiry into a question of responsibility, we are left with the ultimate query: Is R.A. Schwaller de Lubicz responsible for René

Schwaller's ideas and their application, and are Schwaller's ideas still active in de Lubicz's teaching?

We know that there is responsibility, because we know that the seed is responsible for the fruit. We know the nature of the fruit. We are examining the seed.

We are examining the virtuality expressed in the seed, and we watch for germination, a reasonable time after the seed has been implanted in the spiritual humus of Madame Blavatsky's Theosophical Society. Soon there sprouts forth a language that triumphs fully only with the fall of the Third Republic of France.

⊖

As to my leaving his teaching, it was, I believe, truly a choice without decision, the free play of affinities and interdictions, the workings of polarity.

I have mentioned my susceptibility to the *mistral*, a violent wind, cold and dry, that blows through the Rhône Valley. It oppresses me to the point of making breathing difficult. In the summer of 1960, the condition worsened. One time, noticing me gasping for breath: *"Qu'est-ce donc qui veut vous enlever d'ici?"** Aor wondered out loud. Soon thereafter he caught a cold and came down with a touch of pneumonia. He did not leave his room for three weeks, but refused all visits outside the family. I dropped by regularly at first, but the tension with Isha was considerable. I had come to spend very little time alone with her in the preceding two or three months and to my mind she had receded into the *rôle* of "lady of the house," a house where I was frequenting her husband. We had little to say to each other in tête-à-tête now, and neither one of us was used to small talk. After a few short visits consisting of little more than a medical report (and after Isha's insistence that he would not receive visitors in his room), I stayed in contact mainly by telephone. Soon he was well enough to

---

* *What* is *it that wants to drive you away from here?"*

come down for lunch, and we were invited. He promised that we would soon get back to our regular sessions. Breathing difficulties continued to plague him, however, and once I heard him complain about *"cet asthme."* I talked to Doctor Lamy who assured me that Aor's difficulties had nothing to do with asthma at all; he reiterated his displeasure at Aor's continued smoking. A change of climate was decided upon, and the family spent two weeks in Alsace, the land of his childhood and physical ancestry. For the first time in a long while, I found myself left to my own devices once again, and it felt as if I were breathing more freely. I took out some papers I had not looked at for months, *Knowledge and Implicit Functions* among them, and was amazed to find it as solid as before, and entirely compatible with all I had learned since I wrote it. I revised it slightly, added a detail or two, and arrived at the overwhelming conviction that there was a geometric statement still to be made, a statement not issued in *Al-Kemi*, a statement on the *foundations* of Pythagorean geometry. It was the birth of an activity that would lead to *Philosophical Geometry*.

The next day, Madame Robichon delivered a message. They were back, and would we come for lunch.

But soon it was *my* breathing problem that became unbearable. One morning when I was wheezing my way through some geometric considerations in our Cannes apartment, we decided that the best thing to do would be to spend a few days in the mountains where I would be out of reach of the *mistral.* We quickly packed a suitcase and drove toward Grasse. The de Lubicz residence was on our way; I was supposed to go for lunch, and decided to leave a word explaining our absence for a few days. Isha received us, and to my amazement, when I explained our plans, her face darkened.

"Don't you still have my Budge Dictionary?" she asked.

I had borrowed the hieroglyphic vocabulary some time earlier as I was perusing the medical section of *Le Temple de l'Homme*, where hieroglyphic terms were given for anatomical detail. The two volumes were not particularly valuable, and there was at least one more set of Budge in her house as well as some other hieroglyphic dictionaries. In any case, I knew perfectly well that Isha had no need of these books at the moment; she hadn't looked at glyphs in years, not since she had begun to write psycho-spiritual fiction. I explained that we would be gone for just a few days, that the books were safely locked up in our apartment, that I didn't feel particularly well, and I wanted to be on my way. But she persisted. The thought of having to drive back to Cannes for those books, for no particular reason save mistrust, true or contrived for the occasion, made me lose my temper. Suddenly I sensed a pervasive hostility in this house where I had had such excellent moments. There was a meanness in her demand that I was unable to overlook. I told her that if I had to return to Cannes for those books now, I would pack up my things altogether and drive all the way to Paris. I told her I would be back in the afternoon to say farewell to Aor. She seemed satisfied with this solution.

And that is how it went. On the way to Cannes, we noticed heavy storm clouds gathering; the atmosphere became ever more oppressive. It was late afternoon before we were packed and ready to go; on the drive back to Grasse, we were caught in a heavy downpour. Goldian and I arrived at the de Lubicz's pink villa in a Wagnerian setting of thunder and lightning. Our farewell with Aor was brief, adult, and unsentimental, conforming to the gesture appropriate to crucial moments in human relationships. Yet there was a lot of heart in the occasion, as all three of us were sorry that I had to leave. He had wondered earlier what it might be, that unknown force that wanted to take me away from here. I myself was wondering now, and I continued to wonder for many years, while pursuing the inscription of the wealth of experience that had come my way in that house. Admittedly, the foregoing pages were not meant for personal concerns, and so the human relationship between Aor and myself has been largely deleted. That relationship was perhaps best expressed by Dr. Lamy, Aor's stepson, a cold and reserved Frenchman whom I hardly knew

save professionally; he surprised me one day by actually pre-
facing a statement with: *"Puisque nous sommes presque des
frères . . ."* I readily admit that I was far closer to Aor than I
had ever been to my father. I also realize at this writing that
Aor would not have admitted my father into his house. They
would have faced each other and recognized the arch enemy
in one another. Part of me would then have stood with the
one, and part of me with the other. So that there have been
two parts of me that are mortal enemies. Their mutual annihilation is the salary for this work.

The agent of my departure was not a force extrinsic to this
situation, as Aor felt it to be; it was, to the contrary, contained within it, an essential part of it. Truth and falsehood,
right and wrong, knowledge and ignorance, light and shade;
they coexist, they must coexist to give relief to the picture.

Isha, in her *adieu*, graciously controlled her resentment of
me. Our parting, if not friendly, was at least forgiving, *de part
et d'autre.*

We all sat together one more time, some weeks later, after
Goldian and I decided to take up residence in Paris. The
Cannes apartment still had to be cleared out, and we now
went back down to settle our affairs. We had been invited to
lunch. I have no recollection at all of what was said, or done,
or served at that ultimate occasion.

NOTES AND COMMENTS

ABBREVIATIONS:

Temple:	*Le Temple de l'Homme*
Miracle:	*The Egyptian Miracle*
SS:	*Sacred Science*
S&S:	*Symbol and the Symbolic*
E&S:	*Esoterism and Symbol*
NW:	*Nature Word*

Introduction

1. "Aor" was a mystic name received by de Lubicz toward the end of the First World War.

2. *Le Temple de l'Homme: Apet du Sud à Louqsor* (Paris: Caractères, 1958).

Le Roi de la Théocratie Pharaonique (Paris: Flammarion, 1961). American translation: *Sacred Science: The King of Pharaonic Theocracy*, trans. André and Goldian VandenBroeck (New York: Inner Traditions International, 1982).

Le Miracle Egyptien (Paris: Flammarion, 1963). American translation: *The Egyptian Miracle*, trans. André and Goldian VandenBroeck (New York: Inner Traditions International, 1985).

Du Symbole et de la Symbolique (Le Caire: Schindler, 1951). American translation: *Symbol and the Symbolic*, trans. Robert and Deborah Lawlor (New York: Inner Traditions International, 1978).

Propos sur Esoterisme et Symbole (Paris: La Colombe, 1960). American translation: *Esoterism and Symbol*, trans. André and Goldian VandenBroeck (New York: Inner Traditions International, 1985).

Verbe Nature, in Isha Schwaller de Lubicz, *"Aor"* (Paris: La Colombe, 1963). American translation: *Nature Word*, trans. Deborah Lawlor (West Stockbridge, Massachusetts: The Lindisfarne Press, 1982).

3. The term "gnosis" as an English translation of the capitalized *"Connaissance"* had been accepted by the author during my talks with him. As some controversy concerning its use arose in later years, it must be pointed out that even in French, the word *gnose* was considered synonymous with *Connaissance* by the author, cf. *Temple* tome I, p. 26: *"La gnose—ou Connaissance—intrigue."* Also *Miracle* p. 13: ". . . gnosis (which we designate as inborn knowledge concerning the 'secret of becoming') . . ."

4. Cf. my *Philosophical Geometry* (South Otselic, NY: Sadhana Press, 1972). [1987 edition published by Inner Traditions International, Rochester, Vt. Cited pages refer to 1987 edition.] The distinction be-

tween "terms" and "words" is fundamental to theory of language. I have approached the subject at various times from different angles, first in the Introductory Notes to *Philosophical Geometry*. Here the discussion concerned the nature of signs, and various sets of signs have been examined. *"[For] language guarantees its foundation not only by the comprehension which its signs, as terms, afford, but by a formalization through grammar and syntax and through the inventory of a vocabulary. Unless a set of signs is covered by such referential instruments, it must remain in isolation, losing none of its horizontal structuring power, but destined to confine itself to an expression of order: extension beyond terminology is a prerogative of language and does not belong to an isolated set of signs. As a set of terms, language is a structural instrument, but when it anchors to its terms the far-floating meaning of words, it becomes an instrument of knowledge. A language of terms is built on comprehension and order, with general agreement a standing possibility depending only on agreement as to the referential instruments of grammar and syntax. Vocabularies, furthermore, unequivocally show a sign as being or not being a term. In language, the total set of terms as well as all possible orders are present at every moment."*

5. The translation of *"la symbolique"* as "the symbolique" had also been discussed in my talks with de Lubicz, cf. *Sacred Science*, Translators' Note. Rendering *"la symbolique"* by "the symbolic" is a mistranslation, clearly shown by the fact that "the symbolic" has an exact French counterpart, namely *"le symbolique,"* with the sense, in French as well as English, of "that which is symbolic," precisely the sense the author wants to avoid.

6. The nature of "inscription" in de Lubicz's philosophy of evolution is discussed later in the text.

Chapter One

1. See Appendix A.

2. On the English title of this book, see Introduction note #5.

3. "There are two manners of reading and studying the traditional texts of initiation. One is exoteric and deals with the historic meaning that serves in a general way as foundation, or *symbol*, to an esoteric sense expressed by the *symbolique*. People perceived imaged stories in these texts, legends and representations, stories they could understand and eventually disseminate. Had they perceived them as conveying mere nonsense, no esoteric meaning would ever have been transmitted" [my translation].

To give a measure of the author's style, slavishly rendered by a word-for-word translation, I include the published version.

"The traditional texts of initiation can be read and studied in two ways. One of these deals with the exoteric (historic) meaning, which generally serves as a foundation, that is, as a symbol, for the esoteric sense (expressed through the symbolic) which these texts, legends, and representations would not have transmitted had the people seen them as nonsensical rather than as stories forming an image that they could understand and eventually disseminate."

4. In the early fifties, I had made the acquaintance of Andrew Da Passano who had studied with a certain Castellani in Milano. He referred to his work as *travail intérieur,* and it was conducted with the epistemological background of the latest scientific results in the analysis of matter and the probe of the cosmos. Although it embraced psychospiritual self-improvement ethics (as bait, rather, it always seemed to me), physical principles based on the works of Einstein, Bohr, Heisenberg and the like were the main fulcrum of conviction in the proof of the existence of "superior states of consciousness" and in the effort of attaining them. Here also a conviction was expressed of other meanings residing in the scriptures, but while such esoteric themes were reached through a scientific baggage, they in themselves remained of psychological and spiritual import.

5. A seventeenth-century adept. From *De la Nature de l'Oeuf. Epitre certaine de Bernard de T, touchant l'Oeuf des Philosophes.* No bibliographic information available.

6. My text was eventually read by Professor Ferdinand Gonseth, in charge of the department of higher mathematics at the École Polytechnique fédérale of Zurich, and editor of the Swiss review of epistemology, *Dialectica.* It led to an interesting correspondence, an offer of publication, and a meeting at his request. I believe him to have been the only person to have read this paper and to have understood the logical point of view represented by the text. The work undertaken during this encounter, which followed closely upon my departure from Plan-de-Grasse, is slated to become the subject of a separate volume.

7. I must emphasize once again that the moment of this writing lies a quarter of a century this side of the events and of the mentality experiencing them and reacting to them. The "now" of these words has in sight an academic epistemology giving rise to a call for anarchy among its very own, an energetic warning against obsolete methodology (Paul Feyerabend, *Against Method,* London: Verso, 1975). This can only be read as a confirmation of de Lubicz's practice, and, in our time and

to my knowledge, is the first contact of the "two sciences" on their most fundamental *logical* grounds. We are seeing other approaches, not only in medicine, for instance, with acupuncture and other "alternative" practices and "holistic" visions, but also in physics, as a result of the extreme analysis of matter. Cosmology will be the last barricade; it will be conquered by a new world image akin to the symbolique.

8. Cf. note #4.

9. I was to find out that the author disavowed this book. What was good about it, he felt, had been better said by him elsewhere, and what was bad about it was best forgotten. The anachronistic statement on the flyleaf of the New York edition alleging a French 1949 edition entitled *Symbol* (sic) *et Symbolique* is certainly in error. Not only did the author oppose a second edition, but he considered the fortuitous destruction of the first to have been a blessing in disguise. The one and only 1951 Cairo edition, a thin booklet, almost in the pamphlet genre, has an air of sobriety and seriousness that has not been respected in the New York edition. Sole visual presence of Pharaonic Egypt—a logo more than an illustration—the glyph for *Ta-Meri*, beloved name for the land, evokes the earth's affinity.

10. *L'Ouverture du Chemin* (Paris: Caractères, 1957).

11. *Her-Bak Pois Chiche* (Paris: Flammarion, 1955). *Her-Bak Disciple* (Paris: Flammarion, 1956).

12. Isha's account of Aor's deathbed conversion to her cosmogony must encounter the skepticism of anyone who knew the de Lubiczs in their last years.

13. *La Lumière du Chemin* (Paris: La Colombe, 1960).

14. A method combining acupuncture points with the laws of harmony, evolved under de Lubicz's direction. See *Acupuncture: Phonophorèse, Technique-Clinique* (Paris: Maloine, 1967).

15. Cf. *Miracle*, p. 15.

Chapter Two

1. Paris: Pauvert, 1964.

2. *Temple*, tome I, p. 174.

3. Lectures given in 1954-55 in Mexico City to a group of Ouspensky disciples under the direction of Rodney Collin Smith. The musical octave plays a considerable role in this teaching.

4. To this day, the error has not been reported to me, which does not necessarily mean that the intended experience has been entirely missed by the reader.

5. See Feyerabend, *op. cit.* The work is subtitled: *Outline of an Anarchistic Theory of Knowledge.*

6. Particularly *Temple*, tome III, chapters III and IV.

7. *Temple*, tome I, p. 369, also *ibid.*, tome II, plate XLVIII C.

8. *Temple*, tome III, p. 187.

9. No. 358, pp. 323–373.

10. Wife of the architect, Yvonne Robichon had joined the de Lubiczs when they left Egypt for France.

11. See *Aor*, p. 43, for Isha's statement: "Woman does not know abstraction. Her imagination is entirely figurative, which is why metaphysics and abstractive sciences are usually 'strangers' to her."

12. In the tomb of Ramses IX; see *infra* a description of the figuration. Aor spoke of that moment of recognition, when the logical groupings of the figurations suddenly expressed the abstractions he had known in terms of medieval texts and monuments.

13. See Appendix A.

14. *S&S*, p. 59.

15. *SS.*

16. As in the foundations of arithmetic according to Dedekind and Peano.

Chapter Three

1. *Temple*, tome I, p. 425.

2. By which is meant the conception of geometry elaborated by Pythagoras while working in the Pharaonic temple. It must be remembered that for de Lubicz, geometry was dead with Euclid.

3. The Chacornac brothers were publishers of esoterica in Paris.

4. See my *Philosophical Geometry*, pp. 46 and 60.

5. *Hermes the Thief, The Evolution of a Myth* (New York: Vintage Books, 1947).

6. *S&S* p. 29.

7. Cf. his *La Philosophie du Non.* The creative powers he attributes to the act of negation find a distinct resonance in Schwaller de Lubicz's cosmology.

8. The abusive capitalization in the Bachelard quotation is carried through into the English translation of *Du Symbole et de la Symbolique.* Only the broader context of this quotation tells the full story. After noting the young age at which such scientists as Heisenberg,

Dirac, Bohr, Einstein and others made their great contributions, Bachelard speculates that

> the twentieth century has seen a mutation of the brain or of the spirit of man, particularly handy at unraveling the laws of nature, just as in the previous century, the precocity of the likes of Abel, Jacobi, Galois, or Hermite was perhaps due to a mutation of the spirit directed toward an adaptation to the world of mathematical entities. (Le Nouvel Esprit Scientifique, Paris: Presses Universitaires, 1934), p. 178. (Trans. AVB)

We feel de Lubicz straining for confirmation from academic authority, a confirmation for a Spirit that he must deem worth a symbolic sleight of hand. In fact, the quotation shows clearly that Bachelard speaks more of mind or intellect, both legitimate translations of "esprit," than he does of what "Esprit" means to de Lubicz.

9. The book was first announced, on the flyleaf of *Propos sur Esoterisme et Symbole*, as *Le Roi de la Théocratie Pharaonique* (with subtitle: *La Science inhumaine et la Science sacrée*). The subtitle was eliminated by the publisher. The American edition has restored scientific presence to the title.

10. *S&S*, p. 33.

11. *Hermes the Thief*, p. 20.

Chapter Four

1. Some information about those days can be gleaned from Kenneth Rayner Johnson, *The Fulcanelli Phenomenon* (Jersey: Neville Spearman, 1980). As biography, this study never leaves the much belabored level of mystification—with an age-old Fulcanelli wandering across the century—even when it claims to look behind the legend. The author is totally unaware of the de Lubicz connection.

2. Cyliani's *Hermes dévoilé* was published in Paris in 1832, and a reprint of the book in 1915 strongly influenced the Fulcanelli circle.

3. A scientific station established by de Lubicz in Switzerland, above St. Moritz.

4. *Les Douze Clefs*. . . . (Paris: Éditions de Minuit, 1956), p. 107.

5. Paris: La Colombe, 1963.

6. Here is the excerpt from Lucie's letter to me dated February 18, 1974:

> Vous parlez de la relation Aor-Fulcanelli.
> Nous parlions un jour de Fulcanelli au Dr. Rouhier (Véga-Paris) et celui-ci sourit et, plissant malicieusement les yeux, répondit:

"Fulcanelli? Lequel?"

À sa suite, je repète: Qui est Fulcanelli? Le savez-vous? Savez-
vous quelle fut sa relation avec Aor? Vous m'intriguez.

7. His name does appear in biographical works on Milosz, with
whom he was closely associated during the First World War and shortly
thereafter. He is never mentioned in any of the literature concerned
with the Hermetic revival of his time.

8. *Les Cahiers du Sud*, #358.

9. Cf. *Miracle*, p. 59.

10. *NW*, p. 123

11. CF. *Miracle*, pp. 49–50. The author has described mystic perception. He continues by saying:

This is not a priori *knowledge, the knowledge of spatial intelli-*
gence-of-the-heart, for the latter demands that the knower main-
tain a link with our tangible world. Knowledge is to liberate the
individual from restrictive limits while maintaining contact with
the perceptible and ponderable universe.

Such knowledge is a mean term between what is undefinable
and spiritual, and what is finite and perceptible. This requires of
the knower, whom we may call a sage, a tangible means of trans-
mission retaining a character of universality; of the person at
whom this means is directed, it requires an intellective faculty
akin to this means.

The means can only be form, be it number, color, sound, a two-
dimensional image, or a volume. The essential condition, how-
ever, is that this form have no conventional name; for the latter
immediately restricts the universality of the form through the par-
ticular attribution imposed upon it.

12. The necessity of "natural naming" is notably manifest in geometric entities. Cf. *Philosophical Geometry*, p. 3, for "names of facts
given simultaneously with the facts."

13. See notes #10 and #11.

14. To my knowlege, de Lubicz speaks of "functional perception"
only one single time in his writings, in the "Reflections" that follow
the main text of *Nature Word* (p. 136). The context readily shows that
the term "perception" here is a misnomer, for this functional state
(which has variously been described to us as a state of identification)
demands "a momentary elimination . . . of all formal representation."
Such a formal blackout would eliminate the very foundations of what
"perception" *means*, part of which is certainly the sensorium-elements
contact. There is no further need for such blurred terminology, how-

ever, for the author has become aware of a new vocabulary and its liberating power. The discovery crystallizes in the first "verse" of the "poem" *The Way*, an obviously inspired moment: ". . . become *functional consciousness,*" is Aor's viaticum to Nature's wayfarer (p. 135)! The release of tension is notable from here on. All through *Nature Word*, which is replete with definitive attempts on "function," functional consciousness never appears. There is paraphrase, as for instance when psychological consciousness is opposed to "true Consciousness . . . innate in the corporeal bearer" (p. 84), or in the following syntax that comes as close as possible to the term that still escapes the author:

> You look at the world through your senses, but it is impossible to have the Intelligence of what you have observed and compared without the functional identification in yourself with the function revealed by the observed thing.

Subjective identification with revealed function through objective perception must be the leanest definition of functional consciousness we will find. The term itself is not yet realized in language, it eludes the author until after the completion of the text of *Nature Word*. The text speaks of "functional powers" (p. 71), of "functional principles" and "functional rhythm" (p. 77), "functional order" (p. 82), and finally, "functional perception" (p. 136), before the dam breaks with FUNCTIONAL CONSCIOUSNESS, sweeping away all earlier definitions. Lacking all through the body of *Nature Word,* the term does not appear in the first sixty-four pages of the total text (Answers, Reflections, and Conclusion). It then appears thirty-one times in the last nineteen pages! It now demonstrates its power in a stream of definitions, as when it becomes "an abstraction of forms" . . . (p. 138), or "the absolute Cause of everything," a "concretizing impulse" . . . (p. 139). And always, it is opposed to psychological consciousness: "Psychological consciousness selects, functional consciousness unifies" (p. 147). But its first and foremost, its most trenchant definition is deeply significant to whomever knows the author's early work. Here, after its discovery in the "poem," is the very first use of "functional consciousness":

> It is the old story of the fall of paradisal man in the Mosaic Genesis. By accepting rational Knowledge [Savoir] through the complementation of man by his Eve (his shadow, his negation, his other "I," the objective), psychological consciousness comes to obscure functional consciousness.

Nature Word is a communication concerning function; one of his earliest and most direct questions concerns the nature of function (p. 76). The answer is delayed for a warning about error, and the investigation does not really come to grips with the essential, because the language is still missing. It is, in a way, correct that this should be so. For the questions of *Nature Word* are answered by Nature, and the functional consciousness of the "Reflections" is at least a gateway *beyond* nature.

15. Cf. *NW*, p. 135; *Miracle*, pp. 58–59.

16. An emotional content in the object's sound-form was a subject touched on, and usually linked to magical practices.

17. *Miracle*, p. 108.

18. *NW*, pp. 81–82.

19. *SS*, p. 166.

20. *NW*, p. 124.

21. *Ibid.*, p. 107.

22. *Ibid.*, p. 111.

23. *E&S*, p. 9.

Chapter Five

1. *Temple*, tome I, p. 149.

2. For Mercury as substance, see *Miracle*, p. 91 and p. 117.

3. *Ibid.*

4. *Adam, l'Homme Rouge* (Paris: Stock, 1926).

5. See *Miracle*, p. 118 *et seq.*

6. *Ibid.*

7. *Ibid.*, p. 117.

Chapter Six

1. *Aor*, p. 67.

2. *Thematic Origins of Scientific Thought: Kepler to Einstein.* Introduction (Cambridge, Mass: Harvard University Press, 1973).

3. *Les Douze Clefs* . . . , p. 240. (See Plate V.)

4. Cf. *Le Grand Appel: Necessité, in "Aor,"* p. 197.

5. *Ibid.*

6. Cf. Kenneth Rayner Johnson, *op. cit.*

7. Soon after we arrived, Aor told us that on the occasion of a recent literary manifestation involving the history of Surrealism, André Breton had asked him to participate, claiming his *Adam, l'Homme Rouge* (1926) as a contribution to surrealism.

8. Jean Rousselot, *O.V. de L. Milosz* (Paris: Pierre Seghers Éditeur, 1955), p. 88 footnote.

9. *L'Appel du Feu* (Saint Moritz, Switzerland: Éditions Montalia, 1926), p. 3.

10. *Ibid.*

11. *Miracle*, p. 229.

12. *L'Appel du Feu, loc. cit.*

13. *La Doctrine. Trois Conferences faites à Suhalia Noël 1926 par AOR*, (Officina Montalia St. Moritz: Édition Privée, 1926). On the fly-leaf, the following inscription: "This book has been entrusted to . . . . who, by accepting it, pledges on his honor to communicate it to no one and to make arrangements for its return to Suhalia."

14. *Aor*, p. 92.

Chapter Seven

1. Isha Schwaller de Lubicz, *Journey into the Light* (New York: Inner Traditions International, 1984). See note on cover illustration. See also *NW*, Introduction, p.51.

2. The poem was dedicated to René Schwaller.

3. *Aor*, p. 27.

4. *Ibid.*, p. 32.

LETTER TO THE JEWS

To the sole Jews.

It is not one of your own who speaks to you here, but you will listen to me nevertheless, for I speak with knowledge and I know who you are.

Close the book of your history! What does it matter! Do you even have a history, moreover!

As race you are the people chosen by the hidden God *and each site of the earth has been your site, yours, the exiled.*

But hate has pursued you and your spine is bent under all manner of insult, oh great people of Israel!

Yes, you are a great people, Jews, but why do you no longer recognize your Levites! Why now do you disavow your faith in the Saviour—you who are awaiting him still! Why do you not continue to leave at your table the free space for "him who is to come"!

The time has come, people of Abraham who adored the Eternal, Him of the unpronounceable name, the time has come when you must return to the promised land!

And construct the city, which will be yours *at last.*

Now, Jew, the time has come when facing the world, you must reclaim your land!

Go, establish your land and build a square tower in Zion.

Build a square tower in Zion and say:

This is the square tower in Zion, built in honor of the hidden God *and as a sign of his* eternal presence.

Jews, if all of you had recognized the one who has come forth from you, the King *of the Jews, the cornerstone of the temple of universal Faith would have been missing and the edifice would have crumbled.*

You have remained, like the Law remains after its accomplishment, for the beginning of things is remembered in the end.

Christmas 1919

AOR

(Trans. AVB)

5. *Ibid.*

6. *Ibid.*

7. *Ibid.*, p. 19.

8. *Op. cit.*, p. 88. Having brought out that Milosz, in his search for 'superior concepts' "did not even disdain the resurrection of old and soul-staggering initiatic rites," Rousselot adds in a footnote:

> *Witness the creation, by Milosz and the occultist Schwaller, of the group Les Veilleurs. André Lebois alludes to it in a study published March–April 1949, by the magazine* France-Asie *("Presence de Milosz dans son oeuvre"). Toward the end of his life, Milosz implored his friends not to question him concerning Les Veilleurs, and precise information is lacking concerning the nature of this experience which probably belonged among those undertaken in all ages by black magicians and practitioners of conjuring books. As a result of who knows what pact with Milosz, Schwaller had obtained from the latter the right to add to his name half of the poet's name. Thus he called himself Schwaller-Milosz. This 'spiritual' brotherhood remains darkly mysterious, and no less tenebrous are the aims, the means, and the results of this involvement of Milosz with occultism.*

9. *Ibid.*

10. The main source for this politico-spiritual program can be found in the almost contemporary work of Saint-Yves d'Alveydre (1842–1906), cf. J. Saunier, *La Synarchie* (Paris: Grasset, 1971), p. 79 *et seq.*

11. *Temple*, tome III, pp. 178–79. "In light of the transmitted tradi-

tional knowledge concerning the fixation of the indestructible nucleus in the thighbone, the idea expressed by the femur necessarily includes that of inheritor and of regeneration. This must be understood in the sense of a 'personal reincarnation,' transporting the acquirements of a lifetime. This does not concern children engendered during his lifetime by the deceased." (Trans. AVB)

12. *Temple*, tome I, p. 67.

13. *Ibid.*

14. *Temple*, tome III, p. 179.

15. *Ibid.*

16. *Ibid.*

17. See Appendix B.

Chapter Eight

1. See Appendix B.

2. According to Isha's testimony at his death bed, he called himself "a lover of the world of causes." This undoubtedly he was, although it is strangely unlike him to verbalize the fact in these terms, if at all. Isha even has him admitting a "passion for deciphering the laws [of such a world]." Here her terminology goes awry. A passionate lover perhaps, but never a decipherer of *laws*, those lifeless reductions of the only reality: the "general natural disposition" that determines the causal state. Cf. *Miracle*, p. 107 *et seq.;* also *NW*, p. 76. His mini-curriculum vitae in her own terms is a giveaway of inauthenticity:

Thinking that the highest aim of men on this earth was attaining the knowledge of the cosmic laws of genesis, I had dreamt of show-ing them the path.

The path here referred to ("the Path," in Isha's orthography), occurs in the original titles of both of her psycho-spiritual books: *L'Ouverture du Chemin* (1957) and *La Lumière du Chemin* (1960). Aor's desire for disciples ended in 1929, with Suhalia, as we have shown. Isha here is reading her own aspirations into his biography.

3. Cf. *NW*, p. 117.

4. He had the title of Chef des Veilleurs.

5. *Aor*, p. 59. The passage, from a study titled: *Introduction to the Study of the Seven Profound Causes*, must be seen in its full context.

. . . At this time, there is an end to the possibility of an exclu-sively intellectual science. A new domain for human effort is open-ing itself to man: the evolution of intuition, new means of

coordinating observations, new principles of evaluation, a new basis of an ancient science. *However, if the scientist intends to continue applying in this new domain his old mentality, that is, the mentality of experimental observation of the physical world, he will inevitably find himself facing a wall that forms* the unsurmountable partition between one race and another.

Just as it is absolutely impossible for a Senegalese to follow the reasoning of a philosopher such as Kant, similarly it will be impossible for a scholar of our present mentality to penetrate—or even to have an inkling of—the character of an intuitive consideration. (Trans. AVB)

6. *Aor*, p. 21. While it is idle to speculate on an extension of the word "hierarchy" for the editors of *Le Veilleur*, its comprehension here is aided by the stark context in a slogan meant to replace the republican credo, in a counterattack by a monarchic and clerical *ancien régime*. The call for hierarchy to supersede equality is directed at a political and social structure manned by human beings. Hierarchy as a natural phenomenon cannot escape serious observation and will be denied only by blind ideology; on some level or other of understanding, any fair thinker will admit a basically hierarchical structure of nature (see, for instance, Koestler's and other texts in *Beyond Reductionism*, Arthur Koestler & J. R. Smythies, eds., New York: Macmillan, 1969). Nature is rightfully known as a vast repository of first-rate practical advice, but human spirituality in the search for freedom strives beyond such raw data. In nature, human beings are obviously, blatantly, created quite unequal. Considering this creation as divine, they may organize into a hierarchical theocracy according to their divinely assigned differences; unfortunately, as human beings, they will also be motivated by their very human values. It is the aim of spiritual elites to free themselves from the shackles assigned to them by their natural context, and equality, if not yet quite beyond nature, nevertheless belongs to a rationality that stands at the threshold of a free individualism and its responsibilities. Natural hierarchies have never known equality, and are therefore not available to the notion. If man's spiritual work is to go beyond nature, here is a good place to start. Hierarchies will form by necessity, hierarchies of quality, of intellect, of will, through genetic factors, through environmental factors, etc. Such hierarchies will express themselves as long as the liberty factor is respected, as it is more or less in a democratic system. But instituting hierarchy as a principle will restrain liberty as well for those who happen to be at the bottom. Equality must remain the fundamental social and legal principle, and it need never bother the true elite, which is not meant to rule, but to civilize.

7. *NW*, p. 102.

"*Forget 'elites' and recognize the true Elite. It is formed of individuals who have already gone beyond Nature. To be of the Elite is to want to give and to be able to give; it is to know how to draw on the inexhaustible source and give this food to those who are hungry and thirsty in the form which is suited to them. Altruism is the criterion by which to recognize the man who goes beyond humanity.*"

8. *Ibid.*, p. 142.

"*. . . Let your constant prayer be. 'The whole Work of the Universe is in me.'*"

"*I put forward a pure* Individualism, *without egoism, absolute, the source of all true solidarity and of all brotherhood, for it eliminates the 'you and me.'*"

"*Collectivism is 'useful,' but it is of a low nature, being motivated by fear and egoism.*"

"*True solidarity is founded on the consciousness of the responsibility that every man has towards all humanity, his own kind, his species in which he is functionally based.*"

9. *Ibid.*

10. *Ibid.*

11. *NW*, p. 102.

12. George Steiner, *The Portage to San Christobal of A.H.* (New York: Simon & Schuster, 1981), p. 161.

13. *SS*, p. 260, amended translation. I am grateful to Christopher Bamford for reminding me of this passage.

Chapter Nine

1. Louis Allainguillaume in a lecture held in Paris in October 1920, published in *Le Veilleur*, cited in *Aor*, pp. 21–22.

2. *Aor*, p. 20.

3. See note #8, Chapter 6.

4. *NW*, p. 117.

5. Saunier, *op. cit.*, p. 177.

6. *Doctrine, Introduction*, where he condemns the disciples "sowing behind [his] back ideas received in confidence."

7. *L'Appel . . .* , *Prologue*.

8. From *entendre*, to hear, this term is usually translated by "intellect" or "understanding."

9. *Doctrine, Introduction.*

10. *Temple,* tome I, p. 425.

11. Cf. American introduction to *NW,* p. 58.

12. Cf. his deathbed pronouncements according to Isha in *Aor,* p. 118.

13. *Ibid.*

14. *Ibid.,* p. 43.

15. *Ibid.,* p. 20.

16. *Ibid.*

17. *Ibid.*

18. Particularly in a title by Pierre Mariel: *L'Europe païenne du XXème siecle* (Paris: La Palatine, 1964).

19. *Temple,* tome I, p. 65; see Appendix B.

20. *E&S,* p. 38.

21. Fulcanelli, *Demeures,* tome II, p. 249.

22. See my *Philosophical Geometry,* p. 62.

23. *Le Roi . . .*

24. *SS,* p. 6.

25. On the connection of the origins of Nazism and the spiritual, the esoteric, and the occult, cf. Dusty Sklar, *Gods and Beasts: The Nazis and the Occult* (New York: Thomas Y. Crowell Company, 1977).

26. Saunier, *op. cit.,* p. 75.

27. On the back cover of *Aor.*

Chapter Ten

1. Pierre Mariel, *L'Europe païenne . . .,* cited in Saunier, *La Synarchie,* p. 178.

2. *NW,* p. 119. I by far prefer "crudeness" to translator's "rawness."

3. *Ibid.* It is incorrect to translate *"fausse pudeur"* as "false prudishness," thus equating *"pudeur"* with "prudishness." *"Pudeur"* is an attribute of nobility; it is the essence of chivalry, of the Courts of Love. It denotes a discretion, a self-control protective of decency, honesty, refinement (Larousse). There is *pudeur* in dedicated prostitution, inside the temple and out, but fakery destroys the rite. "Prudery" (or "prudishness," in the translator's usage) is an exaggerated, misguided modesty; the term is always to some extent pejorative. "Prudish" is much closer to the French *"prude"* (not surprisingly) than it is to *"pudeur."* False modesty is what the author decries, decorum, the narrow formality of

small minds and sleepy consciousness. *"Fausse pudeur"* could be translated by "prudishness," therefore, but never by *"false* prudishness." "False modesty" is preferable.

4. *NW*, p. 151.

5. *Ibid.*, p. 120.

6. *Ibid.*, p. 139.

7. *Ibid.*, p. 81.

8. *Ibid.*

9. *Ibid.*, p. 86.

10. See p. 167.

11. *NW*, p. 105.

12. *SS*, p. 72.

13. *NW*, p. 120.

14. As publisher of Henry Miller, William Burroughs, Jean Genet, Vladimir Nabokov, Samuel Beckett, as well as lesser lights of Olympia Press and the Travellers' Companion.

15. Vivian du Mas is called "an enigmatic character" by Jean Saunier, who gives us a glimpse at his work (*op. cit.*, p. 178 *et seq.*), while Girodias offers a more intimate look at the private individual and his milieu. Vivian du Mas' *Schéma de l'archétype social* (Paris: undated), "presents itself as a systematic analysis of all the levels of the visible and invisible universe." There is a system of "universal spheres of decreasing Consciousness creating the different vehicles of collective consciousness." Vivian du Mas distinguishes five worlds: spiritual, intuitional, rational, emotional, and material, each of which is in relation with a "spirit-element," namely Ether, Air, Fire, Water, and Earth respectively. Saunier emphasizes that these considerations are by no means restricted to the philosophical, but are extended to man's constitution and social organization. He finds that many of the ideas can be traced to the "doctrines of the Theosophical Society" on the one hand, and to Saint-Yves d'Alveydre on the other (see note #10, Chapter 7). Considering that Saint-Yves' work "partakes both of personal revelation and of para-scientific interpretation of age-old traditions" (Saunier, p. 79), and knowing the role played by René Schwaller in the Theosophical Society, the origin and descent of this body of ideas from occult to political are easily established, with Les Veilleurs as central hinge.

16. Maurice Girodias, *The Frog Prince* (New York: Crown Publishers, Inc., 1980). On his first encounter with the group, at a Krishnamurti lecture in Paris, the author comments on their attire, noticing the riding boots. "Who are they: God's own Storm Troopers?" (p. 145)

17. Girodias, who was present at the "foundation of the Synarchist Order" (*Ibid.*, p. 250 *et seq.*), gives us his tongue-in-cheek account of the event at which Vivian du Mas presented his treatise, *Le Pacte Synarchique*, sequel to his *Schéma de l'archétype social*. In an inaugural address, du Mas explains that "synarchy is founded upon four orders that correspond to the Hindu caste system; which itself is inspired by a recognition of the basic psychological differences between four very distinct categories of humans. (. . .) Each order has its own hierarchy, and government is exercised in common by their elected delegates. This division of the people into orders is natural and conforms with tradition. (. . .) Thus synarchy restores a natural order within societies, which befits the spiritual classification of individuals . . ."

Whatever the merits of such rhetoric and however grotesque the occasion, the document itself seems to have made its way in the corridors of the Third Republic and during the Occupation. It enters our theme only for its direct descent from occultistic sociopolitical speculations, and for its author's link to Les Veilleurs.

18. *La Synarchie*, p. 177.

19. See note # 25, Chapter 9.

20. *La Synarchie*, p. 73.

21. *Ibid.*

22. *Gods and Beasts*, p. 3.

23. *Ibid.*

24. *Aor*, p. 43.

25. *SS*, p. 49.

26. *NW*, p. 83; *Miracle*, p. 162.

27. *Miracle, ibid.*

28. After Madame Blavatsky, who had it incorporated into a mystical brooch. *Gods . . .*, pp. 66, 38, 28 *et al.*

29. *Aor*, p. 31.

30. *Gods . . .*, p. 29.

31. *Ibid.*, p. 6.

32. Cf. *Pacific Shift* (San Francisco: Sierra Club Books, 1985). Chapter 4, Gaia Politique, *passim*, in particular p. 163. ". . . I do not see the noetic polity of the future as an authoritarian state, and I would strongly disagree with those scholars, such as Schwaller de Lubicz, Alain Dánelieu [*sic*], and Robert Lawlor, who celebrate ancient theocracies and caste systems as the form of society that is appropriate for a mystically enlightened civilization."

33. As Mr. Thompson found out with Aurobindo, Yogananda, Gopi

Krishna *et al.*, cf. *Passages about Earth* (New York: Harper & Row, 1973), p. 88.

34. *Pacific Shift,* p. 23.

35. *Aor,* p. 72.

36. *Passages,* p. 180.

37. *Pacific Shift,* p. 157.

38. *Le Roi* . . . See back cover.

39. *Pacific Shift,* p. 158.

40. *Ibid.,* p. 157.

41. *Ibid.,* p. 24.

42. Cf. Introduction to *NW,* p. 51.

APPENDIX A

KNOWLEDGE AND IMPLICIT FUNCTIONS

Given the notion of "knowledge" as a variable of indeterminate value, and given that such knowledge is conceivable only in function of the method that brings it into existence or a method to which it corresponds, a relationship is established which can be satisfied by the expression

$$y = f(x)$$

where (y), knowledge, exists in function of (x), method.

Method, however, can only be syntactics * of knowledge, while knowledge, in turn, exists in function of its underlying method. We obtain a structure

$$y_1 = f(x_1)$$
$$y_2 = f(x_2)$$
$$y_3 = f(x_3)$$
$$\ldots \text{etc.}$$

where every (x), such as (x₁, x₂, x₃, . . . etc.) is syntactics of knowledge (y₁, y₂, y₃, . . . etc.)

As each and every method comprises syntactics of knowledge, and as all knowledge refers to a method, these relations can be expressed by

$$y_n = f(x_n)$$

where the possibility of (n + 1) is ever present.

By definition, the equation

$$y_n = f(x_n)$$

reveals an interior structure of the type

$$y = f(x)$$

---

* The term "syntactics" is used to translate "la syntactique" according to André Lalande's *Vocabulaire de la Philosophie*, (Paris, 1956), p. 1090. The reference is from Cournot, *Traité de l'Enchaînement*, where the term is defined as "science of combinations and of order." Beyond denoting the discipline, the term will also be used here to denote the combinations and the order in themselves.

$$y_1 = f(x_1)$$
$$y_2 = f(x_2)$$
$$y_3 = f(x_3)$$
$$\cdots\cdots$$
$$\cdots\cdots$$
$$y_n = f(x_n)$$

an architectonic structure which in itself is syntactical.

It should be noted that the scaffolding signified by

$$y_n = f(x_n)$$

is perpetuated by *explicit functions*, i.e., functions that allow us to know (y) whenever (x) is known. In the presence of explicit functions, there exists a tendency to valorize the right side of the equation as antecedent, given that (x) furnishes the means of knowing (y), whereas even if (y) were known, (x) would remain inaccessible. An explicit function thus indicates that a method has generated knowledge, and it excludes the possibility of knowledge giving rise to method.

It would be contrary to the spirit of

$$y_n = f(x_n)$$

to impose *content* upon such a scaffolding, and therefore to substitute in the place of (x) on the right side of the equation a well-defined magnitude (k), knowing that in these syntactics, any given magnitude attributed to (x) occurs, as (y, y_1, y_2, y_3, . . . etc.), in function of a variable. The syntactics of explicit functions are useful as structure providing this structure remains devoid of content.

Implicit functions inform us differently. In this case, we tend to valorize the antecedence of the left side of the equation, and here a given magnitude (k) can indeed be substituted in the place of (y) in the equation, leading to a determination of (x). Knowledge can determine method. It would be frivolous to maintain that knowledge is also method in itself, as this would be saying that y = x, whereas we know that y = f(x). Substitution of (k) in the place of (y) becomes possible. *Implicit functions, when recognized,* can thus intervene and arrest the sequence (n) with (n + 1) as constant possibility. Such a function can be designated by

$$y_k = f(x_k)$$

where (k) within syntactics of equations, shows the *intervention* of
an implicit equation and where no possibility of (k + 1) exists. We
retain the above expression for functions which have been *recognized* as being implicit, whereas we continue to express by

$$y_n = f(x_n)$$

syntactics of explicit equations *as well as* equations the nature of
which has not been ascertained. Alone *implicit equations* which
have been *recognized* as such shall be designated by

$$y_k = f(x_k)$$

where no possibility of (k + 1) exists.

The synthetic character of the variable (y) should be noted, since
this synthesis is what lends an implicit function the possibility of
content. The variable (x), on the other hand, could be qualified as
being analytic.

The syntactics presented above are epitomized in the examination of an analytic discipline. Let us observe the analytic mind
aiming at knowledge: in this particular instance of $y_n = f(x_n)$, an
instance we shall name $y_a = f(x_a)$, no inquisitiveness is manifest
concerning the nature of the function, since all notion of implicit
functions is absent. By definition, the analytical mind valorizes the
right side of the equation as antecedent, thereby *creating* an explicit
function. As this analytic effort aims at specific knowledge, it bur-
dens the right side of the equation with content by substituting a
constant in the place of the variable (x_a), thus obtaining specific
knowledge in the place of (y_a). This is the manner by which knowledge is acquired through an analytic method (x_a) which is a particular instance (a) in a strucure (n) of explicit functions. In terms of a
logic abhorrent to reason, a logic we are indeed attempting here to
eradicate, we would say that the function $y_a = f(x_a)$ is an explicit
function even though it could be considered to be an "unrecognized
implicit function." *

It suffices to recall the definitions $y_n = f(x_n)$ and $y_k = f(x_k)$ and to
repeat that $y_a = f(x_a)$ is a particular instance of $y_n = f(x_n)$, a particular
instance for which the notion of *ascertainment* (of the nature of the
function) does not exist. For the analytical mind, the notion of given

---

* Korzybski, in *Science and Sanity,* has applied himself to the rectification of this type of lunacy, and we retain his syntactics of "plenum" as
stabilizing a concept hitherto cluttered by structureless formulas.

knowledge does not exist, and therefore the notion of ascertainment is absent as well. It is by definition that $y_a = f(x_a)$ is a particular instance of $y_n = f(x_n)$.

Is the analytical mind thus irrevocably condemned to a vicious circle of systematic error? Evidently not, as the concept of this error exists. However, before we examine the subtle dialectics of such a rehabilitation of thinking, it might be useful to examine more closely the error itself.

(x_a) is a variable whose complex variability could be represented by a set of "points," all variable and all interdependent. When the free play of a certain number of these "points" is arrested, the variable is oppressed; it ceases to breathe freely. This partial or total determination saddles it with a measure; it is burdened with a quantity, and an evaluation of this quantity is established according to its relation with another quantity of the same kind, taken as term of comparison (Larousse under "measure"). Now this other quantity of the same kind can only be (y_a), as no other term exists. By definition, a relation x/y is created which is the measure of a magnitude (x), the magnitude (y) being taken as a unit (Lalande under "relation"). By definition again, the relation x/y is a constant, and we may say that $x/y = r$, where (r) is the constant relation between (x) and (y). Since (x) and (y) are "of the same kind" (Larousse), in other words, since their structure is similar, and since one is measured in relation to the other, one is thought of as being part of the other. Close scrutiny of the relation $x/y = r$ seems indeed to communicate just such a circumstance.

After this glance at relation in general, we now return to the specific case of $x_a/y_a = r$, an expression which infers that method is part of knowledge. This inference, arbitrary and *blind*, can in no way be accepted as cognitive and has no place in a method which is syntactics of knowledge. Yet it inevitably makes itself felt in the expression $y_a = f(x_a)$.

We may note that since (r) is not designated as having a value either smaller or larger than 1, nor as having the value of 1, the concept exists of an (x_a) greater than (y_a). Yet the formula of the relation $x_a/y_a = r$ dictates a structure where (x_a) is a part of (y_a), and we express this fact by the formula $y_a = x_a + p$, where (p) designates the part of (y_a) which is *not* (x_a).

We need not examine these formulas in greater detail. It is sufficient at this time to ascertain that the synthetic character of (y_a) has vanished. Therefore (y_a) will vanish in its entirety.

$$(x_a + p) = f(x_a)$$
$$p = f(x_a) - x_a$$

We might call the above expression an *interference formula*. It is always preceded by

$$x_a/y_a = r, \quad x_a = (y_a)r, \quad y_a = x_a/r$$

an *inference formula* in one of its three aspects.

While $y = f(x)$ exemplifies an equation creative of structural relations, the inference formula appears as a principle destructive to such relations. The movement it implies (its three expressions being but snapshots of critical moments) is circular, creating a closed system in perfect equilibrium but having lost any and all relations with a similar structure. It is a perfectly isolated system. A detailed study of the ratio as relation, constant by definition, such as it is expressed in general by $x/y = 1$, would show this expression as a formula of the absurd. It is for the moment sufficient to show method standing with knowledge not in a constant ratio, but in a structural relation which is expressed, in general, by $y = f(x)$.

The path leading to a rehabilitation of the idea of $y_a = f(x_a)$ need now be traced. As the concept of systematized error exists in this *plenum*, and as this error stems from an action upon (x_a) (the action of loading (x_a) with content, thus producing a formula of interference), the concept of action must give way not to its negation which could be termed "non-action," but to the positive concept of *inaction*. Whereas non-action contradicts the positive nature of the plenum expressed by $y = f(x)$, the very live concept of inaction is most suitable to it. This inaction is contemplation of structure. For as soon as action upon (x_a) has ceased, the latter term regains its variability, and the structure forms into the expression $y_n = f(x_n)$, replacing $y_a = f(x_a)$. Now in the structure $y_n = f(x_n)$, the intervention of an implicit function $y_k = f(x_k)$ is *conceivable*, though becoming *possible* only by means of *recognition*, a concept without existence in the idea of $y_n = f(x_n)$. There exists however the concept of structured contemplation, of *inaction, and this concept has become knowledge*, a (y) which remains to be named. But have we not named it already, and is this not *given knowledge?* Indeed, is it possible to point to a method having generated this knowledge? If we retrace our steps in trying to discover such a method, determining knowledge as a *knowledge of structure*, and method as *syntac-*

tics of inaction, we realize that we have created an implicit function of the type

$$y_k = f(x_k)$$

where (y_k), given knowledge, has determined a method (x_k), a particular case of $y_k = f(x_k)$ which can be termed

$$y_s = f(x_s)$$

in order to underline its character of synthesis. It is also to be noted that in the expression $y_s = f(x_s)$, the concept of recognition (ascertainment) exists.

If $(k + 1)$ does not exist for the expression $y_k = f(x_k)$, it must be that the latter finds syntactics of structure in the concept $(k - 1)$. Having indicated for $y_n = f(x_n)$ an internal structure of

$$y = f(x)$$
$$y_1 = f(x_1)$$
$$y_2 = f(x_2)$$
$$y_3 = f(x_3)$$
$$\cdots \cdots$$
$$\cdots \cdots$$
$$y_n = f(x_n)$$

we shall indicate for $y_k = f(x_k)$ an internal structure as follows:

$$y_k = f(x_k)$$
$$y_{k-1} = f(x_{k-1})$$
$$y_{k-2} = f(x_{k-2})$$
$$y_{k-3} = f(x_{k-3})$$
$$\cdots \cdots$$
$$\cdots \cdots$$

where the possibility of $y_{k-k} = f(x_{k-k})$ is a concept which remains to be studied.

Bruges, 1959.
Cannes, 1960.

APPENDIX B

from *Temple*, tome I, p. 65 *et seq.*

Evolution or *expansion of consciousness* is manifested bodily by the form and organism *of the individual.* In perpetuating himself, the individual does no more than multiply the unit he represents. *Adaptations* to the milieu through "the struggle for life" make for the varieties among groups of individuals, varieties that are classified according to race and species. The classification is made from bottom to top, from the individual to the general. This concerns the transmission of characteristics *by the individual's seed.*

Therefore it is in the individual itself that we must seek the passage in the development of consciousness, *and beside the fact of any seminal proliferation.*

A reexamination is in order regarding the possible transformations of specificities and their transmission.

According to a precept as old as wisdom: *"A form cannot pass to another form unless it be by integral decomposition of the first into its essential component elements."*

A second precept of the same wisdom asserts: *"Every thing and every being contain a fixed nucleus which neither putrefaction nor fire can destroy."*

Our biologists have not been aware of these principles, and therefore their attempts at presenting a coherent theory of evolution have failed. And yet, the facts of nature demand such a theory.

If we leave aside the moral character attributed to the "soul," reserving for "psyche" the sense of specificity—admittedly a term difficult to define—then *metempsychosis* exists. It is to the principle of metempsychosis, moreover, that the legendary vegetal *palingenesis* refers, based as it is on the fixed residue contained in the ashes.

Through putrefaction, every plant or animal body is reduced to two separable states, one volatile, the other constituting a fixed residue. Once dessicated, the fixed part reveals an alkaline salt.

Similarly, but by violent means, combustion divides all vegetal or organic bodies into volatile parts, leaving an ash which contains a fixed alkaline salt. "Dust thou art, and unto dust shalt thou return." Thus, each and every thing is essentially composed of a volatile part and of a fixed part, generative principle epitomized by Pharaonic theology, for example, in its instruction concerning *Ba* and *Ka.*

If the ashes of a plant that has been burned are sown into earth along with seed of the same plant, qualities of this vegetal entity can be exalted or its typical qualities can be modified. These same ashes can impede the growth of plants "complementary" to it. The legendary vegetal palingenesis as well as the legend of the Phoenix are initiatory traditions revealing a mode of generation *the "cellular" seed cannot realize.*

It follows that transformations can be accomplished *only by and for the same individual* having undergone during his lifetime a profound modification of his being. He must *reincarnate*, for his *seed* is incapable of transmitting these new characteristics to another being. Ignorance of this fact makes it impossible to establish a definitive law of heredity.

The fixed salt, which is extremely fixed indeed—it can even be said to be indestructible in comparison with the chromosome—is the true bearer of the individual's specificity; it preserves his *personal* characteristics, including those that have been acquired during his lifetime.

For the chemist, one living cell is like any other, just as one residual salt of putrefaction or combustion is like any other, but *from the vital point of view*, there obviously are materially indistinguishable nuances in the parts of each individual, because the latter is always characterized. One leaf of a tree is never identical to another leaf of the same tree; an individual—and what he might be composed of—is never identical to another individual, except in certain rare cases of twins born of the same egg.

The nucleus that *fixes* the psyche of an individual must join the *organic* nucleus of a seed-cell in order that "reincarnation" take place. By itself, the fixed nucleus cannot engender a new organized being, as it cannot recede in the evolutionary lineage in order to start anew the entire cycle leading to organic life. A kinship is indispensable between the two nuclei, the fixed mineral and the cellular animal or vegetal. Metempsychosis is the history of the avatars of this fixed nucleus seeking to rediscover the living being corresponding to its rhythm. . . .

The natural path of metempsychosis is through the plant, because during its growth, the plant is first to resorb the fixed salt. It is through the food chain that the fixed salt returns to the individual carrying the regenerative seed. Here lies one of the causes of genetic mutation.

In man, the absolute fixed salt of his being is formed in the thighbone, basis and support of the physical body (the Egyptian *men.t*).

The arms of Eze-s/mer (A.M.) France *

The animal or vegetal seed-cell maintains the qualities typical of a species, including its adaptations; on the other hand, the fixed salt transports—sometimes through lengthy periods of *invisibility*—the *consciousness acquired* by an individual demanding a modification of form in order to provide to his consciousness the means of expressing itself.

The sudden appearance of new forms, seemingly without transition (gene mutation), is actually a continual sequence of the *evolution of consciousness.*

In this succession, the regenerative seed is necessary; thus the plant and animal stay confined to their respective realms; the mineral cannot pass to the vegetable kingdom without the pre-existence of the latter. Now in order to understand the passage of one realm to another, that is, the expansion of consciousness, two essential principles must be kept in mind: first, that there is transmission of consciousness by reincarnation, meaning that there has been a previous destruction of form; second, that it is the energetic milieu that fashions the organ.

In order to facilitate the development of this idea, the terms

*Drawing by Lucie Lamy.

"fixed" and "volatile" are used here to represent fixed and volatile "principles." In nuclear science, one would speak summarily of nucleus and negative electrons. The fixed salt is the neutral neutron of the fixed nucleus. Its alkaline mineral character is but the bearer of the psyche's energetic characteristics. Its specificity is energetic and represents *a puissance which is consciousness.* . . .

At the time of destruction of the form, the fixed and the volatile separate. We call this death. At the moment of disjunction, energetic influences of the milieu (such as light or sound) are able to act and make an impression, as the form is no longer an obstacle.*

The rebirth of a form demands the reconjunction of the volatile with the fixed. The fixed is determined, the volatile is feminine and indeterminate, while nevertheless being of a general "rhythm" analogous to the rhythm of the fixed part. Thus it is the fixed which must recover its volatile for reincarnation to occur, whatever its form, be it physical or more subtle.

That which brings the fixed is paternal, that which brings the volatile is maternal. At the same time as regeneration, there is reconjunction of the volatile and the fixed parts of a determined state. It is at this moment that the influence of the environment comes into play to modify the *instrument* of the individual's consciousness.

This is the mysterious Hermetic thesis that claims to demonstrate that the vital destruction of a mineral can render it vegetative, that is to say, make it capable of nourishing and multiplying itself.

The principle is correct and can be controlled in the plant and animal kingdoms; this suffices to give credence to what has been claimed for the mineral. Perhaps the continuation of atomic research will make it possible to confirm this fact, so that the understanding of it can become generally accessible.

There exists a transmission of the characteristics of the species, a maintenance of that species through the seed; there also exists evolutionary transformation and transmutation, and passage of the realms through the nucleus or fixed center. (Trans. AVB)

---

* The disjunction of elements *that belong to one another* creates the energetic milieu of the thing. This energy is in some way the "desire" for reunion, affinity.

ACKNOWLEDGMENT

To Christopher Bamford, I am indebted
for a creative reading of the manuscript,
for believing in the book, and for
giving generously of his capacities
at every stage of its realization.